HERETIC

ROBBIE MORRISON

CHARLIE ADLARD

"For my dad who passed away a few
years ago—he would've loved this one!"
—Charlie

"In memory of my much-missed Aunt Evelyn,
whose smile and sense of humour could brighten
up even the dreichest of Scottish days."
—Robbie

IMAGE COMICS, INC.

Robert Kirkman – Chief Operating Officer
Erik Larsen – Chief Financial Officer
Todd McFarlane – President
Marc Silvestri – Chief Executive Officer
Jim Valentino – Executive Vice President
Eric Stephenson – Publisher / Chief Creative Officer

Nicole Lapalme – Vice President of Finance
Leanna Caunter – Accounting Analyst
Sue Korpela – Accounting & HR Manager
Alex Cox – Vice President of Direct Market Sales
Margot Wood – Vice President of Book Market Sales
Chloe Ramos – Book Market & Library Sales Manager
Kat Salazar – Vice President of PR & Marketing
Deanna Phelps – Marketing Design Manager
Jim Viscardi – Vice President of Business Development
Lorelei Bunjes – Vice President of Digital Strategy
Emilio Bautista – Digital Sales Coordinator
Dirk Wood – Vice President of International Sales & Licensing
Ryan Brewer – International Sales & Licensing Manager
Drew Gill – Art Director
Heather Doornink – Vice President of Production
Ian Baldessari – Print Manager
Melissa Gifford – Content Manager
Drew Fitzgerald – Content Manager
Erika Schnatz – Senior Production Artist
Wesley Griffith – Production Artist
Rich Fowlks – Production Artist
Jon Schlaffman – Production Artist

IMAGECOMICS.COM

WRITER
ROBBIE MORRISON

ARTIST
CHARLIE ADLARD

LETTERER
RUS WOOTON

SCRIPT EDITOR
DEBORAH TATE

PRODUCTION
DREW GILL

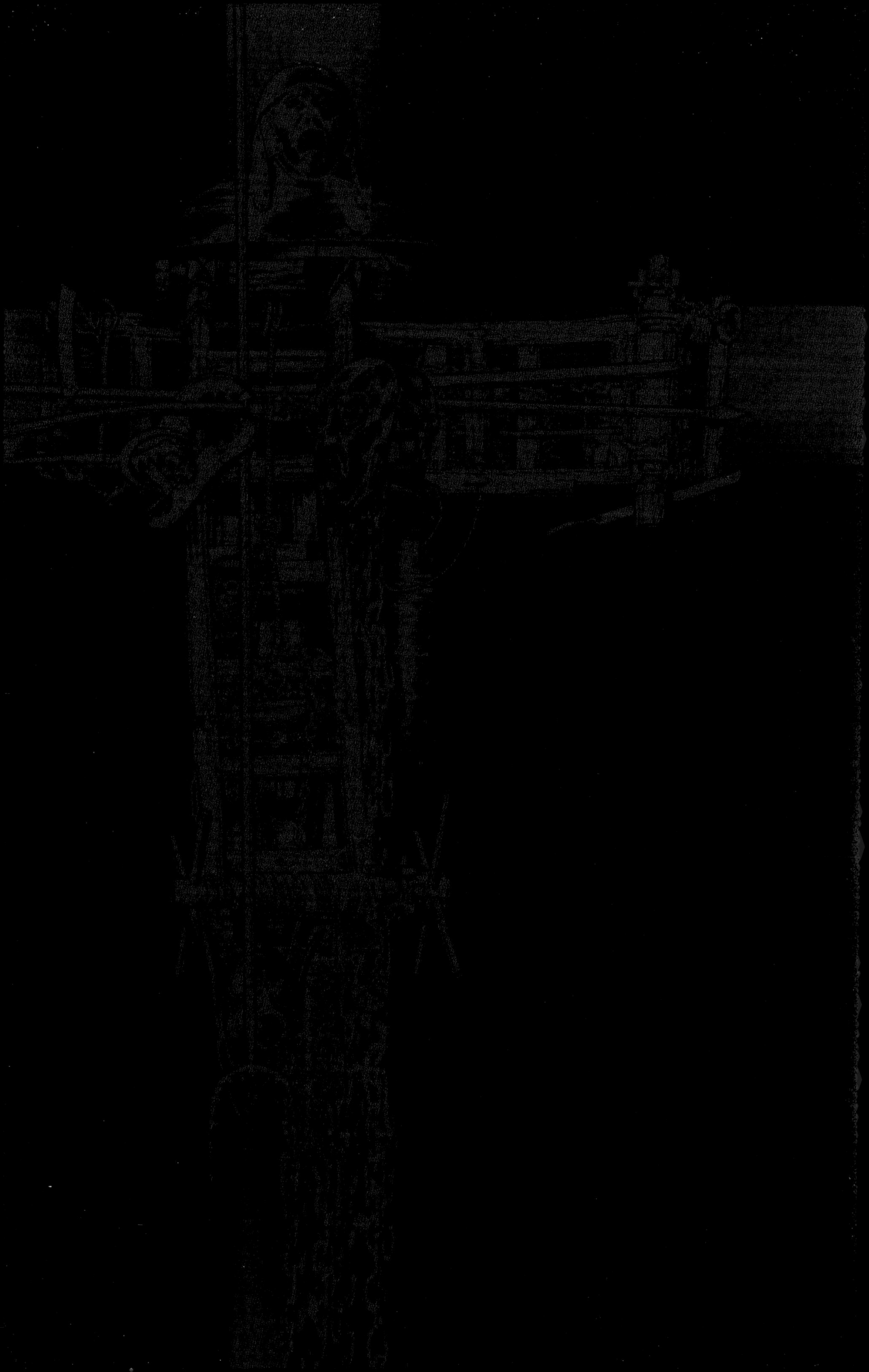

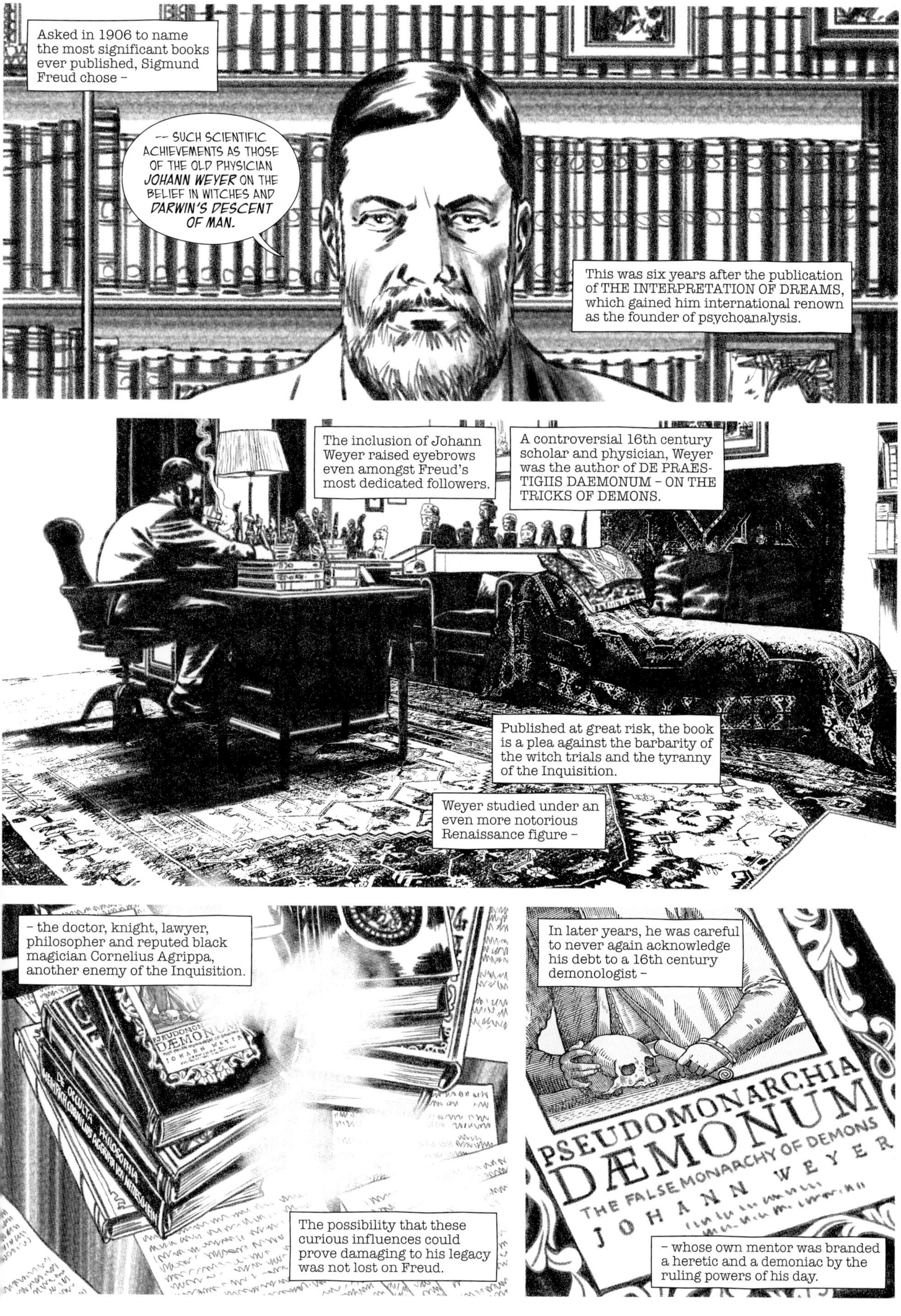
Asked in 1906 to name the most significant books ever published, Sigmund Freud chose –
-- SUCH SCIENTIFIC ACHIEVEMENTS AS THOSE OF THE OLD PHYSICIAN *JOHANN WEYER* ON THE BELIEF IN WITCHES AND *DARWIN'S DESCENT OF MAN.*
This was six years after the publication of THE INTERPRETATION OF DREAMS, which gained him international renown as the founder of psychoanalysis.
The inclusion of Johann Weyer raised eyebrows even amongst Freud's most dedicated followers.
A controversial 16th century scholar and physician, Weyer was the author of DE PRAESTIGIIS DAEMONUM – ON THE TRICKS OF DEMONS.
Published at great risk, the book is a plea against the barbarity of the witch trials and the tyranny of the Inquisition.
Weyer studied under an even more notorious Renaissance figure –
– the doctor, knight, lawyer, philosopher and reputed black magician Cornelius Agrippa, another enemy of the Inquisition.
DE OCCULTA PHILOSOPHIA
The possibility that these curious influences could prove damaging to his legacy was not lost on Freud.
In later years, he was careful to never again acknowledge his debt to a 16th century demonologist –
PSEUDOMONARCHIA DÆMONUM
THE FALSE MONARCHY OF DEMONS
JOHANN WEYER
– whose own mentor was branded a heretic and a demoniac by the ruling powers of his day.

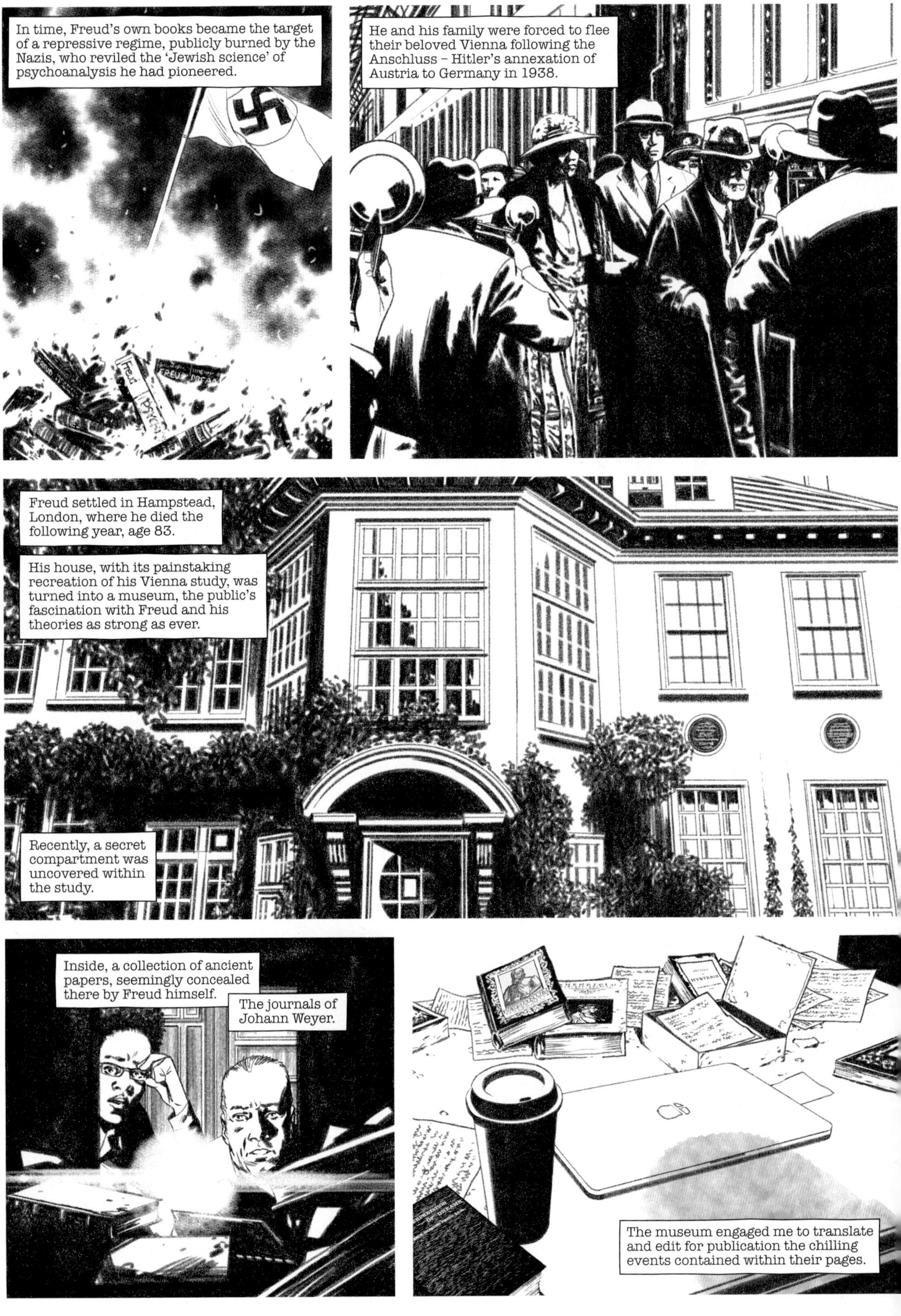
In time, Freud's own books became the target of a repressive regime, publicly burned by the Nazis, who reviled the 'Jewish science' of psychoanalysis he had pioneered.
He and his family were forced to flee their beloved Vienna following the Anschluss – Hitler's annexation of Austria to Germany in 1938.
Freud settled in Hampstead, London, where he died the following year, age 83.
His house, with its painstaking recreation of his Vienna study, was turned into a museum, the public's fascination with Freud and his theories as strong as ever.
Recently, a secret compartment was uncovered within the study.
Inside, a collection of ancient papers, seemingly concealed there by Freud himself.
The journals of Johann Weyer.
The museum engaged me to translate and edit for publication the chilling events contained within their pages.

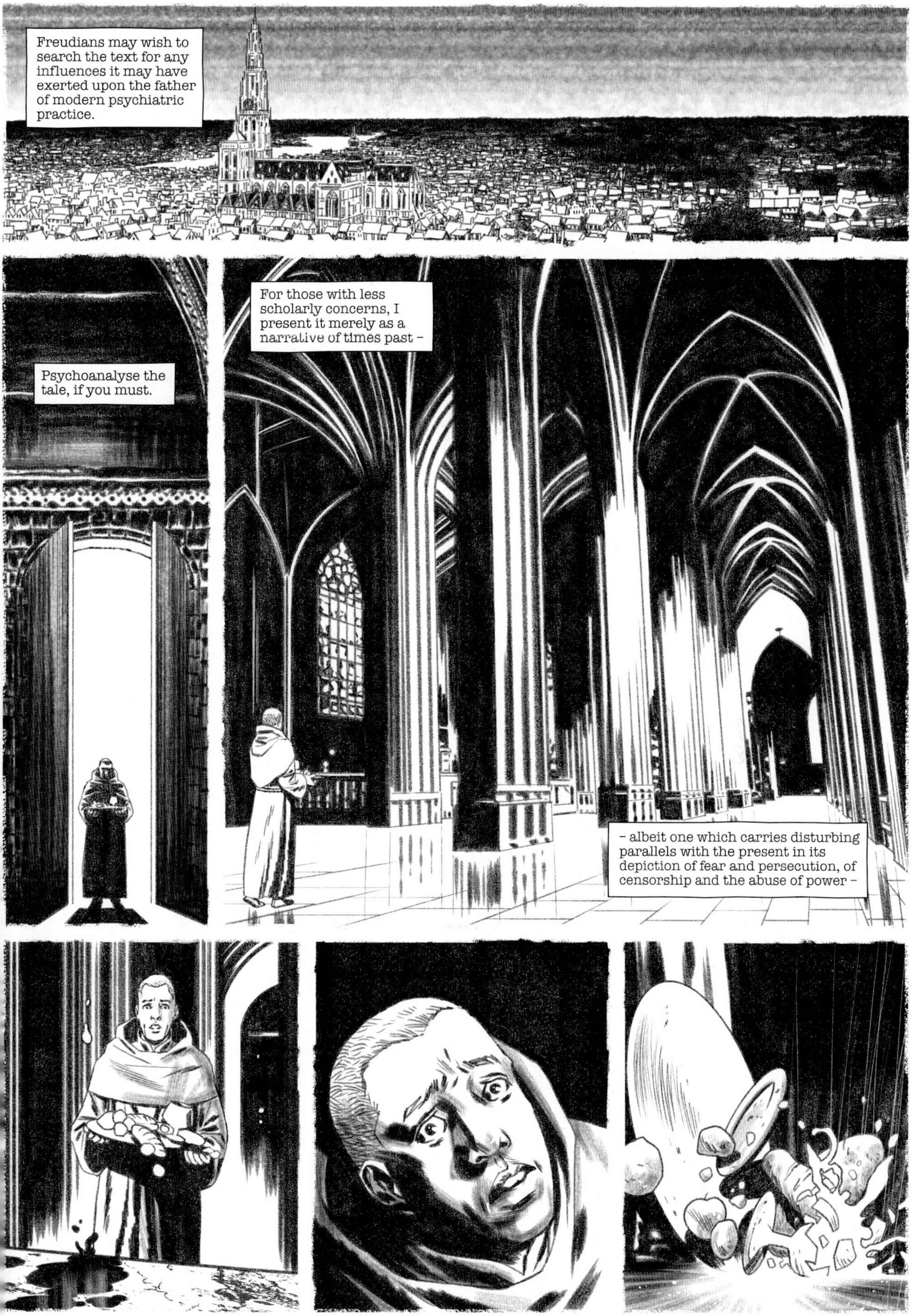

Freudians may wish to search the text for any influences it may have exerted upon the father of modern psychiatric practice.
Psychoanalyse the tale, if you must.
For those with less scholarly concerns, I present it merely as a narrative of times past –
– albeit one which carries disturbing parallels with the present in its depiction of fear and persecution, of censorship and the abuse of power –

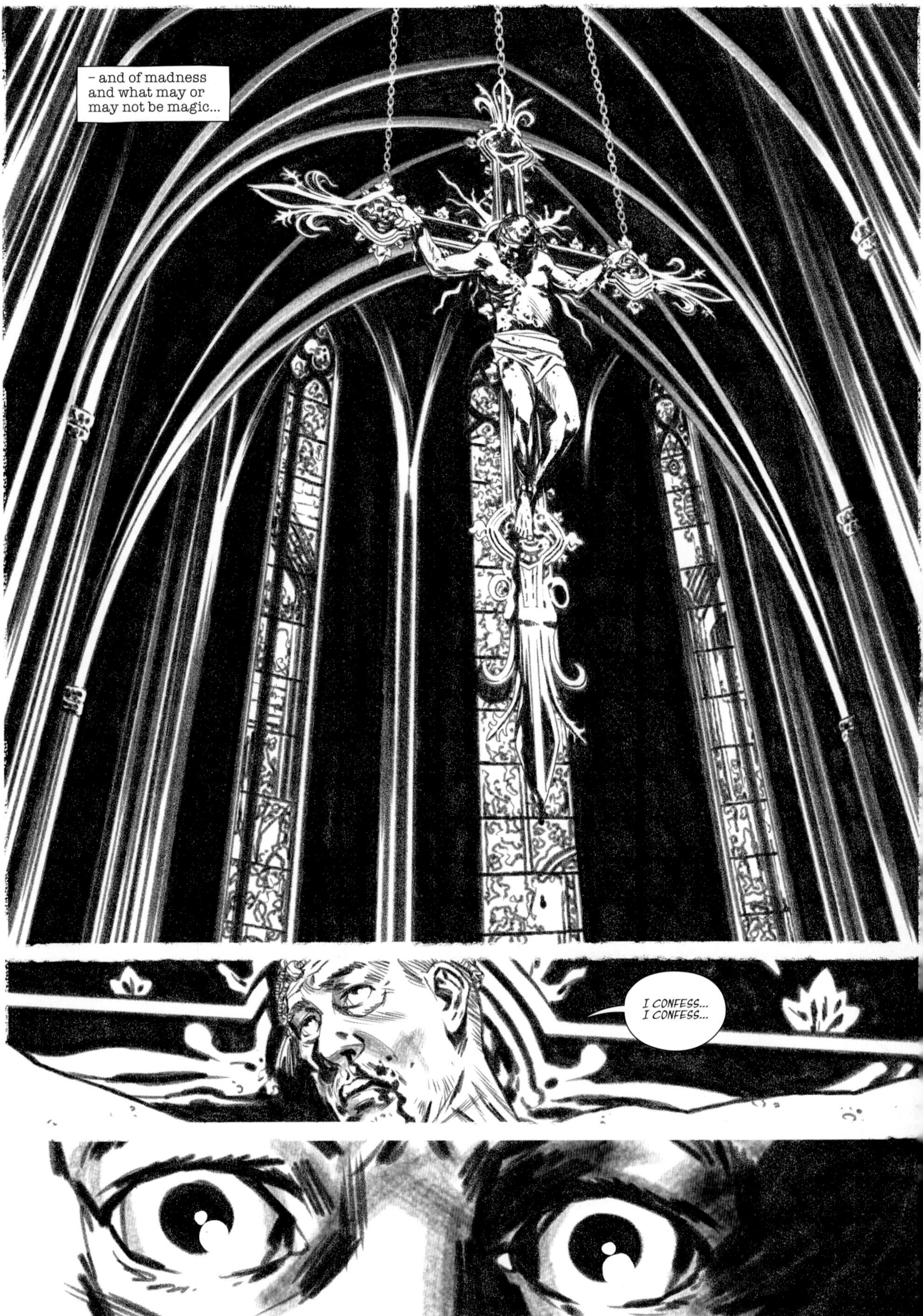
– and of madness and what may or may not be magic...
I CONFESS... I CONFESS...

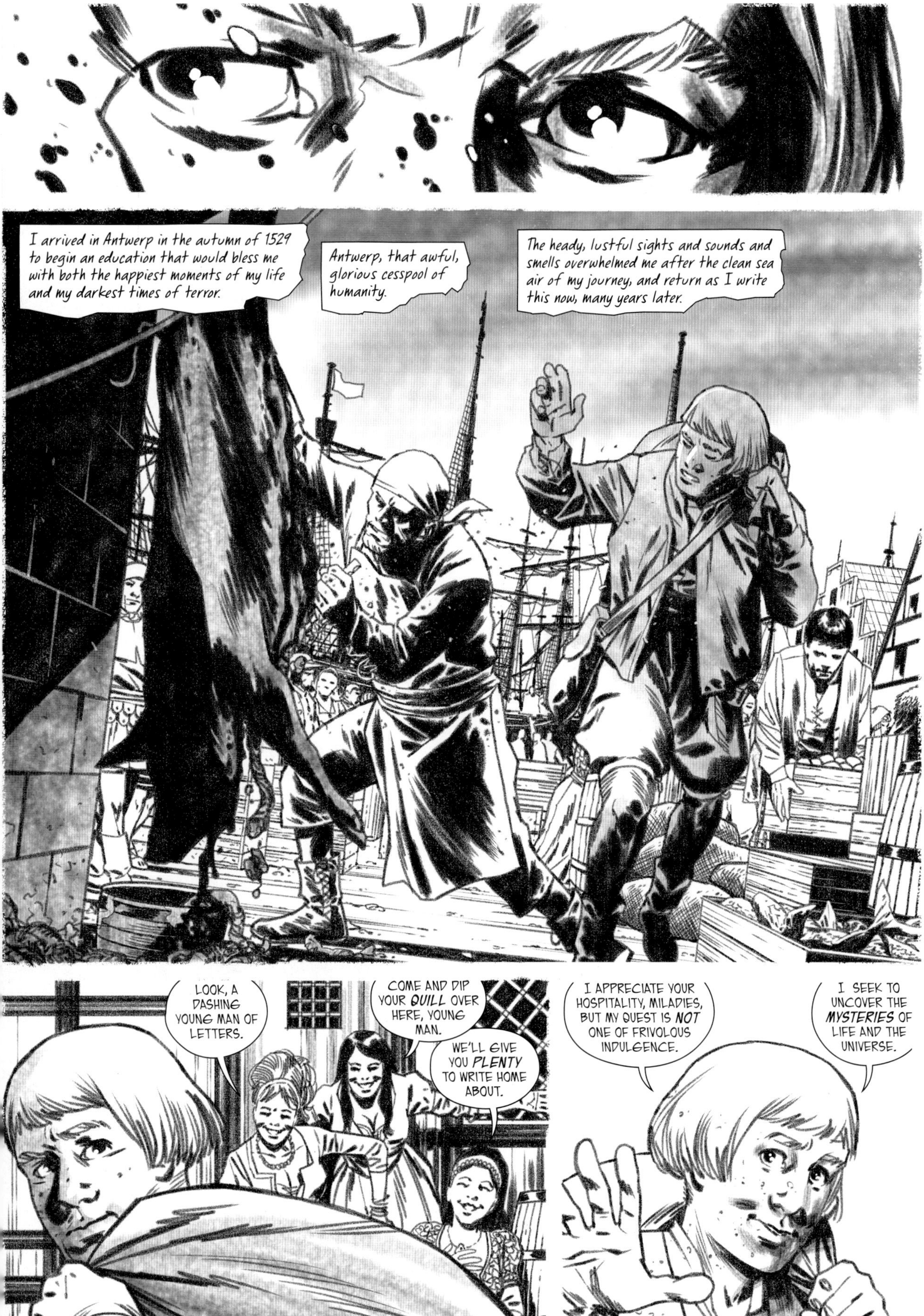
I arrived in Antwerp in the autumn of 1529 to begin an education that would bless me with both the happiest moments of my life and my darkest times of terror.
Antwerp, that awful, glorious cesspool of humanity.
The heady, lustful sights and sounds and smells overwhelmed me after the clean sea air of my journey, and return as I write this now, many years later.
LOOK, A DASHING YOUNG MAN OF LETTERS.
COME AND DIP YOUR QUILL OVER HERE, YOUNG MAN.
WE'LL GIVE YOU PLENTY TO WRITE HOME ABOUT.
I APPRECIATE YOUR HOSPITALITY, MILADIES, BUT MY QUEST IS NOT ONE OF FRIVOLOUS INDULGENCE.
I SEEK TO UNCOVER THE MYSTERIES OF LIFE AND THE UNIVERSE.

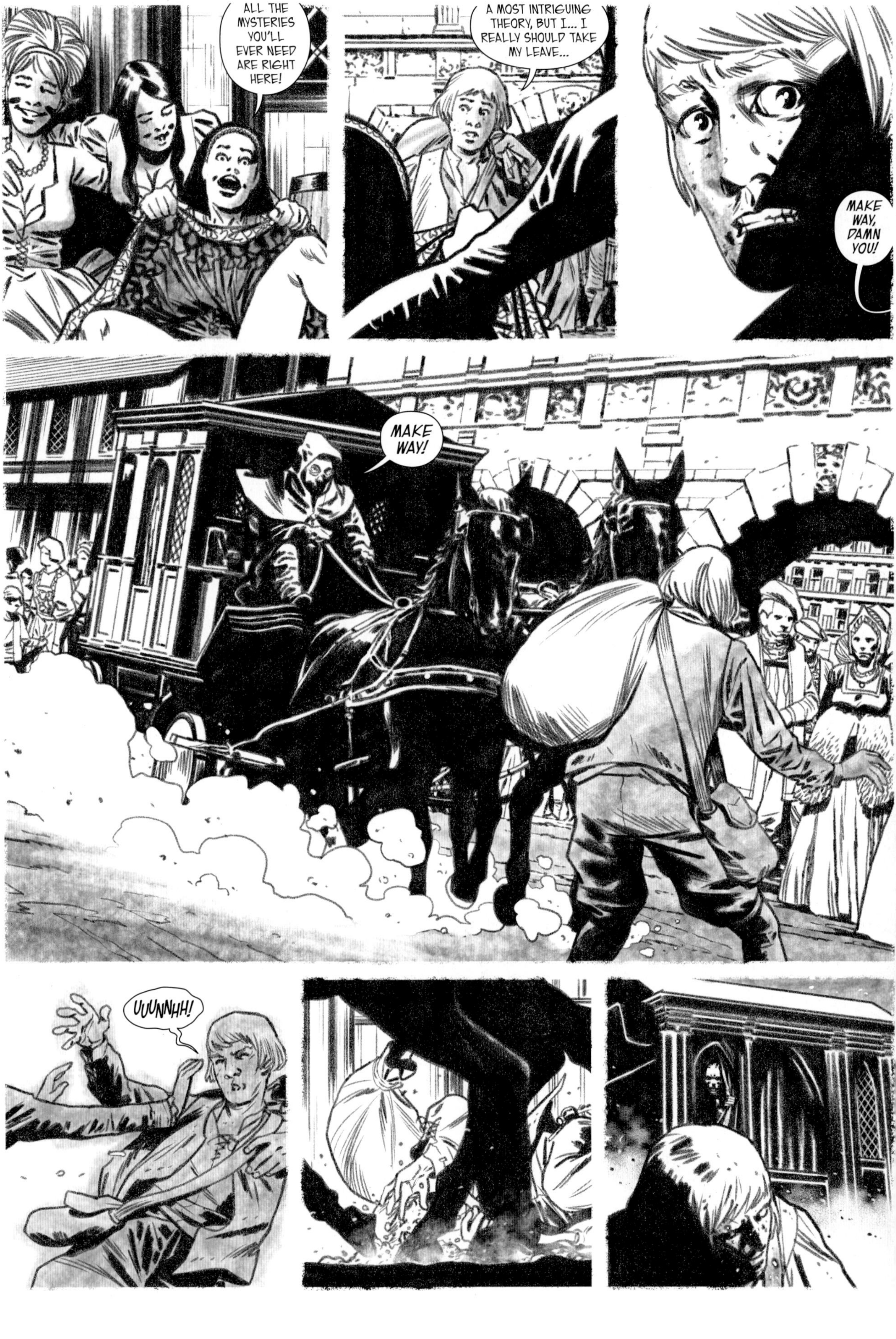
ALL THE MYSTERIES YOU'LL EVER NEED ARE RIGHT HERE!
A MOST INTRIGUING THEORY, BUT I... I REALLY SHOULD TAKE MY LEAVE...
MAKE WAY, DAMN YOU!
MAKE WAY!
UUUNNHH!

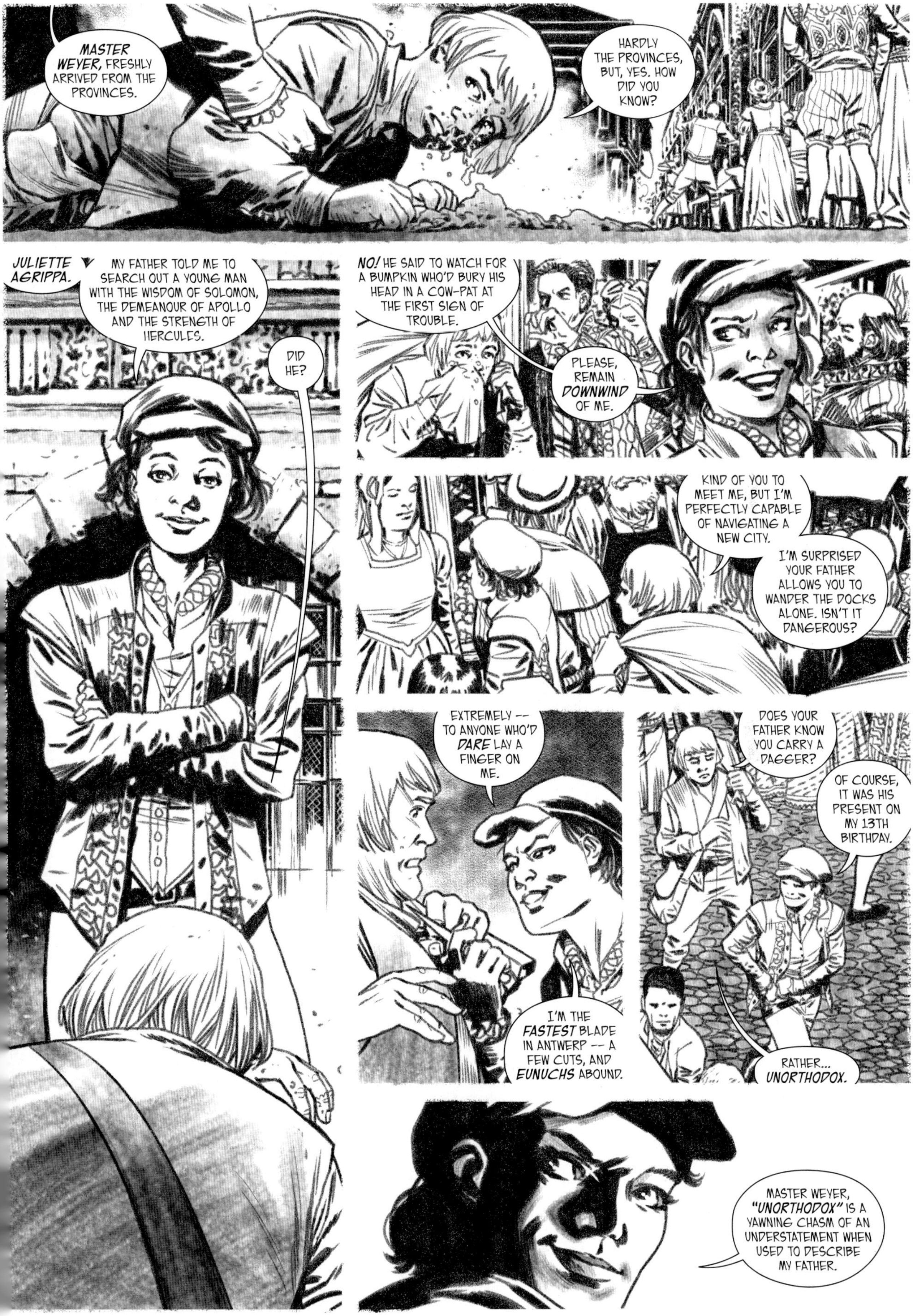
MASTER WEYER, FRESHLY ARRIVED FROM THE PROVINCES.
HARDLY THE PROVINCES, BUT, YES. HOW DID YOU KNOW?
JULIETTE AGRIPPA.
MY FATHER TOLD ME TO SEARCH OUT A YOUNG MAN WITH THE WISDOM OF SOLOMON, THE DEMEANOUR OF APOLLO AND THE STRENGTH OF HERCULES.
DID HE?
NO! HE SAID TO WATCH FOR A BUMPKIN WHO'D BURY HIS HEAD IN A COW-PAT AT THE FIRST SIGN OF TROUBLE.
PLEASE, REMAIN DOWNWIND OF ME.
KIND OF YOU TO MEET ME, BUT I'M PERFECTLY CAPABLE OF NAVIGATING A NEW CITY.
I'M SURPRISED YOUR FATHER ALLOWS YOU TO WANDER THE DOCKS ALONE. ISN'T IT DANGEROUS?
EXTREMELY -- TO ANYONE WHO'D DARE LAY A FINGER ON ME.
I'M THE FASTEST BLADE IN ANTWERP -- A FEW CUTS, AND EUNUCHS ABOUND.
DOES YOUR FATHER KNOW YOU CARRY A DAGGER?
OF COURSE, IT WAS HIS PRESENT ON MY 13TH BIRTHDAY.
RATHER... UNORTHODOX.
MASTER WEYER, "UNORTHODOX" IS A YAWNING CHASM OF AN UNDERSTATEMENT WHEN USED TO DESCRIBE MY FATHER.

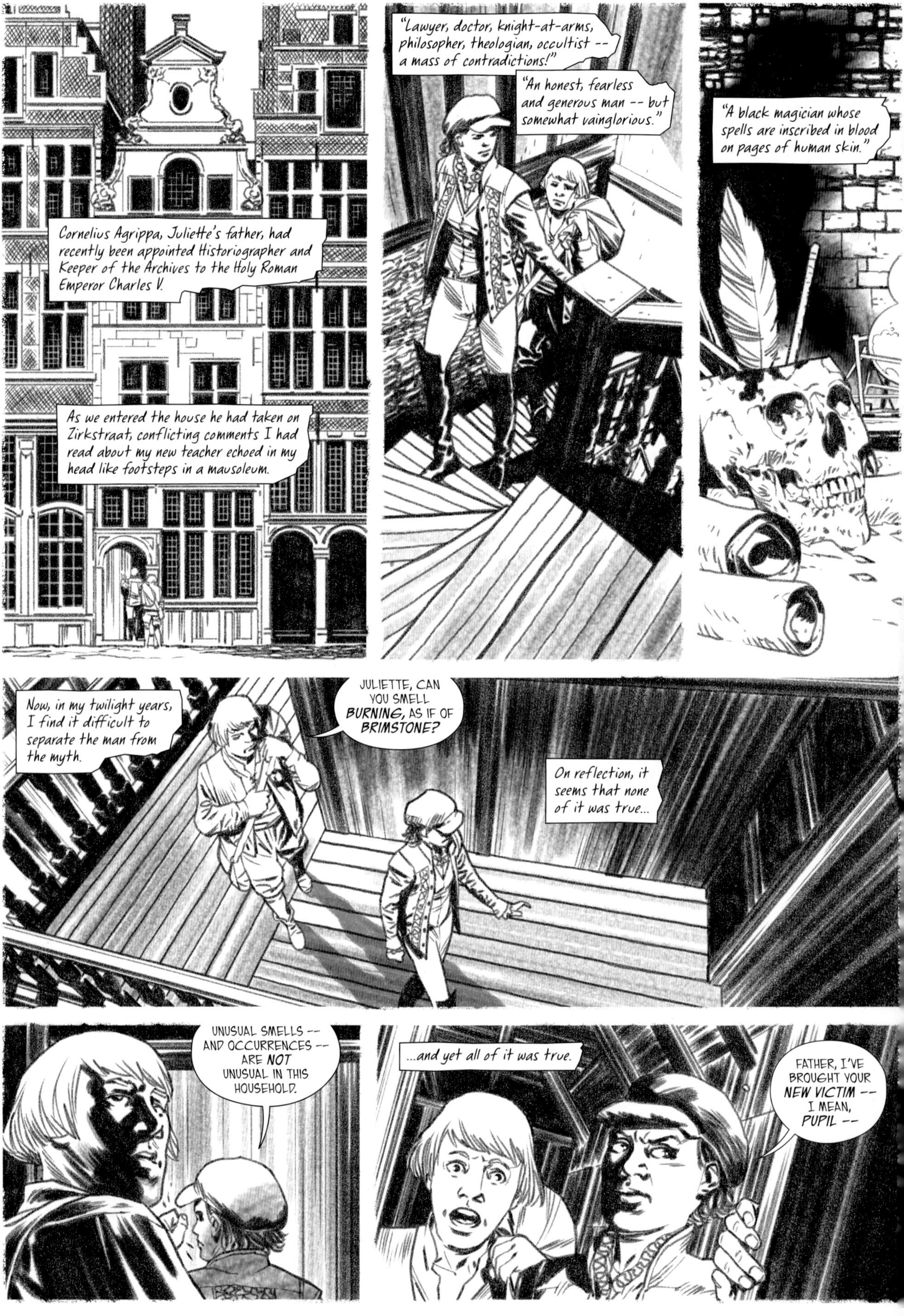

Cornelius Agrippa, Juliette's father, had recently been appointed Historiographer and Keeper of the Archives to the Holy Roman Emperor Charles V.
As we entered the house he had taken on Zirkstraat, conflicting comments I had read about my new teacher echoed in my head like footsteps in a mausoleum.
"Lawyer, doctor, knight-at-arms, philosopher, theologian, occultist -- a mass of contradictions!"
"An honest, fearless and generous man -- but somewhat vainglorious."
"A black magician whose spells are inscribed in blood on pages of human skin."
Now, in my twilight years, I find it difficult to separate the man from the myth.
JULIETTE, CAN YOU SMELL **BURNING,** AS IF OF **BRIMSTONE?**
On reflection, it seems that none of it was true...
UNUSUAL SMELLS -- AND OCCURRENCES -- ARE **NOT** UNUSUAL IN THIS HOUSEHOLD.
...and yet all of it was true.
FATHER, I'VE BROUGHT YOUR **NEW VICTIM** -- I MEAN, **PUPIL** --

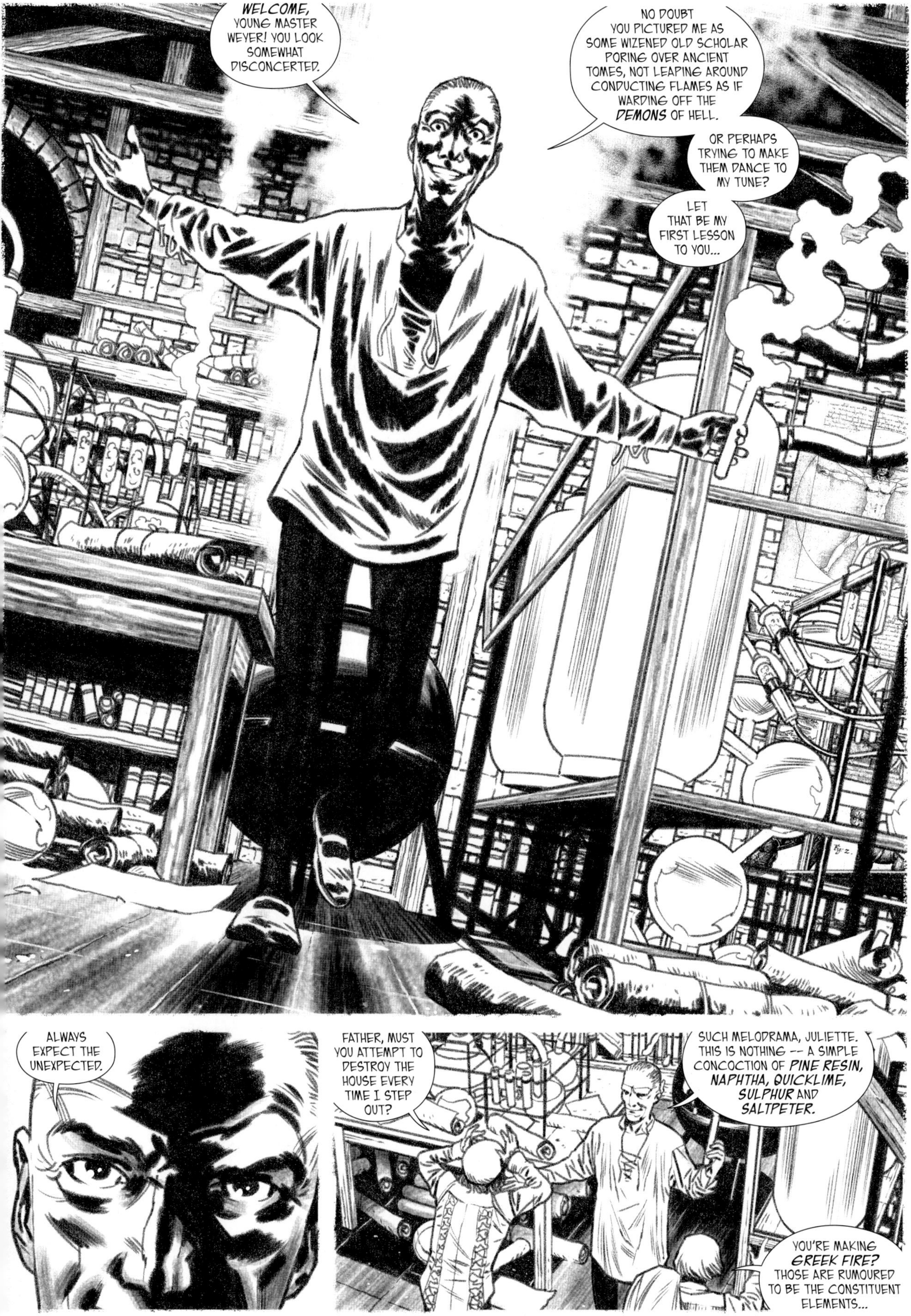
WELCOME, YOUNG MASTER WEYER! YOU LOOK SOMEWHAT DISCONCERTED.
NO DOUBT YOU PICTURED ME AS SOME WIZENED OLD SCHOLAR PORING OVER ANCIENT TOMES, NOT LEAPING AROUND CONDUCTING FLAMES AS IF WARDING OFF THE DEMONS OF HELL.
OR PERHAPS TRYING TO MAKE THEM DANCE TO MY TUNE?
LET THAT BE MY FIRST LESSON TO YOU...
ALWAYS EXPECT THE UNEXPECTED.
FATHER, MUST YOU ATTEMPT TO DESTROY THE HOUSE EVERY TIME I STEP OUT?
SUCH MELODRAMA, JULIETTE. THIS IS NOTHING -- A SIMPLE CONCOCTION OF PINE RESIN, NAPHTHA, QUICKLIME, SULPHUR AND SALTPETER.
YOU'RE MAKING GREEK FIRE? THOSE ARE RUMOURED TO BE THE CONSTITUENT ELEMENTS...

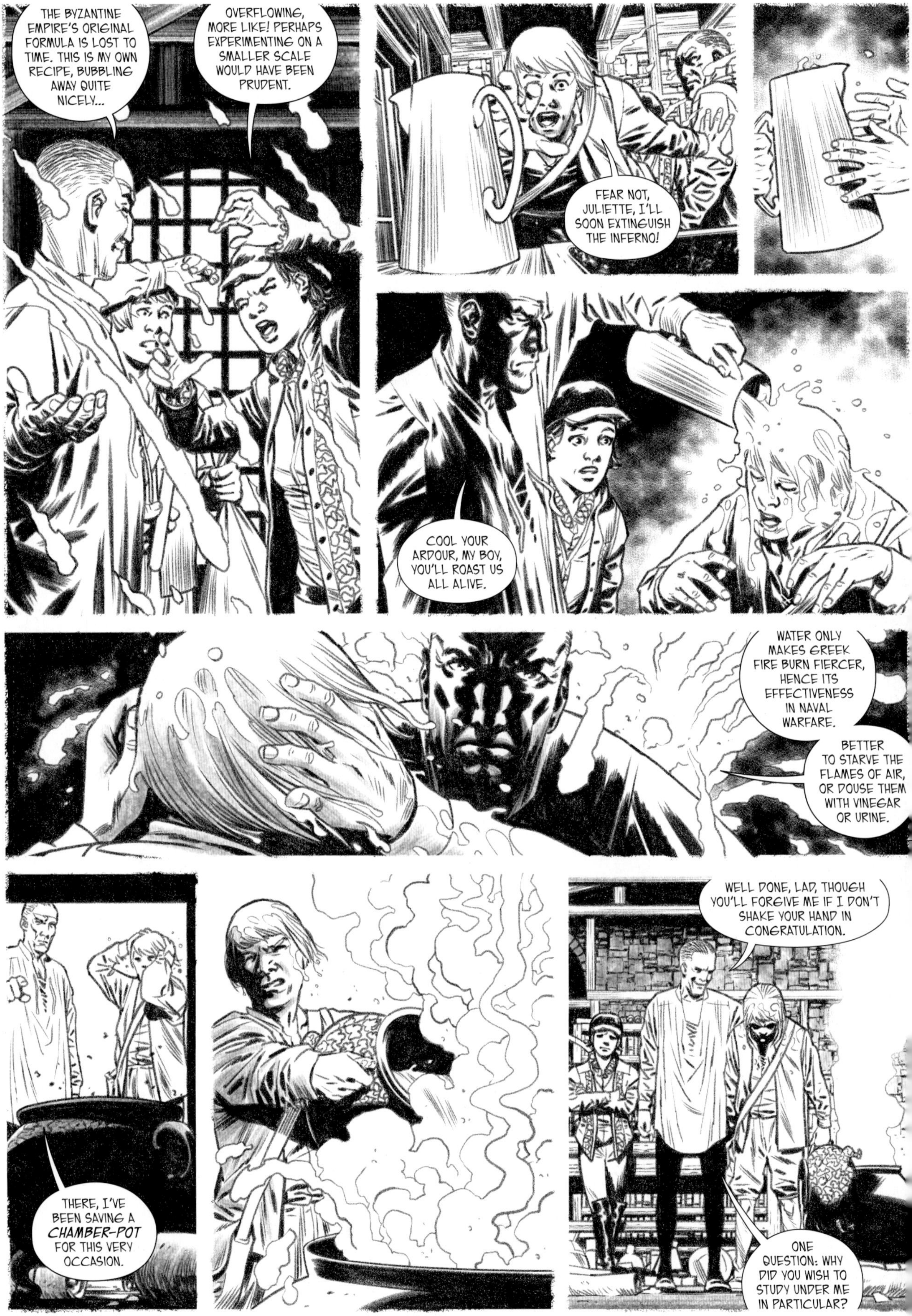
THE BYZANTINE EMPIRE'S ORIGINAL FORMULA IS LOST TO TIME. THIS IS MY OWN RECIPE, BUBBLING AWAY QUITE NICELY...
OVERFLOWING, MORE LIKE! PERHAPS EXPERIMENTING ON A SMALLER SCALE WOULD HAVE BEEN PRUDENT.
FEAR NOT, JULIETTE, I'LL SOON EXTINGUISH THE INFERNO!
COOL YOUR ARDOUR, MY BOY, YOU'LL ROAST US ALL ALIVE.
WATER ONLY MAKES GREEK FIRE BURN FIERCER, HENCE ITS EFFECTIVENESS IN NAVAL WARFARE.
BETTER TO STARVE THE FLAMES OF AIR, OR DOUSE THEM WITH VINEGAR OR URINE.
THERE, I'VE BEEN SAVING A *CHAMBER-POT* FOR THIS VERY OCCASION.
WELL DONE, LAD, THOUGH YOU'LL FORGIVE ME IF I DON'T SHAKE YOUR HAND IN CONGRATULATION.
ONE QUESTION: WHY DID YOU WISH TO STUDY UNDER ME IN PARTICULAR?

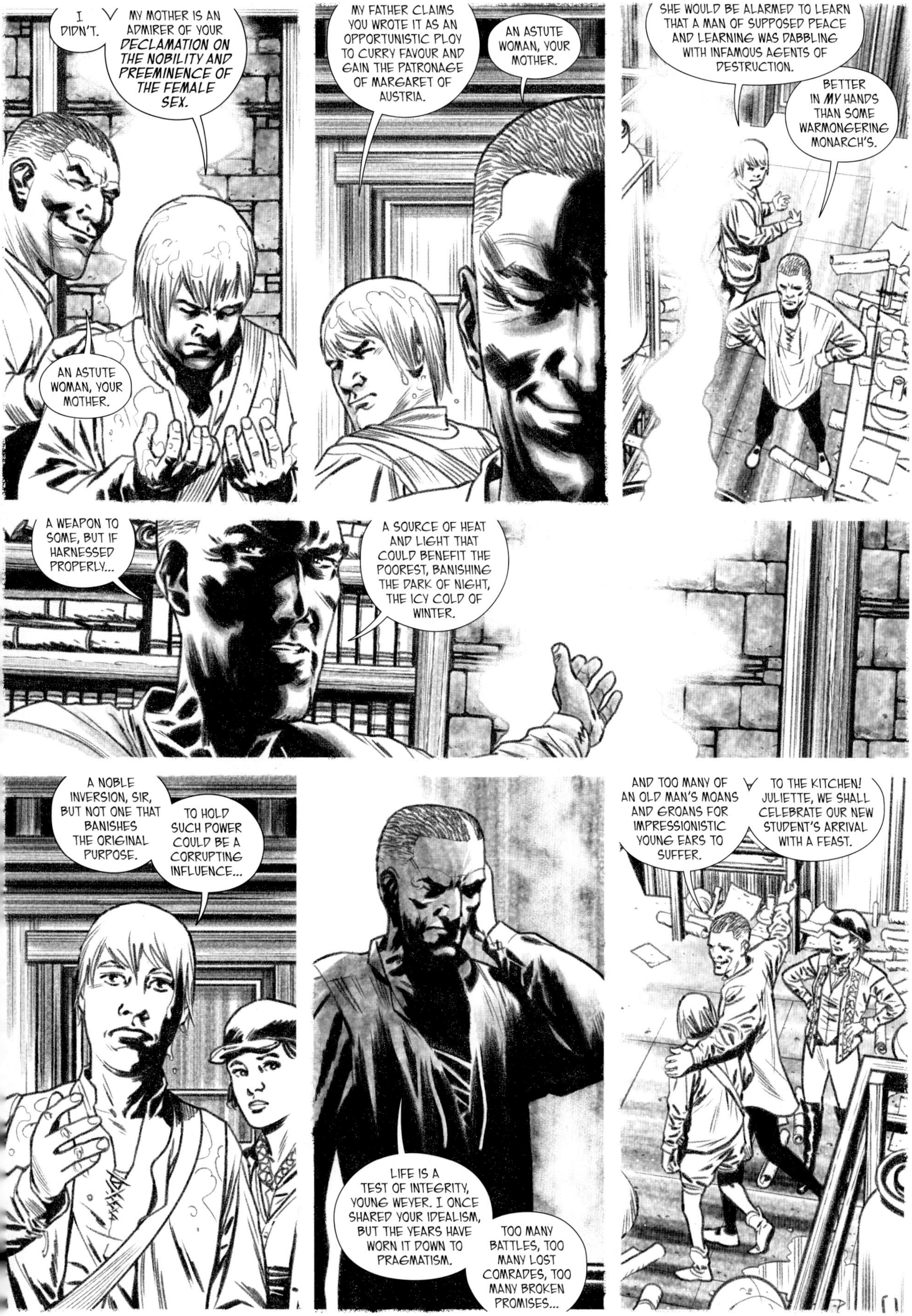
I DIDN'T.
MY MOTHER IS AN ADMIRER OF YOUR DECLAMATION ON THE NOBILITY AND PREEMINENCE OF THE FEMALE SEX.
AN ASTUTE WOMAN, YOUR MOTHER.
MY FATHER CLAIMS YOU WROTE IT AS AN OPPORTUNISTIC PLOY TO CURRY FAVOUR AND GAIN THE PATRONAGE OF MARGARET OF AUSTRIA.
AN ASTUTE WOMAN, YOUR MOTHER.
SHE WOULD BE ALARMED TO LEARN THAT A MAN OF SUPPOSED PEACE AND LEARNING WAS DABBLING WITH INFAMOUS AGENTS OF DESTRUCTION.
BETTER IN MY HANDS THAN SOME WARMONGERING MONARCH'S.
A WEAPON TO SOME, BUT IF HARNESSED PROPERLY...
A SOURCE OF HEAT AND LIGHT THAT COULD BENEFIT THE POOREST, BANISHING THE DARK OF NIGHT, THE ICY COLD OF WINTER.
A NOBLE INVERSION, SIR, BUT NOT ONE THAT BANISHES THE ORIGINAL PURPOSE.
TO HOLD SUCH POWER COULD BE A CORRUPTING INFLUENCE...
LIFE IS A TEST OF INTEGRITY, YOUNG WEYER. I ONCE SHARED YOUR IDEALISM, BUT THE YEARS HAVE WORN IT DOWN TO PRAGMATISM.
TOO MANY BATTLES, TOO MANY LOST COMRADES, TOO MANY BROKEN PROMISES...
AND TOO MANY OF AN OLD MAN'S MOANS AND GROANS FOR IMPRESSIONISTIC YOUNG EARS TO SUFFER.
TO THE KITCHEN! JULIETTE, WE SHALL CELEBRATE OUR NEW STUDENT'S ARRIVAL WITH A FEAST.

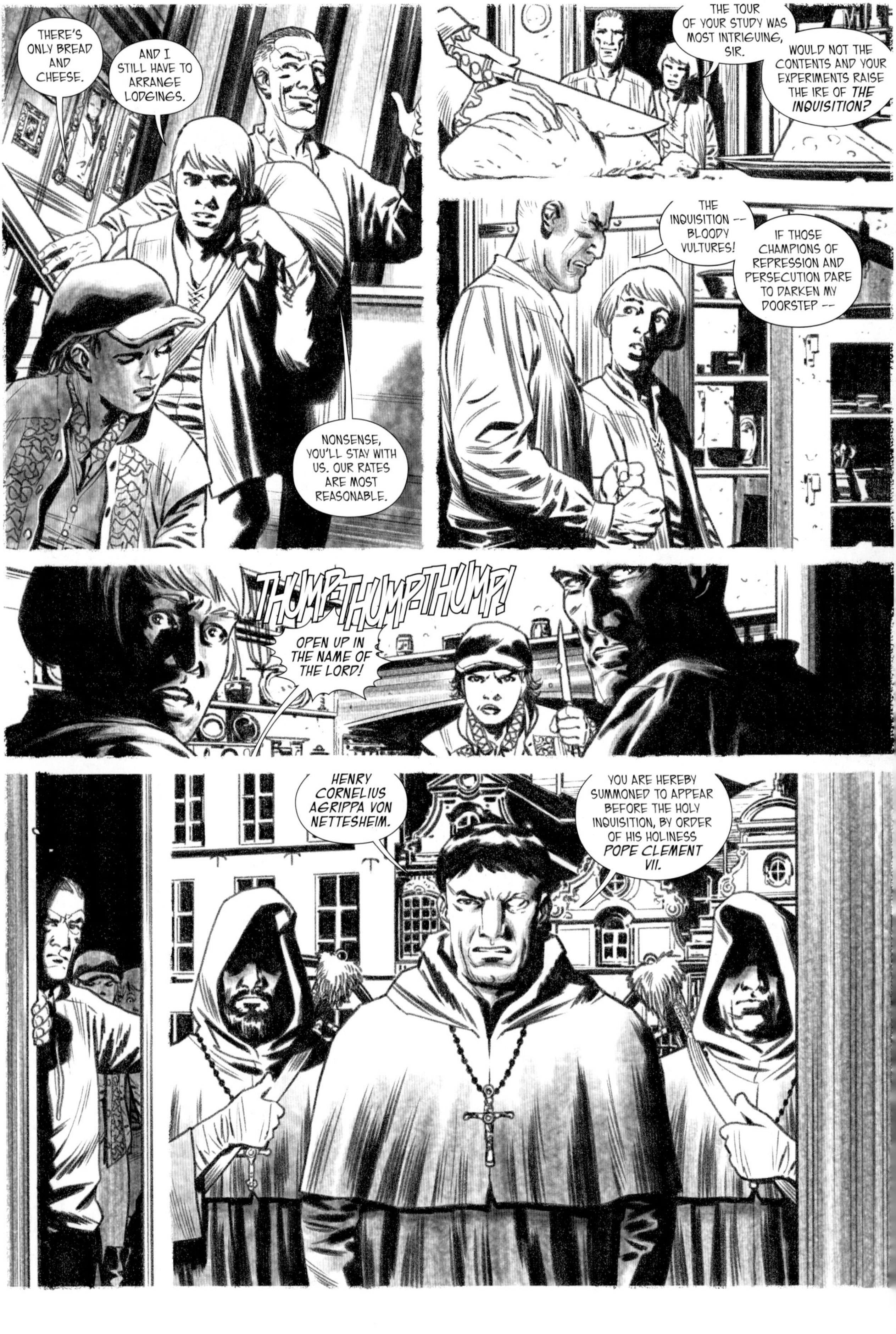
THERE'S ONLY BREAD AND CHEESE.
AND I STILL HAVE TO ARRANGE LODGINGS.
NONSENSE, YOU'LL STAY WITH US. OUR RATES ARE MOST REASONABLE.
THE TOUR OF YOUR STUDY WAS MOST INTRIGUING, SIR.
WOULD NOT THE CONTENTS AND YOUR EXPERIMENTS RAISE THE IRE OF *THE INQUISITION?*
THE INQUISITION -- BLOODY VULTURES!
IF THOSE CHAMPIONS OF REPRESSION AND PERSECUTION DARE TO DARKEN MY DOORSTEP --
THUMP-THUMP-THUMP!
OPEN UP IN THE NAME OF THE LORD!
HENRY CORNELIUS AGRIPPA VON NETTESHEIM.
YOU ARE HEREBY SUMMONED TO APPEAR BEFORE THE HOLY INQUISITION, BY ORDER OF HIS HOLINESS *POPE CLEMENT VII.*

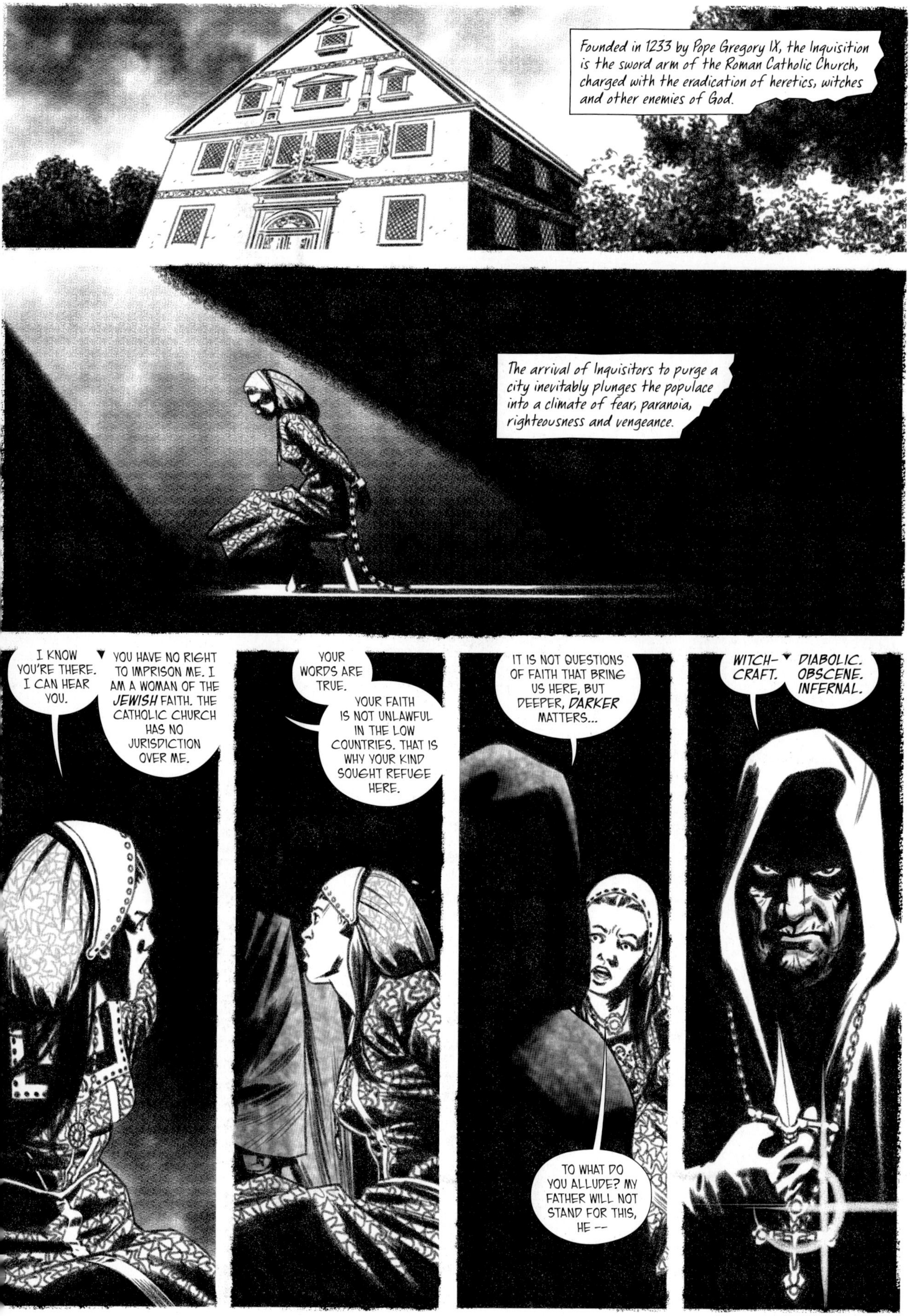
Founded in 1233 by Pope Gregory IX, the Inquisition is the sword arm of the Roman Catholic Church, charged with the eradication of heretics, witches and other enemies of God.
The arrival of Inquisitors to purge a city inevitably plunges the populace into a climate of fear, paranoia, righteousness and vengeance.
I KNOW YOU'RE THERE. I CAN HEAR YOU.
YOU HAVE NO RIGHT TO IMPRISON ME. I AM A WOMAN OF THE JEWISH FAITH. THE CATHOLIC CHURCH HAS NO JURISDICTION OVER ME.
YOUR WORDS ARE TRUE.
YOUR FAITH IS NOT UNLAWFUL IN THE LOW COUNTRIES. THAT IS WHY YOUR KIND SOUGHT REFUGE HERE.
IT IS NOT QUESTIONS OF FAITH THAT BRING US HERE, BUT DEEPER, DARKER MATTERS...
TO WHAT DO YOU ALLUDE? MY FATHER WILL NOT STAND FOR THIS, HE --
WITCH-CRAFT.
DIABOLIC. OBSCENE. INFERNAL.

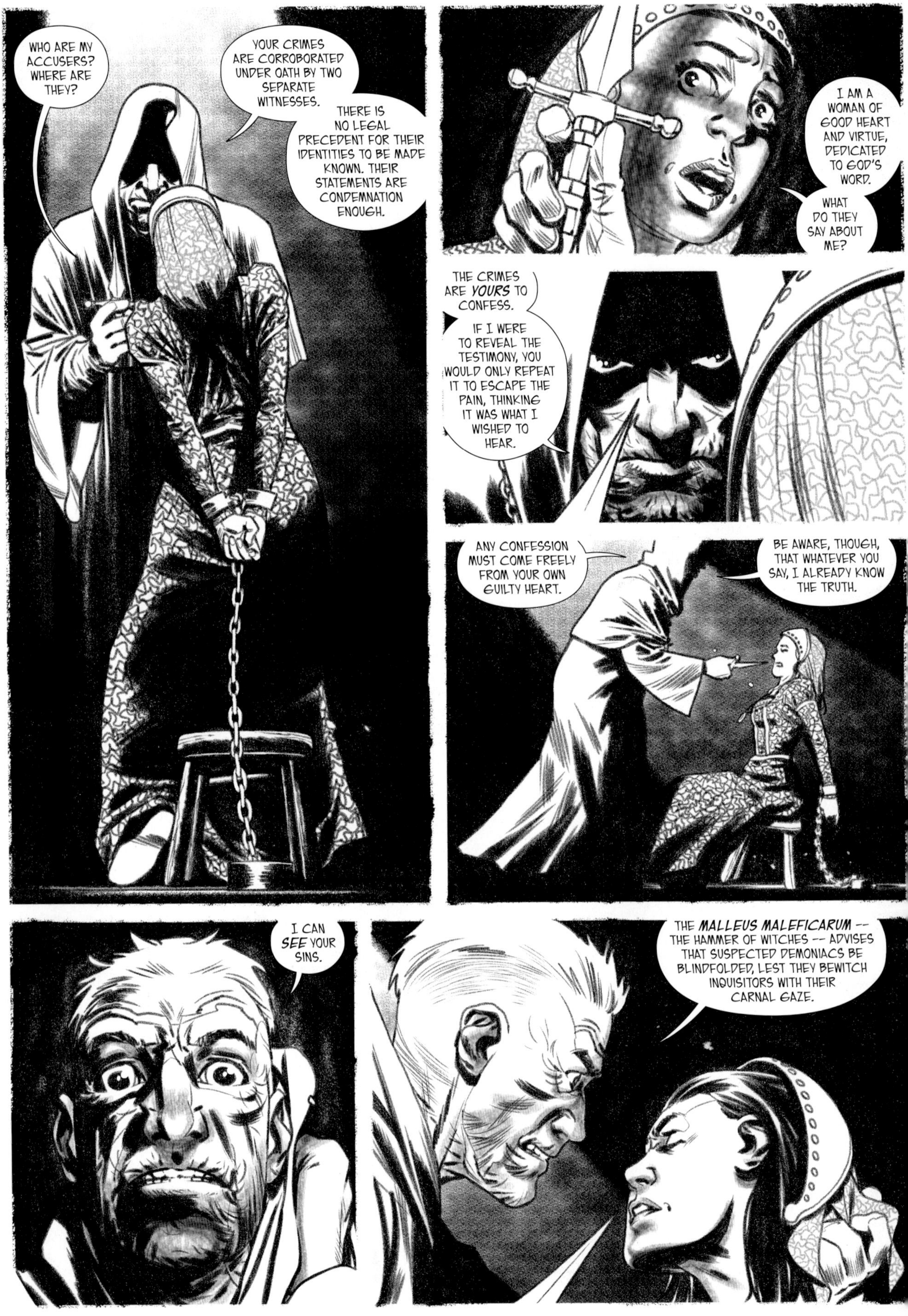
WHO ARE MY ACCUSERS? WHERE ARE THEY?
YOUR CRIMES ARE CORROBORATED UNDER OATH BY TWO SEPARATE WITNESSES.
THERE IS NO LEGAL PRECEDENT FOR THEIR IDENTITIES TO BE MADE KNOWN. THEIR STATEMENTS ARE CONDEMNATION ENOUGH.
I AM A WOMAN OF GOOD HEART AND VIRTUE, DEDICATED TO GOD'S WORD.
WHAT DO THEY SAY ABOUT ME?
THE CRIMES ARE YOURS TO CONFESS.
IF I WERE TO REVEAL THE TESTIMONY, YOU WOULD ONLY REPEAT IT TO ESCAPE THE PAIN, THINKING IT WAS WHAT I WISHED TO HEAR.
ANY CONFESSION MUST COME FREELY FROM YOUR OWN GUILTY HEART.
BE AWARE, THOUGH, THAT WHATEVER YOU SAY, I ALREADY KNOW THE TRUTH.
I CAN SEE YOUR SINS.
THE MALLEUS MALEFICARUM -- THE HAMMER OF WITCHES -- ADVISES THAT SUSPECTED DEMONIACS BE BLINDFOLDED, LEST THEY BEWITCH INQUISITORS WITH THEIR CARNAL GAZE.

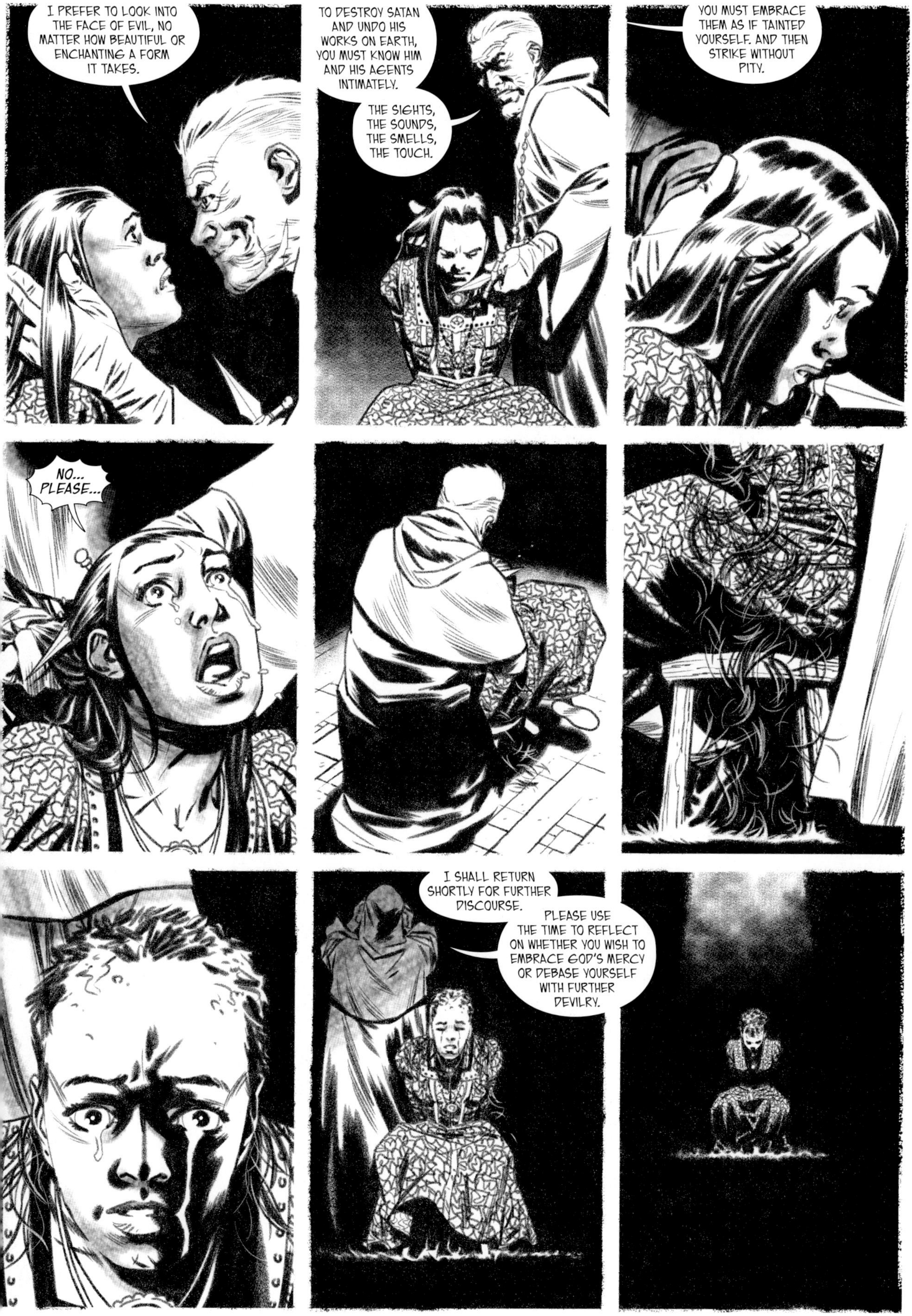
I PREFER TO LOOK INTO THE FACE OF EVIL, NO MATTER HOW BEAUTIFUL OR ENCHANTING A FORM IT TAKES.
TO DESTROY SATAN AND UNDO HIS WORKS ON EARTH, YOU MUST KNOW HIM AND HIS AGENTS INTIMATELY.
THE SIGHTS, THE SOUNDS, THE SMELLS, THE TOUCH.
YOU MUST EMBRACE THEM AS IF TAINTED YOURSELF. AND THEN STRIKE WITHOUT PITY.
NO... PLEASE...
I SHALL RETURN SHORTLY FOR FURTHER DISCOURSE.
PLEASE USE THE TIME TO REFLECT ON WHETHER YOU WISH TO EMBRACE GOD'S MERCY OR DEBASE YOURSELF WITH FURTHER DEVILRY.

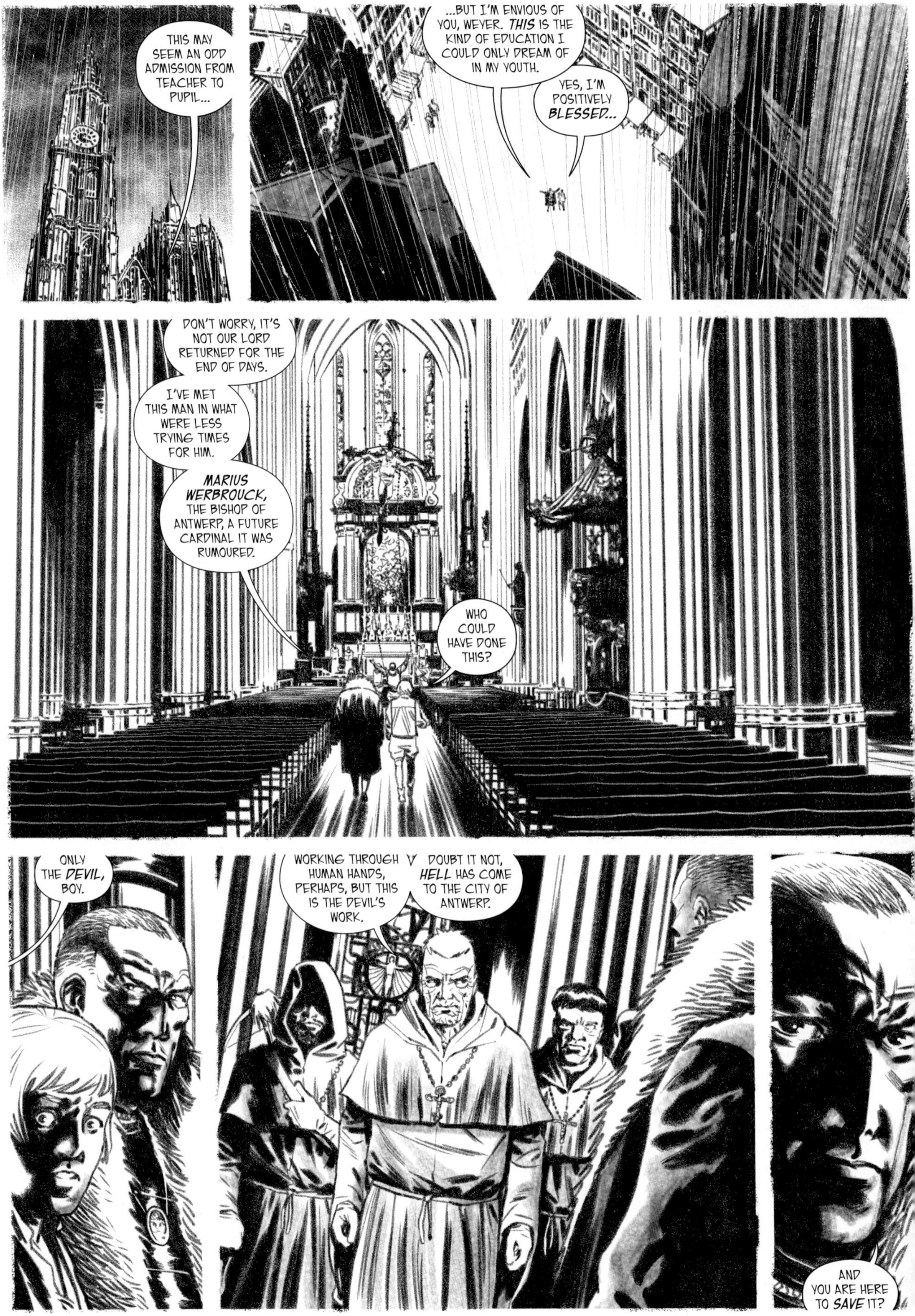
THIS MAY SEEM AN ODD ADMISSION FROM TEACHER TO PUPIL...
...BUT I'M ENVIOUS OF YOU, WEYER. THIS IS THE KIND OF EDUCATION I COULD ONLY DREAM OF IN MY YOUTH.
YES, I'M POSITIVELY BLESSED...
DON'T WORRY, IT'S NOT OUR LORD RETURNED FOR THE END OF DAYS.
I'VE MET THIS MAN IN WHAT WERE LESS TRYING TIMES FOR HIM.
MARIUS WERBROUCK, THE BISHOP OF ANTWERP, A FUTURE CARDINAL IT WAS RUMOURED.
WHO COULD HAVE DONE THIS?
ONLY THE DEVIL, BOY.
WORKING THROUGH HUMAN HANDS, PERHAPS, BUT THIS IS THE DEVIL'S WORK.
DOUBT IT NOT, HELL HAS COME TO THE CITY OF ANTWERP.
AND YOU ARE HERE TO SAVE IT?

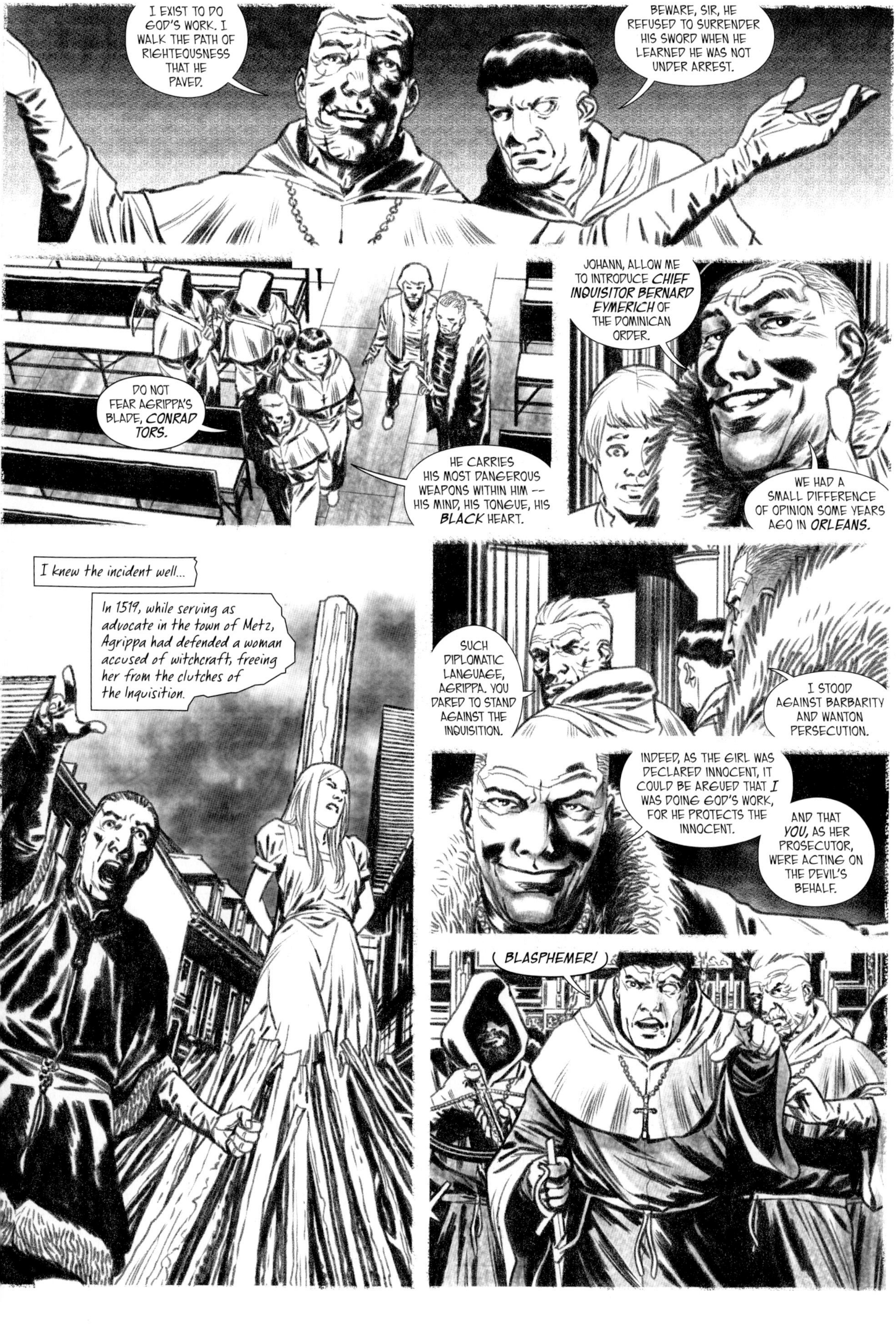

I EXIST TO DO GOD'S WORK. I WALK THE PATH OF RIGHTEOUSNESS THAT HE PAVED.
BEWARE, SIR, HE REFUSED TO SURRENDER HIS SWORD WHEN HE LEARNED HE WAS NOT UNDER ARREST.
DO NOT FEAR AGRIPPA'S BLADE, CONRAD TORS.
HE CARRIES HIS MOST DANGEROUS WEAPONS WITHIN HIM -- HIS MIND, HIS TONGUE, HIS BLACK HEART.
JOHANN, ALLOW ME TO INTRODUCE CHIEF INQUISITOR BERNARD EYMERICH OF THE DOMINICAN ORDER.
WE HAD A SMALL DIFFERENCE OF OPINION SOME YEARS AGO IN ORLEANS.
I knew the incident well...
In 1519, while serving as advocate in the town of Metz, Agrippa had defended a woman accused of witchcraft, freeing her from the clutches of the Inquisition.
SUCH DIPLOMATIC LANGUAGE, AGRIPPA. YOU DARED TO STAND AGAINST THE INQUISITION.
I STOOD AGAINST BARBARITY AND WANTON PERSECUTION.
INDEED, AS THE GIRL WAS DECLARED INNOCENT, IT COULD BE ARGUED THAT I WAS DOING GOD'S WORK, FOR HE PROTECTS THE INNOCENT.
AND THAT YOU, AS HER PROSECUTOR, WERE ACTING ON THE DEVIL'S BEHALF.
BLASPHEMER!

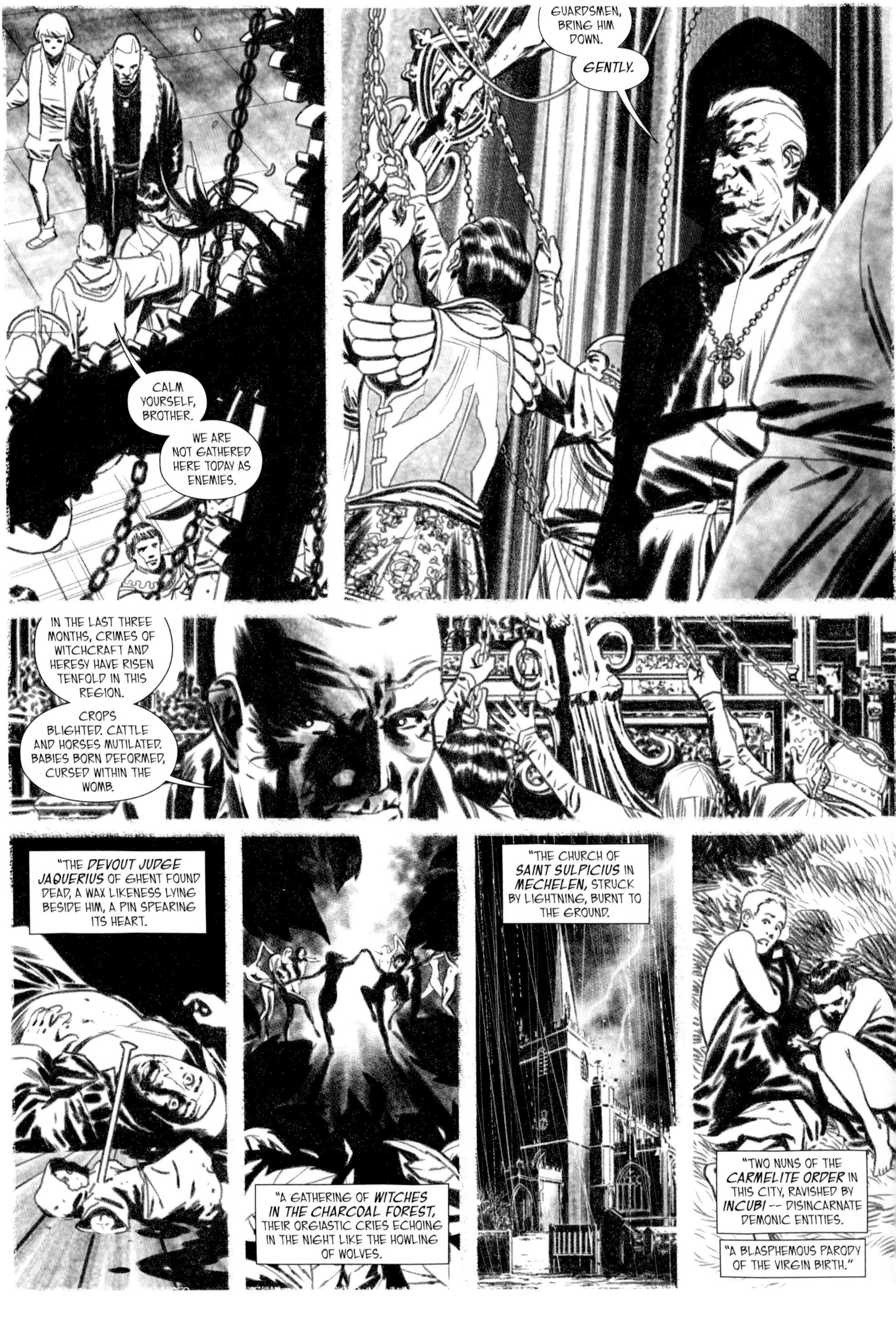
GUARDSMEN, BRING HIM DOWN.
GENTLY.
CALM YOURSELF, BROTHER.
WE ARE NOT GATHERED HERE TODAY AS ENEMIES.
IN THE LAST THREE MONTHS, CRIMES OF WITCHCRAFT AND HERESY HAVE RISEN TENFOLD IN THIS REGION.
CROPS BLIGHTED. CATTLE AND HORSES MUTILATED. BABIES BORN DEFORMED, CURSED WITHIN THE WOMB.
"THE DEVOUT JUDGE JAQUERIUS OF GHENT FOUND DEAD, A WAX LIKENESS LYING BESIDE HIM, A PIN SPEARING ITS HEART.
"A GATHERING OF WITCHES IN THE CHARCOAL FOREST, THEIR ORGIASTIC CRIES ECHOING IN THE NIGHT LIKE THE HOWLING OF WOLVES.
"THE CHURCH OF SAINT SULPICIUS IN MECHELEN, STRUCK BY LIGHTNING, BURNT TO THE GROUND.
"TWO NUNS OF THE CARMELITE ORDER IN THIS CITY, RAVISHED BY INCUBI -- DISINCARNATE DEMONIC ENTITIES.
"A BLASPHEMOUS PARODY OF THE VIRGIN BIRTH."

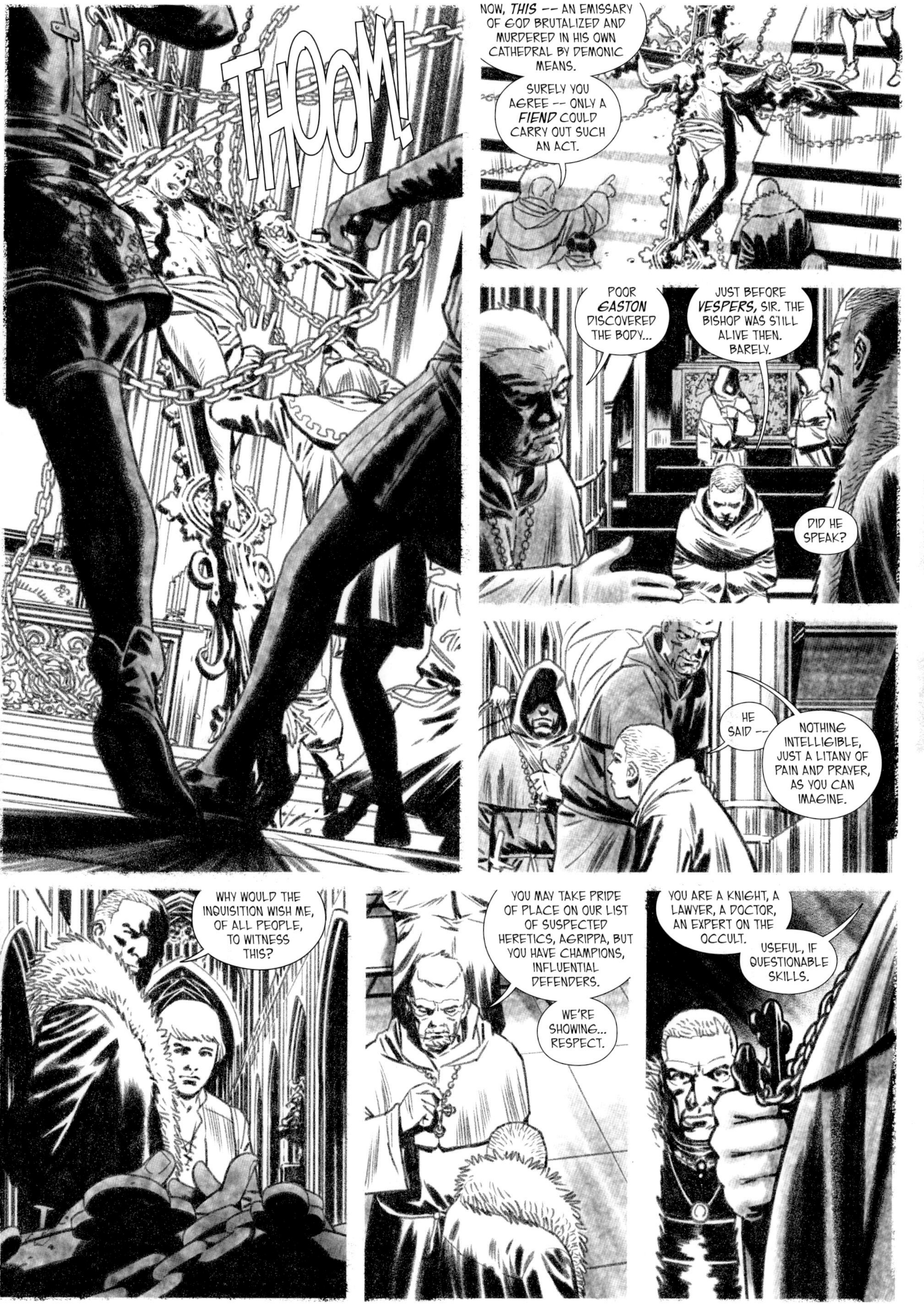
THOOM!
NOW, THIS -- AN EMISSARY OF GOD BRUTALIZED AND MURDERED IN HIS OWN CATHEDRAL BY DEMONIC MEANS.
SURELY YOU AGREE -- ONLY A FIEND COULD CARRY OUT SUCH AN ACT.
POOR GASTON DISCOVERED THE BODY...
JUST BEFORE VESPERS, SIR. THE BISHOP WAS STILL ALIVE THEN. BARELY.
DID HE SPEAK?
HE SAID --
NOTHING INTELLIGIBLE, JUST A LITANY OF PAIN AND PRAYER, AS YOU CAN IMAGINE.
WHY WOULD THE INQUISITION WISH ME, OF ALL PEOPLE, TO WITNESS THIS?
YOU MAY TAKE PRIDE OF PLACE ON OUR LIST OF SUSPECTED HERETICS, AGRIPPA, BUT YOU HAVE CHAMPIONS, INFLUENTIAL DEFENDERS.
WE'RE SHOWING... RESPECT.
YOU ARE A KNIGHT, A LAWYER, A DOCTOR, AN EXPERT ON THE OCCULT.
USEFUL, IF QUESTIONABLE SKILLS.

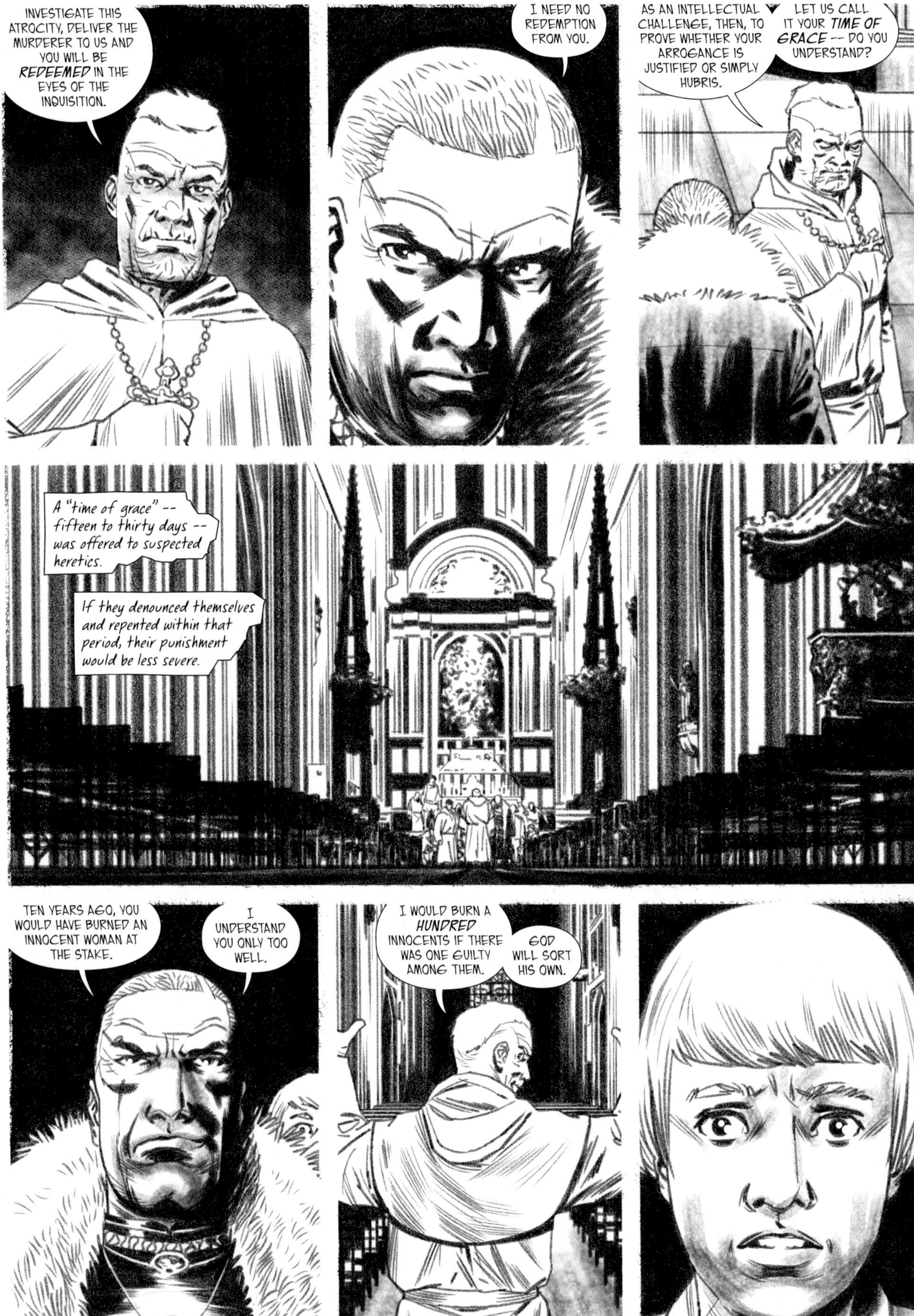
INVESTIGATE THIS ATROCITY, DELIVER THE MURDERER TO US AND YOU WILL BE *REDEEMED* IN THE EYES OF THE INQUISITION.
I NEED NO REDEMPTION FROM YOU.
AS AN INTELLECTUAL CHALLENGE, THEN, TO PROVE WHETHER YOUR ARROGANCE IS JUSTIFIED OR SIMPLY HUBRIS.
LET US CALL IT YOUR *TIME OF GRACE* -- DO YOU UNDERSTAND?
A "time of grace" -- fifteen to thirty days -- was offered to suspected heretics.
If they denounced themselves and repented within that period, their punishment would be less severe.
TEN YEARS AGO, YOU WOULD HAVE BURNED AN INNOCENT WOMAN AT THE STAKE.
I UNDERSTAND YOU ONLY TOO WELL.
I WOULD BURN A *HUNDRED* INNOCENTS IF THERE WAS ONE GUILTY AMONG THEM.
GOD WILL SORT HIS OWN.

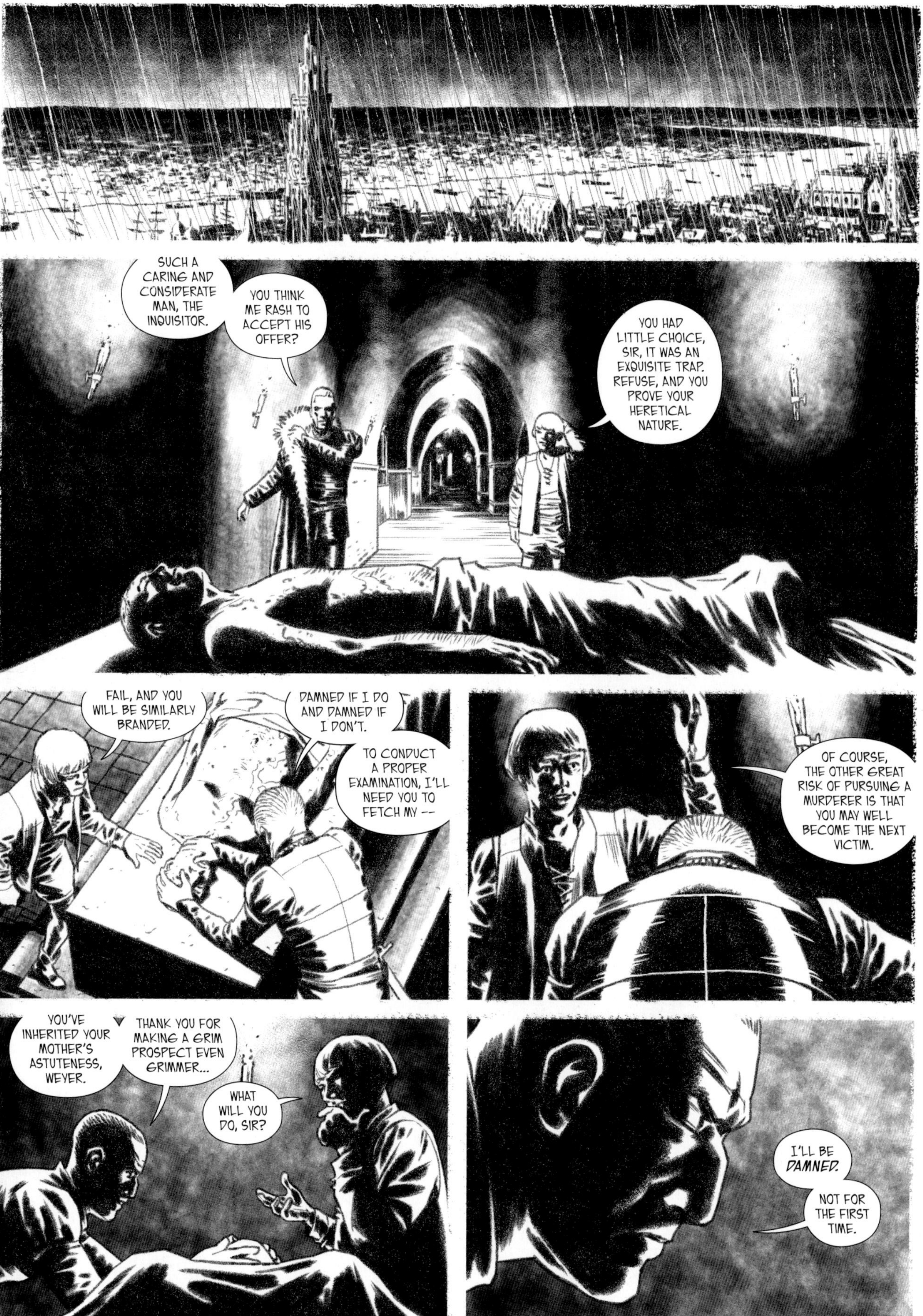

SUCH A CARING AND CONSIDERATE MAN, THE INQUISITOR.
YOU THINK ME RASH TO ACCEPT HIS OFFER?
YOU HAD LITTLE CHOICE, SIR, IT WAS AN EXQUISITE TRAP. REFUSE, AND YOU PROVE YOUR HERETICAL NATURE.
FAIL, AND YOU WILL BE SIMILARLY BRANDED.
DAMNED IF I DO AND DAMNED IF I DON'T.
TO CONDUCT A PROPER EXAMINATION, I'LL NEED YOU TO FETCH MY --
OF COURSE, THE OTHER GREAT RISK OF PURSUING A MURDERER IS THAT YOU MAY WELL BECOME THE NEXT VICTIM.
YOU'VE INHERITED YOUR MOTHER'S ASTUTENESS, WEYER.
THANK YOU FOR MAKING A GRIM PROSPECT EVEN GRIMMER...
WHAT WILL YOU DO, SIR?
I'LL BE *DAMNED.*
NOT FOR THE FIRST TIME.

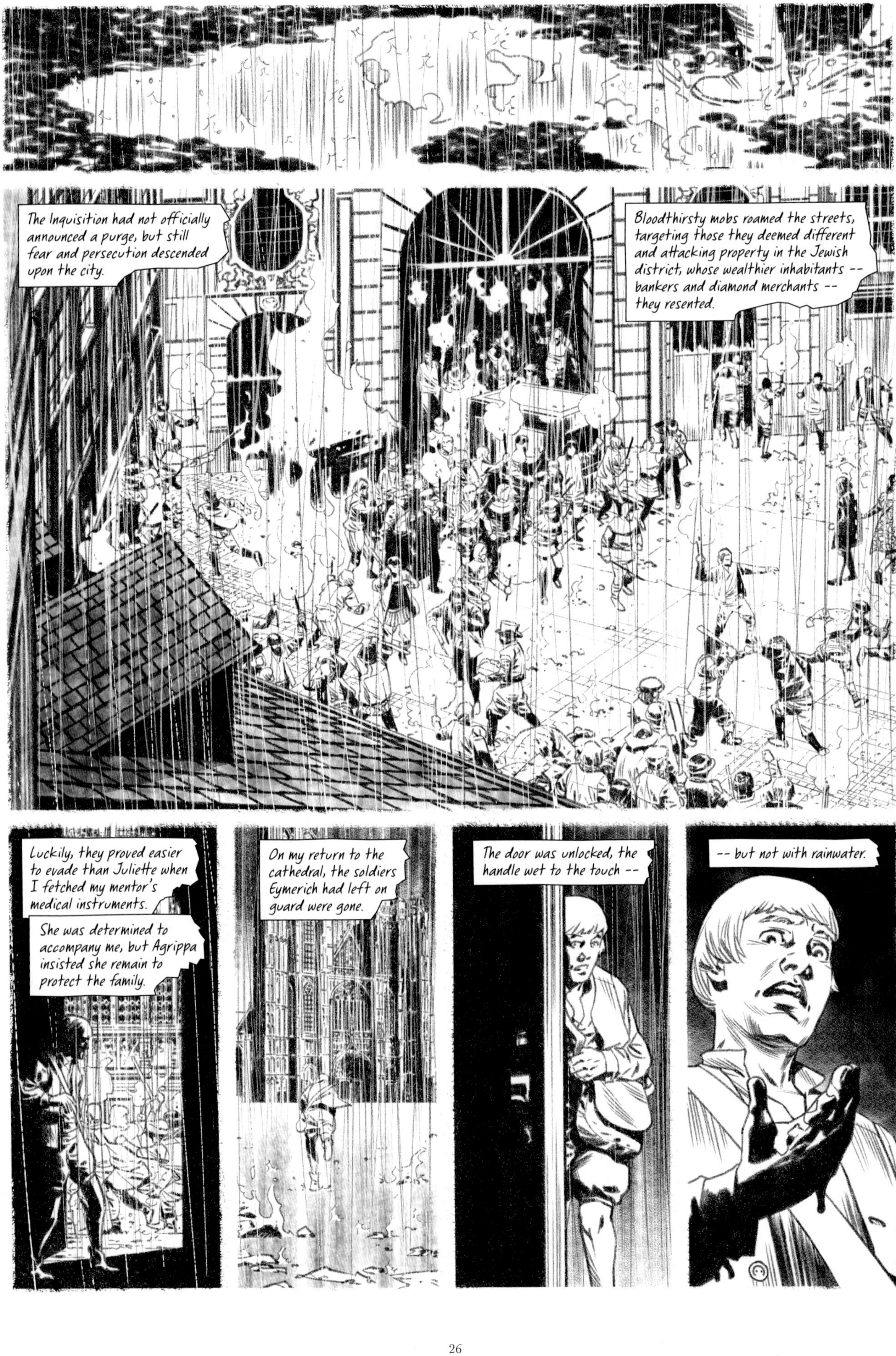
The Inquisition had not officially announced a purge, but still fear and persecution descended upon the city.
Bloodthirsty mobs roamed the streets, targeting those they deemed different and attacking property in the Jewish district, whose wealthier inhabitants -- bankers and diamond merchants -- they resented.
Luckily, they proved easier to evade than Juliette when I fetched my mentor's medical instruments.
She was determined to accompany me, but Agrippa insisted she remain to protect the family.
On my return to the cathedral, the soldiers Eymerich had left on guard were gone.
The door was unlocked, the handle wet to the touch --
-- but not with rainwater.

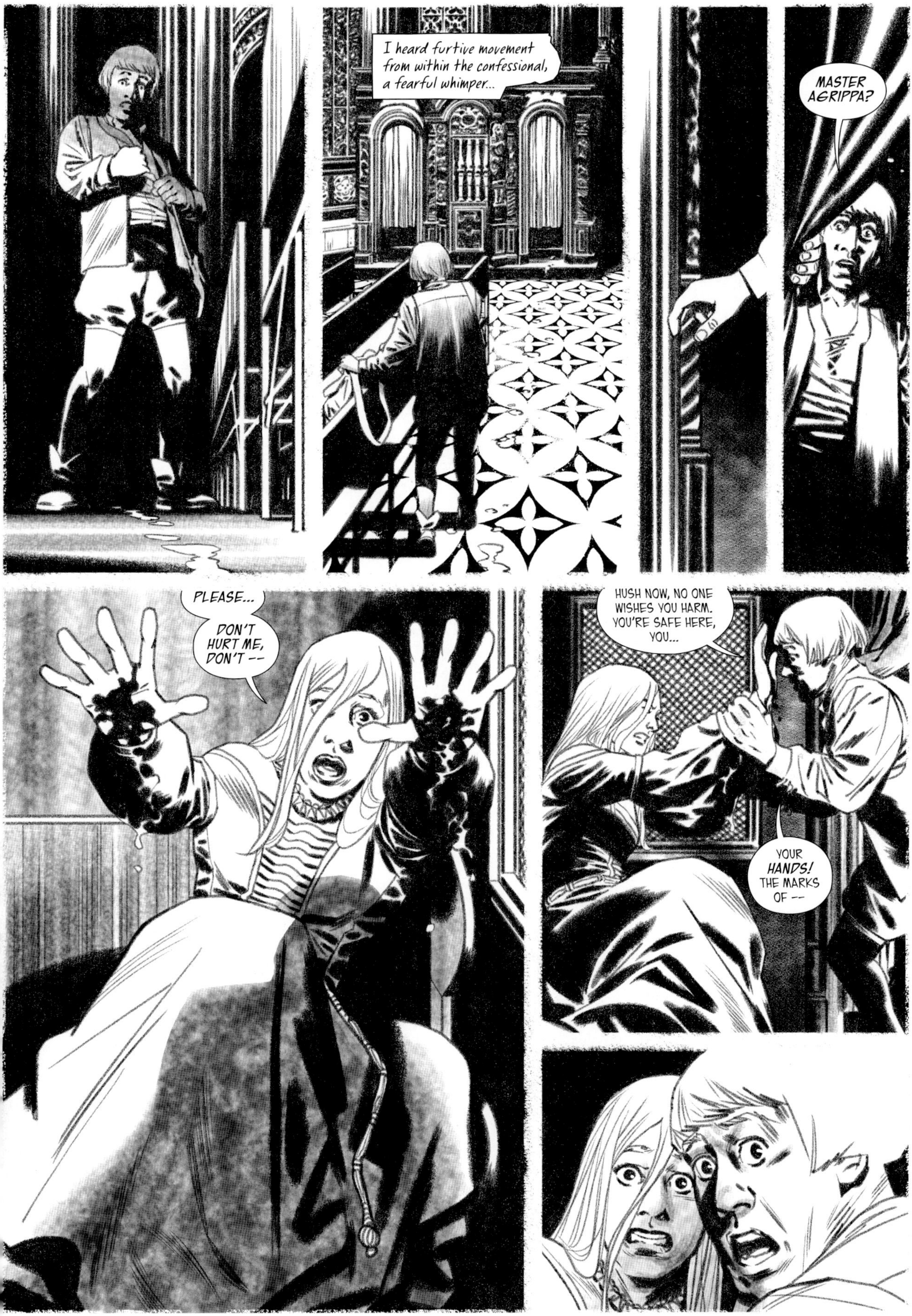
I heard furtive movement from within the confessional, a fearful whimper...
MASTER AGRIPPA?
PLEASE...
DON'T HURT ME, DON'T --
HUSH NOW, NO ONE WISHES YOU HARM. YOU'RE SAFE HERE, YOU...
YOUR HANDS! THE MARKS OF --

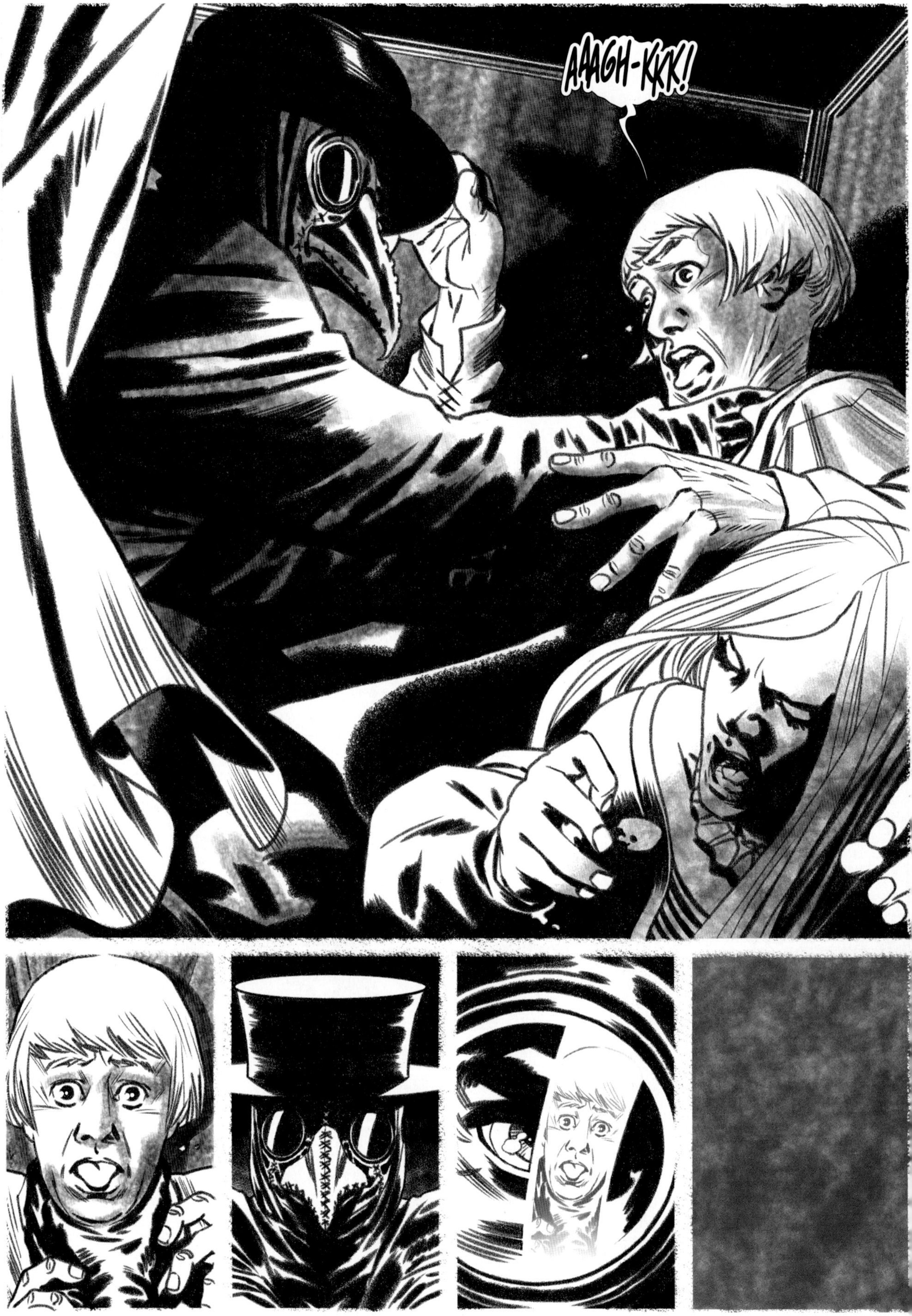
AAAGH-KKK!

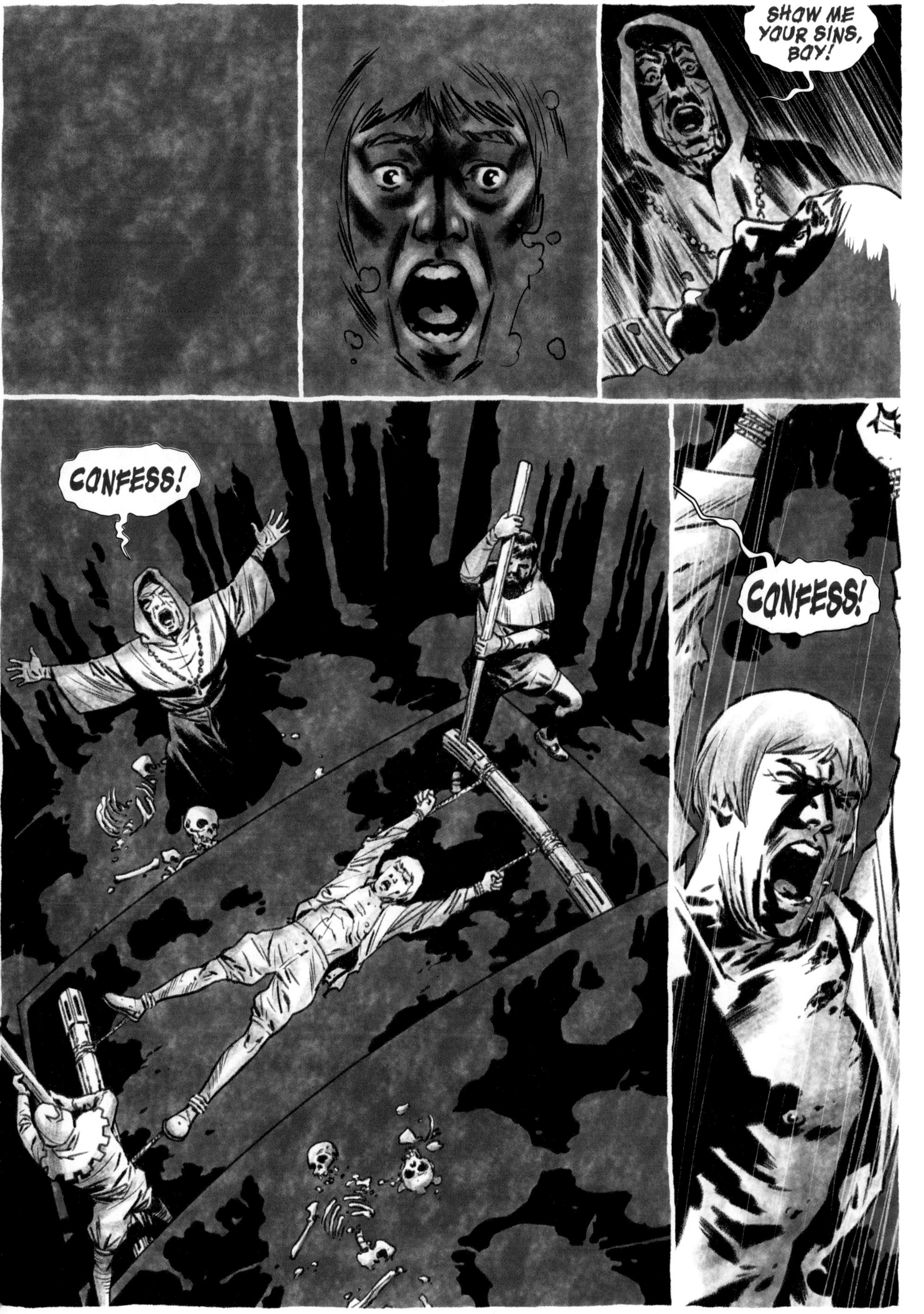
SHOW ME YOUR SINS, BOY!
CONFESS!
CONFESS!

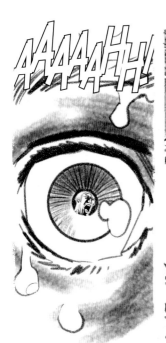

AAAAAHH!

TOLD YOU HE WAS ALIVE.

LIAR! YOU SAID PAPA WAS GOING TO DISSECT HIM, LIKE THAT FROG.

I'LL TURN HIM INTO A FROG WITH ONE OF PAPA'S SPELLS IF HE DOESN'T GET OUT OF MY BED.

OUT!

TELL FATHER OUR GUEST IS AWAKE.

THERE WAS A GIRL WITH BLOODY HANDS AND A... A CREATURE...

HUSH, CHILD, YOU'RE SAFE NOW. I'M ISABELLA, CORNELIUS'S WIFE.

MY WICKED STEPMOTHER.

YOU'RE LUCKY SHE ONLY PUT YOU TO BED. SHE LOCKS ME IN THE CELLAR.

IT'S THE ONLY WAY TO KEEP YOU OUT OF TROUBLE, JULIETTE.

YOU'VE KEPT US IN GREAT SUSPENSE SINCE I DISCOVERED YOU UNCONSCIOUS IN THE CONFESSIONAL, LAD.

EITHER YOU WERE OVERWHELMED BY THE WEIGHT OF YOUR SINS OR YOU HAVE QUITE THE STORY TO TELL...

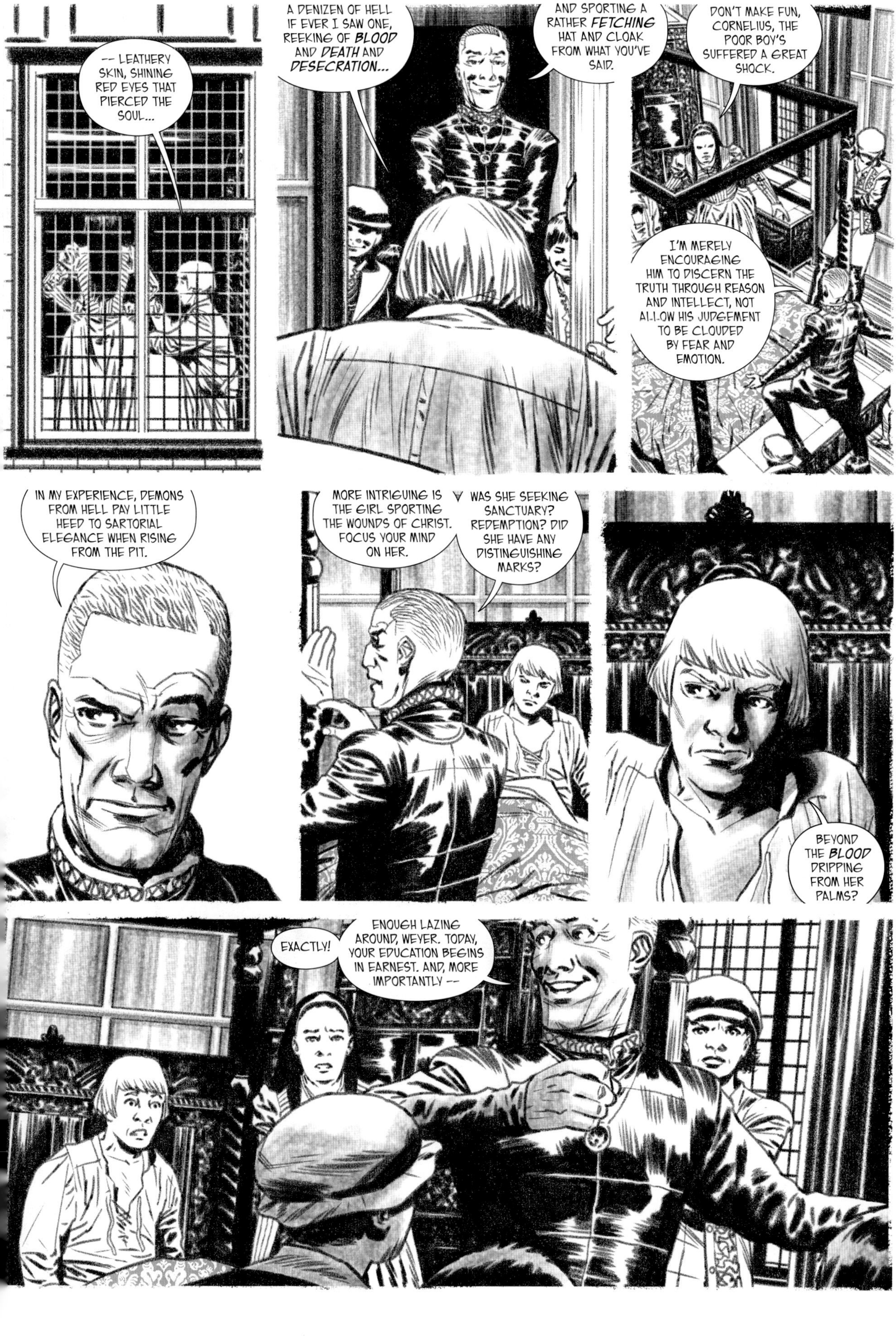
-- LEATHERY SKIN, SHINING RED EYES THAT PIERCED THE SOUL...
A DENIZEN OF HELL IF EVER I SAW ONE, REEKING OF BLOOD AND DEATH AND DESECRATION...
AND SPORTING A RATHER FETCHING HAT AND CLOAK FROM WHAT YOU'VE SAID.
DON'T MAKE FUN, CORNELIUS, THE POOR BOY'S SUFFERED A GREAT SHOCK.
I'M MERELY ENCOURAGING HIM TO DISCERN THE TRUTH THROUGH REASON AND INTELLECT, NOT ALLOW HIS JUDGEMENT TO BE CLOUDED BY FEAR AND EMOTION.
IN MY EXPERIENCE, DEMONS FROM HELL PAY LITTLE HEED TO SARTORIAL ELEGANCE WHEN RISING FROM THE PIT.
MORE INTRIGUING IS THE GIRL SPORTING THE WOUNDS OF CHRIST. FOCUS YOUR MIND ON HER.
WAS SHE SEEKING SANCTUARY? REDEMPTION? DID SHE HAVE ANY DISTINGUISHING MARKS?
BEYOND THE BLOOD DRIPPING FROM HER PALMS?
EXACTLY!
ENOUGH LAZING AROUND, WEYER. TODAY, YOUR EDUCATION BEGINS IN EARNEST. AND, MORE IMPORTANTLY --

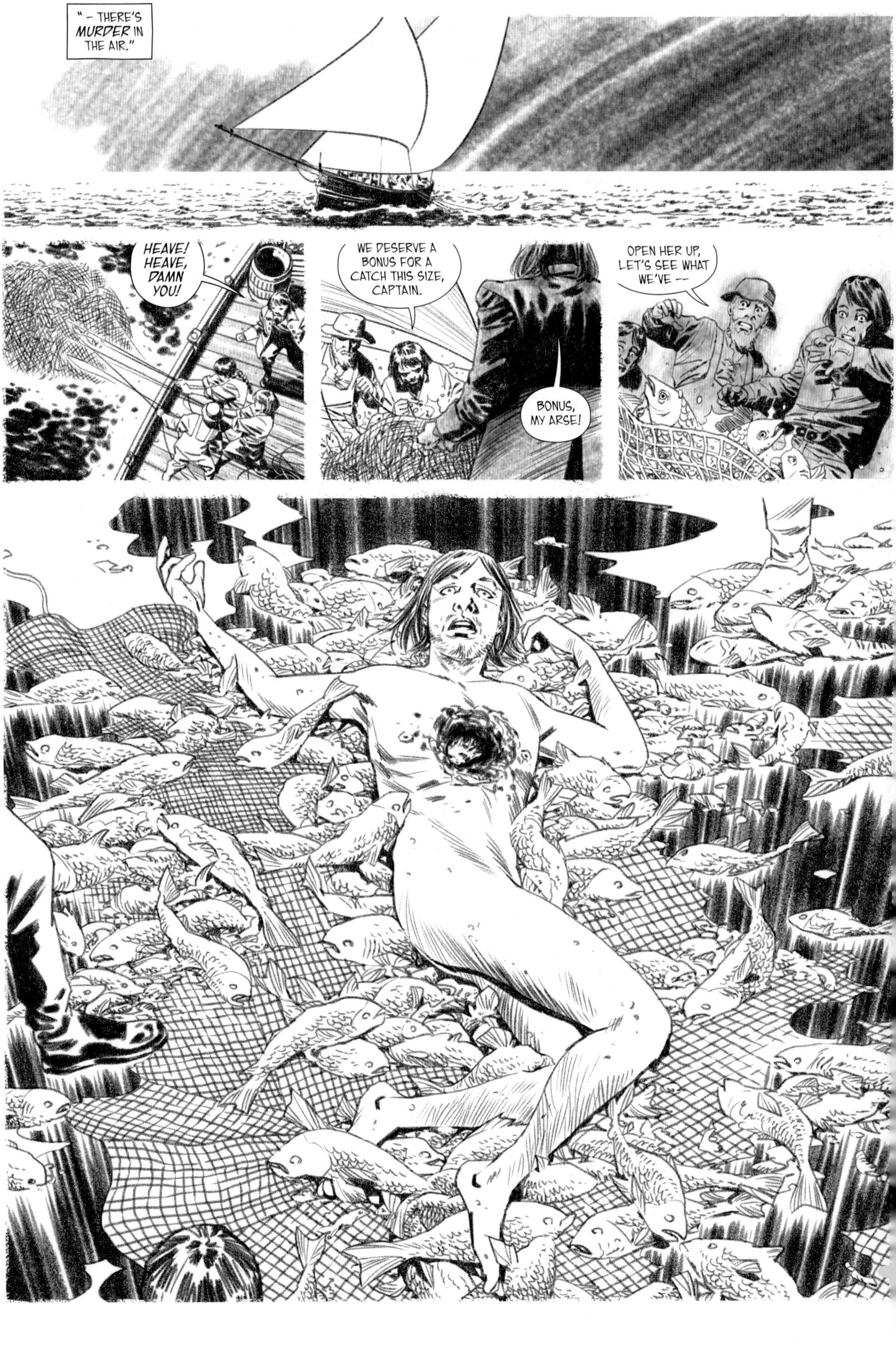
"– THERE'S MURDER IN THE AIR."
HEAVE! HEAVE, DAMN YOU!
WE DESERVE A BONUS FOR A CATCH THIS SIZE, CAPTAIN.
BONUS, MY ARSE!
OPEN HER UP, LET'S SEE WHAT WE'VE --

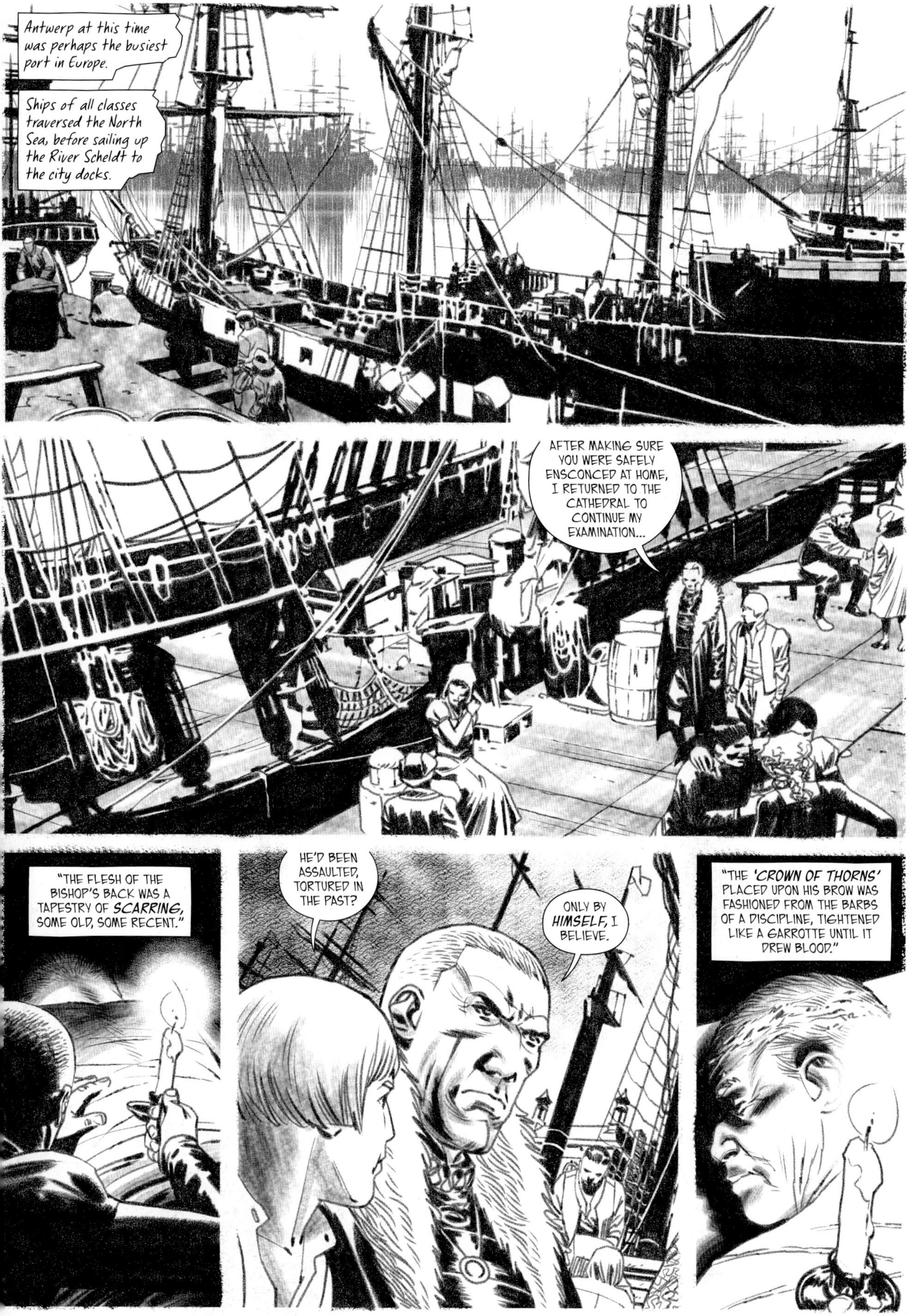
Antwerp at this time was perhaps the busiest port in Europe.
Ships of all classes traversed the North Sea, before sailing up the River Scheldt to the city docks.
AFTER MAKING SURE YOU WERE SAFELY ENSCONCED AT HOME, I RETURNED TO THE CATHEDRAL TO CONTINUE MY EXAMINATION...
"THE FLESH OF THE BISHOP'S BACK WAS A TAPESTRY OF SCARRING, SOME OLD, SOME RECENT."
HE'D BEEN ASSAULTED, TORTURED IN THE PAST?
ONLY BY HIMSELF, I BELIEVE.
"THE 'CROWN OF THORNS' PLACED UPON HIS BROW WAS FASHIONED FROM THE BARBS OF A DISCIPLINE, TIGHTENED LIKE A GARROTTE UNTIL IT DREW BLOOD."

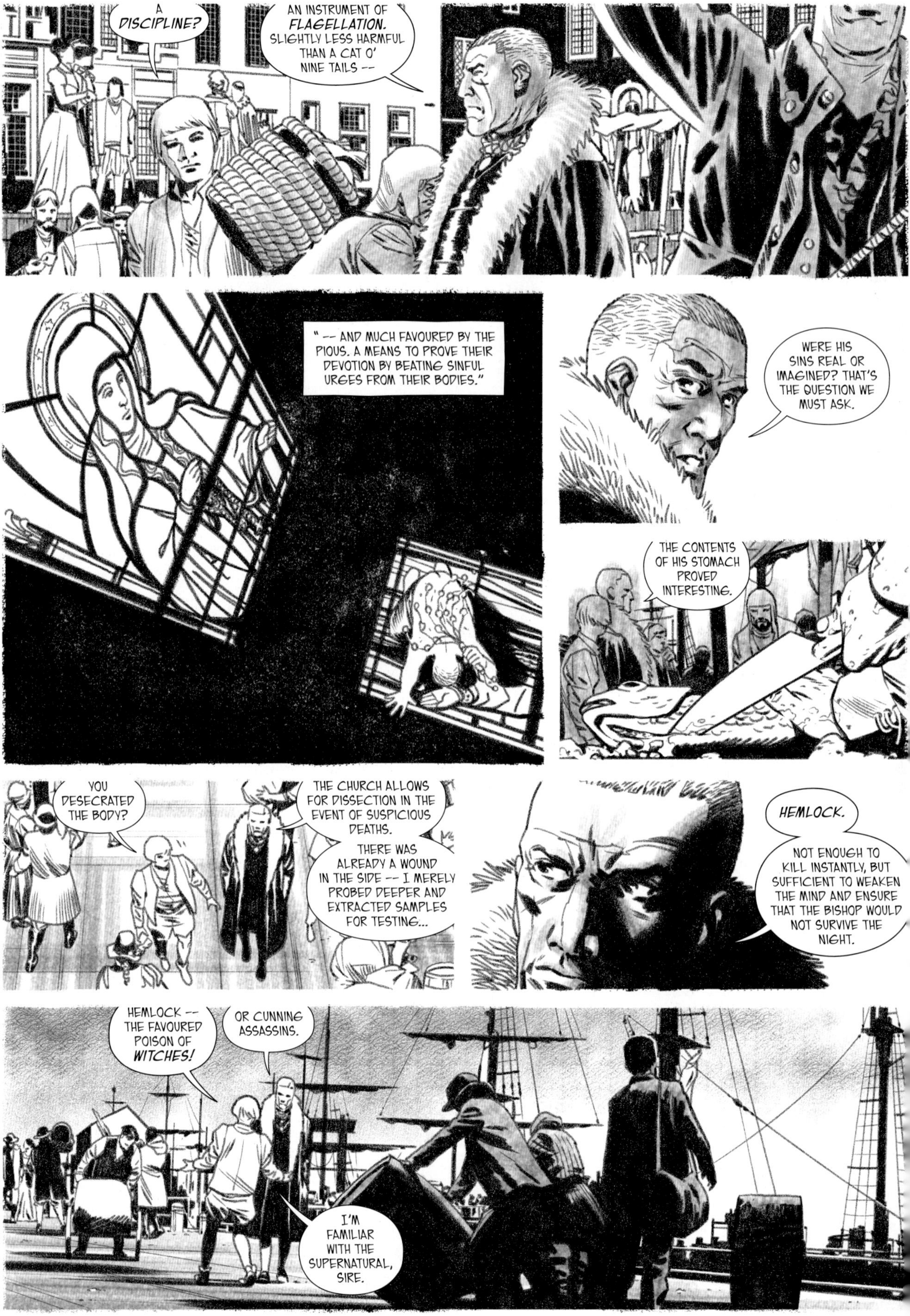
A DISCIPLINE?
AN INSTRUMENT OF FLAGELLATION. SLIGHTLY LESS HARMFUL THAN A CAT O' NINE TAILS --
" -- AND MUCH FAVOURED BY THE PIOUS. A MEANS TO PROVE THEIR DEVOTION BY BEATING SINFUL URGES FROM THEIR BODIES."
WERE HIS SINS REAL OR IMAGINED? THAT'S THE QUESTION WE MUST ASK.
THE CONTENTS OF HIS STOMACH PROVED INTERESTING.
YOU DESECRATED THE BODY?
THE CHURCH ALLOWS FOR DISSECTION IN THE EVENT OF SUSPICIOUS DEATHS.
THERE WAS ALREADY A WOUND IN THE SIDE -- I MERELY PROBED DEEPER AND EXTRACTED SAMPLES FOR TESTING...
HEMLOCK.
NOT ENOUGH TO KILL INSTANTLY, BUT SUFFICIENT TO WEAKEN THE MIND AND ENSURE THAT THE BISHOP WOULD NOT SURVIVE THE NIGHT.
HEMLOCK -- THE FAVOURED POISON OF WITCHES!
OR CUNNING ASSASSINS.
I'M FAMILIAR WITH THE SUPERNATURAL, SIRE.

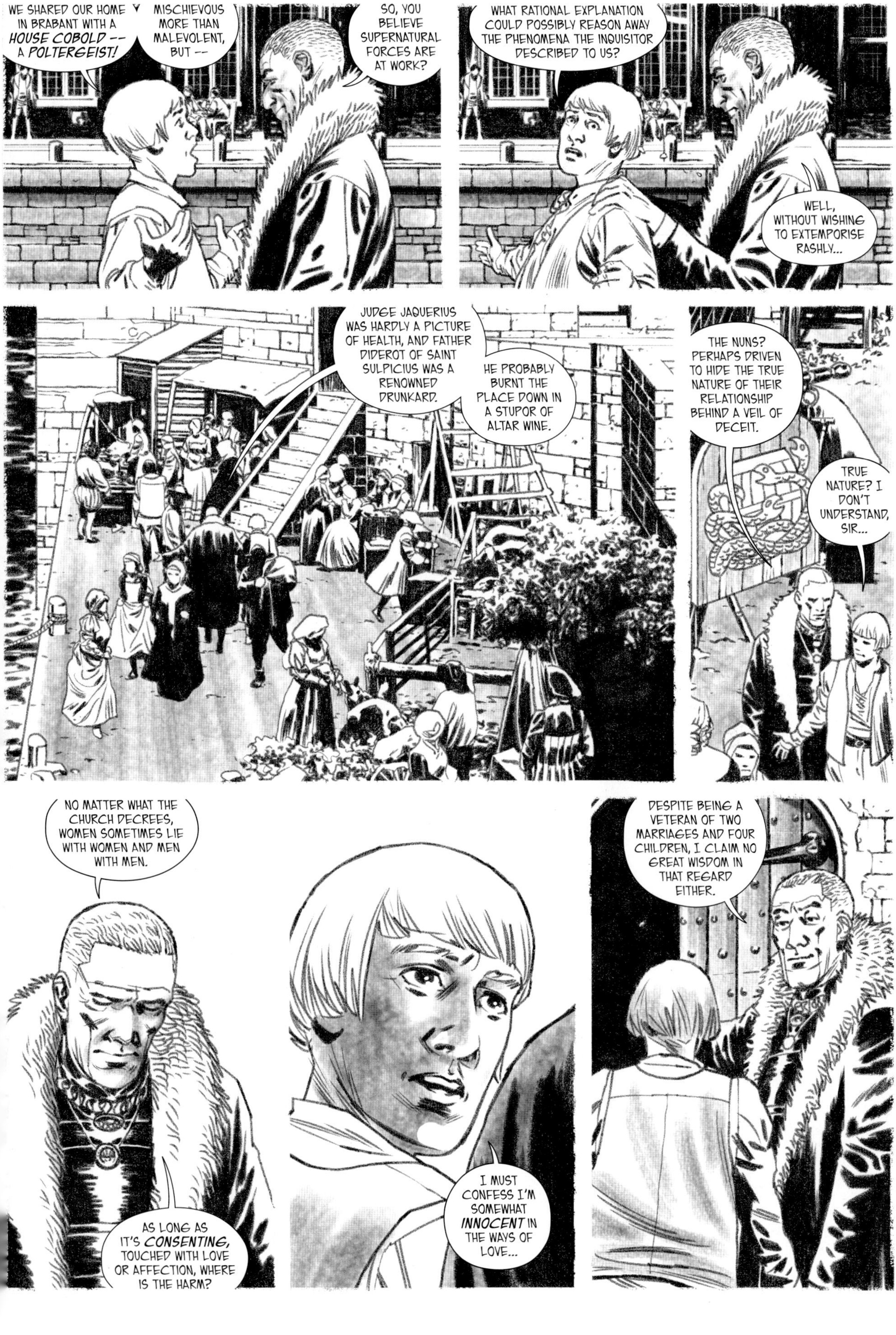
WE SHARED OUR HOME IN BRABANT WITH A *HOUSE COBOLD* -- A *POLTERGEIST!*
MISCHIEVOUS MORE THAN MALEVOLENT, BUT --
SO, YOU BELIEVE SUPERNATURAL FORCES ARE AT WORK?
WHAT RATIONAL EXPLANATION COULD POSSIBLY REASON AWAY THE PHENOMENA THE INQUISITOR DESCRIBED TO US?
WELL, WITHOUT WISHING TO EXTEMPORISE RASHLY...
JUDGE JAQUERIUS WAS HARDLY A PICTURE OF HEALTH, AND FATHER DIDEROT OF SAINT SULPICIUS WAS A RENOWNED DRUNKARD.
HE PROBABLY BURNT THE PLACE DOWN IN A STUPOR OF ALTAR WINE.
THE NUNS? PERHAPS DRIVEN TO HIDE THE TRUE NATURE OF THEIR RELATIONSHIP BEHIND A VEIL OF DECEIT.
TRUE NATURE? I DON'T UNDERSTAND, SIR...
NO MATTER WHAT THE CHURCH DECREES, WOMEN SOMETIMES LIE WITH WOMEN AND MEN WITH MEN.
AS LONG AS IT'S *CONSENTING,* TOUCHED WITH LOVE OR AFFECTION, WHERE IS THE HARM?
I MUST CONFESS I'M SOMEWHAT *INNOCENT* IN THE WAYS OF LOVE...
DESPITE BEING A VETERAN OF TWO MARRIAGES AND FOUR CHILDREN, I CLAIM NO GREAT WISDOM IN THAT REGARD EITHER.

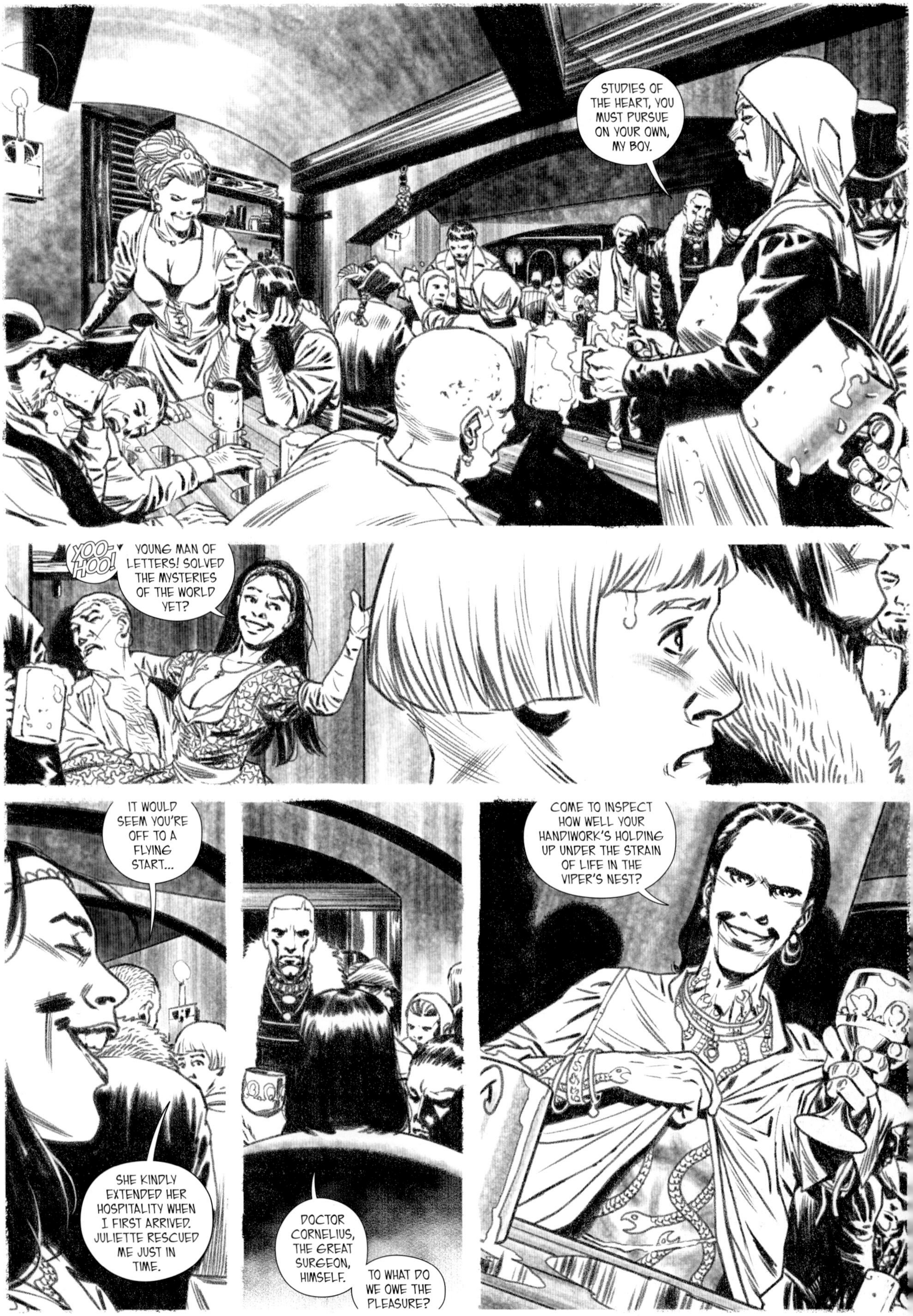
STUDIES OF THE HEART, YOU MUST PURSUE ON YOUR OWN, MY BOY.
YOO-HOO!
YOUNG MAN OF LETTERS! SOLVED THE MYSTERIES OF THE WORLD YET?
IT WOULD SEEM YOU'RE OFF TO A FLYING START...
SHE KINDLY EXTENDED HER HOSPITALITY WHEN I FIRST ARRIVED. JULIETTE RESCUED ME JUST IN TIME.
DOCTOR CORNELIUS, THE GREAT SURGEON, HIMSELF.
TO WHAT DO WE OWE THE PLEASURE?
COME TO INSPECT HOW WELL YOUR HANDIWORK'S HOLDING UP UNDER THE STRAIN OF LIFE IN THE VIPER'S NEST?

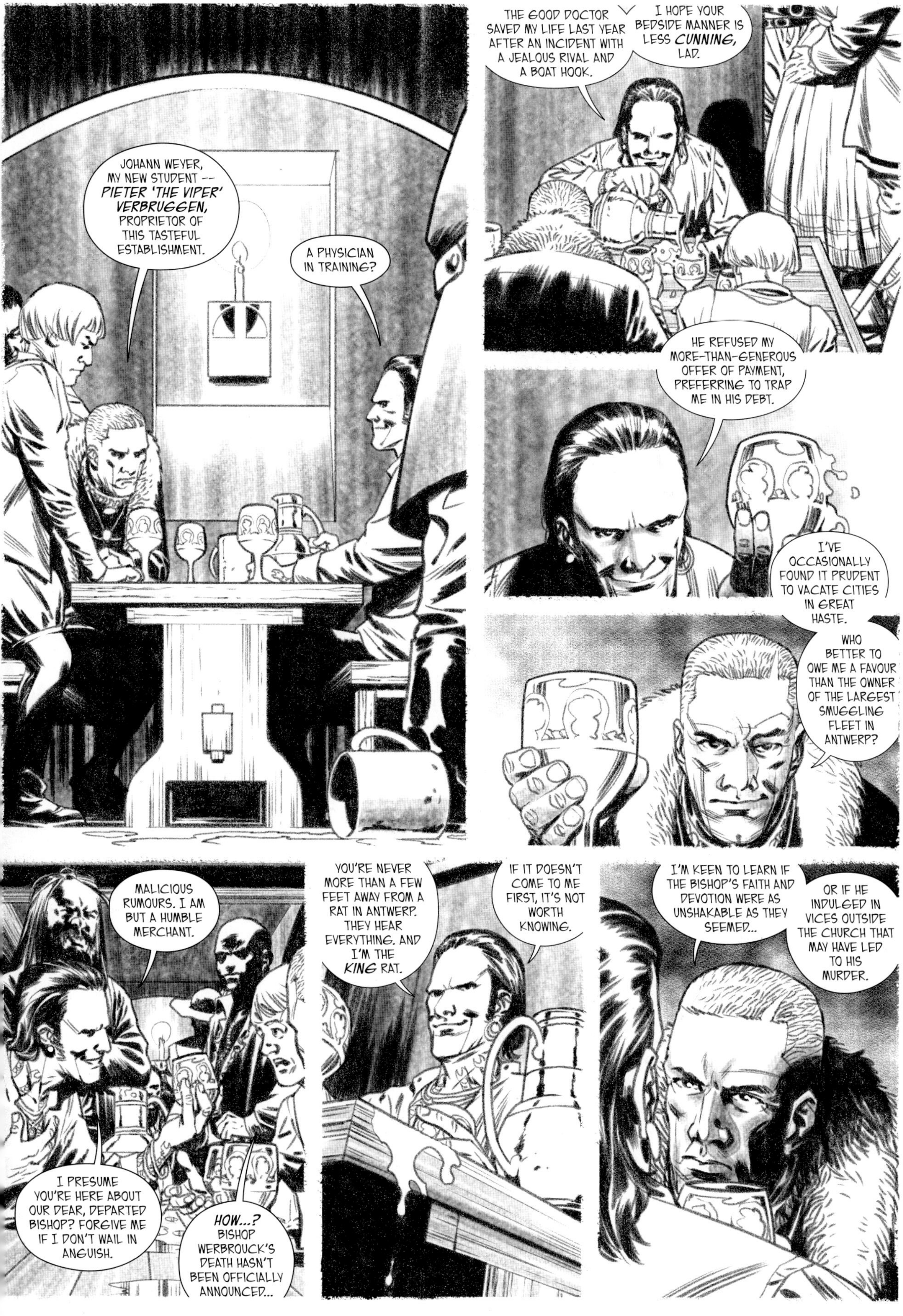
JOHANN WEYER, MY NEW STUDENT -- PIETER 'THE VIPER' VERBRUGGEN, PROPRIETOR OF THIS TASTEFUL ESTABLISHMENT.
A PHYSICIAN IN TRAINING?
THE GOOD DOCTOR SAVED MY LIFE LAST YEAR AFTER AN INCIDENT WITH A JEALOUS RIVAL AND A BOAT HOOK.
I HOPE YOUR BEDSIDE MANNER IS LESS CUNNING, LAD.
HE REFUSED MY MORE-THAN-GENEROUS OFFER OF PAYMENT, PREFERRING TO TRAP ME IN HIS DEBT.
I'VE OCCASIONALLY FOUND IT PRUDENT TO VACATE CITIES IN GREAT HASTE.
WHO BETTER TO OWE ME A FAVOUR THAN THE OWNER OF THE LARGEST SMUGGLING FLEET IN ANTWERP?
MALICIOUS RUMOURS. I AM BUT A HUMBLE MERCHANT.
I PRESUME YOU'RE HERE ABOUT OUR DEAR, DEPARTED BISHOP? FORGIVE ME IF I DON'T WAIL IN ANGUISH.
HOW...? BISHOP WERBROUCK'S DEATH HASN'T BEEN OFFICIALLY ANNOUNCED...
YOU'RE NEVER MORE THAN A FEW FEET AWAY FROM A RAT IN ANTWERP. THEY HEAR EVERYTHING. AND I'M THE KING RAT.
IF IT DOESN'T COME TO ME FIRST, IT'S NOT WORTH KNOWING.
I'M KEEN TO LEARN IF THE BISHOP'S FAITH AND DEVOTION WERE AS UNSHAKABLE AS THEY SEEMED...
OR IF HE INDULGED IN VICES OUTSIDE THE CHURCH THAT MAY HAVE LED TO HIS MURDER.

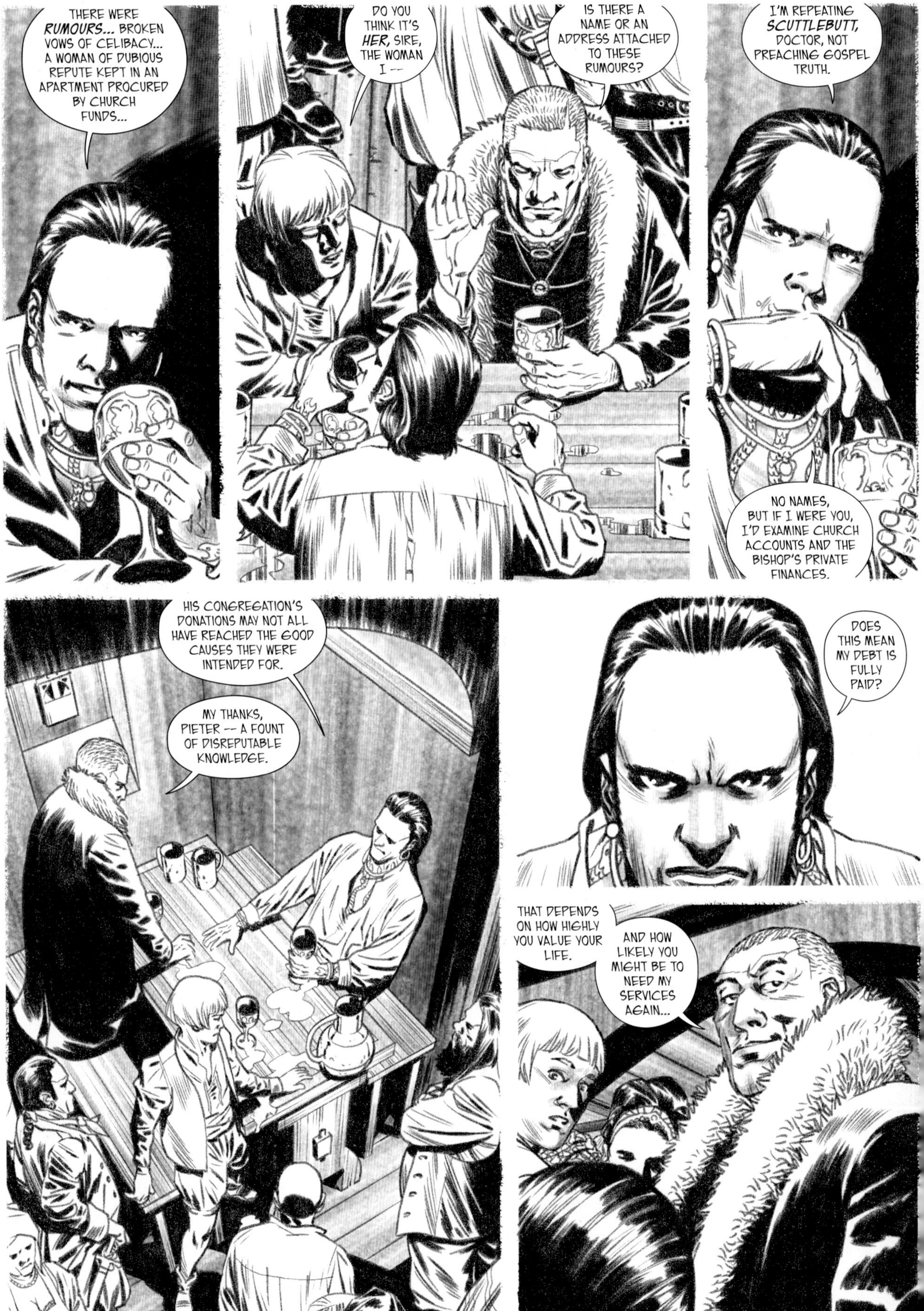
THERE WERE RUMOURS... BROKEN VOWS OF CELIBACY... A WOMAN OF DUBIOUS REPUTE KEPT IN AN APARTMENT PROCURED BY CHURCH FUNDS...
DO YOU THINK IT'S HER, SIRE, THE WOMAN I --
IS THERE A NAME OR AN ADDRESS ATTACHED TO THESE RUMOURS?
I'M REPEATING SCUTTLEBUTT, DOCTOR, NOT PREACHING GOSPEL TRUTH.
NO NAMES, BUT IF I WERE YOU, I'D EXAMINE CHURCH ACCOUNTS AND THE BISHOP'S PRIVATE FINANCES.
HIS CONGREGATION'S DONATIONS MAY NOT ALL HAVE REACHED THE GOOD CAUSES THEY WERE INTENDED FOR.
MY THANKS, PIETER -- A FOUNT OF DISREPUTABLE KNOWLEDGE.
DOES THIS MEAN MY DEBT IS FULLY PAID?
THAT DEPENDS ON HOW HIGHLY YOU VALUE YOUR LIFE.
AND HOW LIKELY YOU MIGHT BE TO NEED MY SERVICES AGAIN...

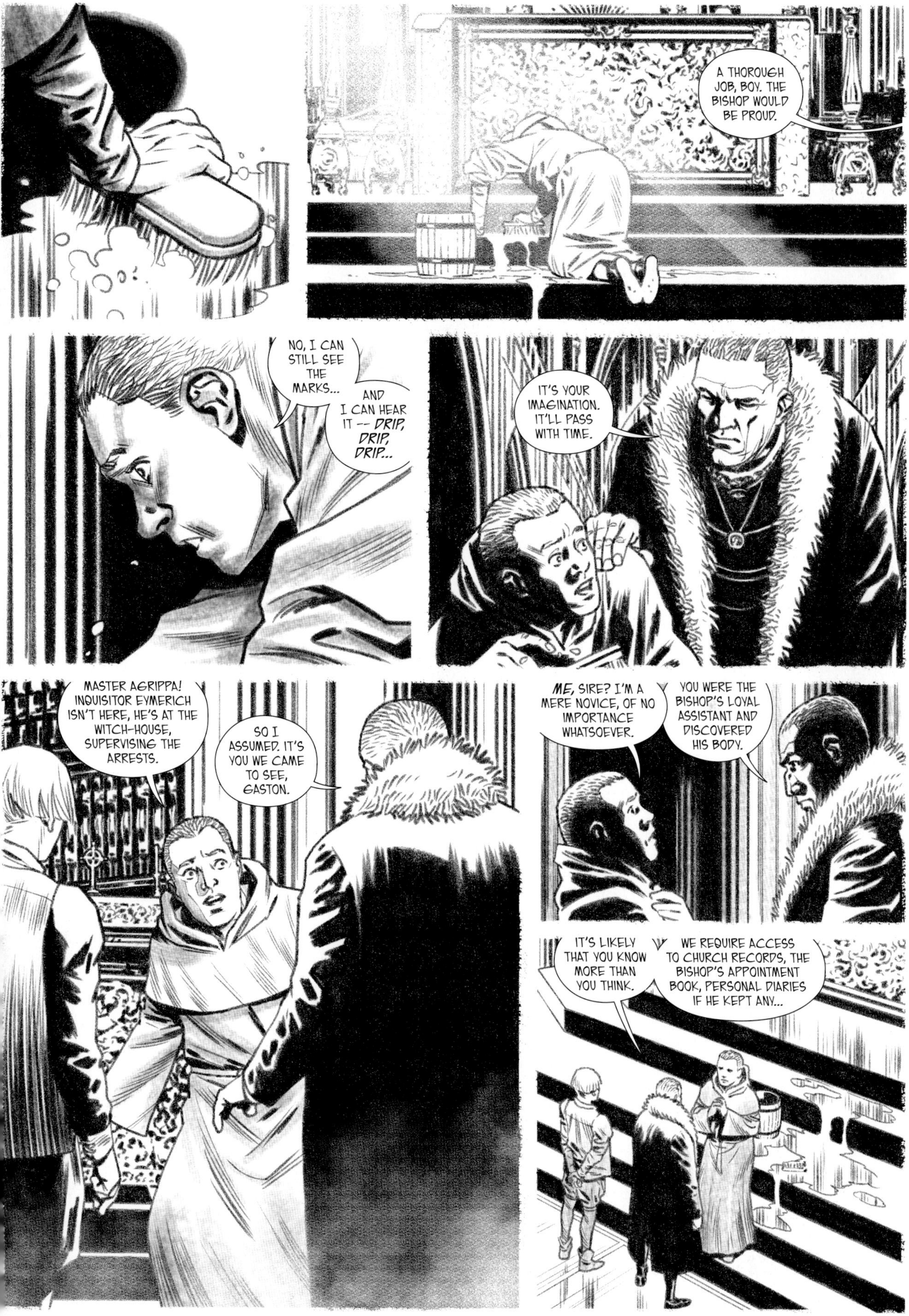
A THOROUGH JOB, BOY. THE BISHOP WOULD BE PROUD.
NO, I CAN STILL SEE THE MARKS...
AND I CAN HEAR IT -- DRIP, DRIP, DRIP...
IT'S YOUR IMAGINATION. IT'LL PASS WITH TIME.
MASTER AGRIPPA! INQUISITOR EYMERICH ISN'T HERE, HE'S AT THE WITCH-HOUSE, SUPERVISING THE ARRESTS.
SO I ASSUMED. IT'S YOU WE CAME TO SEE, GASTON.
ME, SIRE? I'M A MERE NOVICE, OF NO IMPORTANCE WHATSOEVER.
YOU WERE THE BISHOP'S LOYAL ASSISTANT AND DISCOVERED HIS BODY.
IT'S LIKELY THAT YOU KNOW MORE THAN YOU THINK.
WE REQUIRE ACCESS TO CHURCH RECORDS, THE BISHOP'S APPOINTMENT BOOK, PERSONAL DIARIES IF HE KEPT ANY...

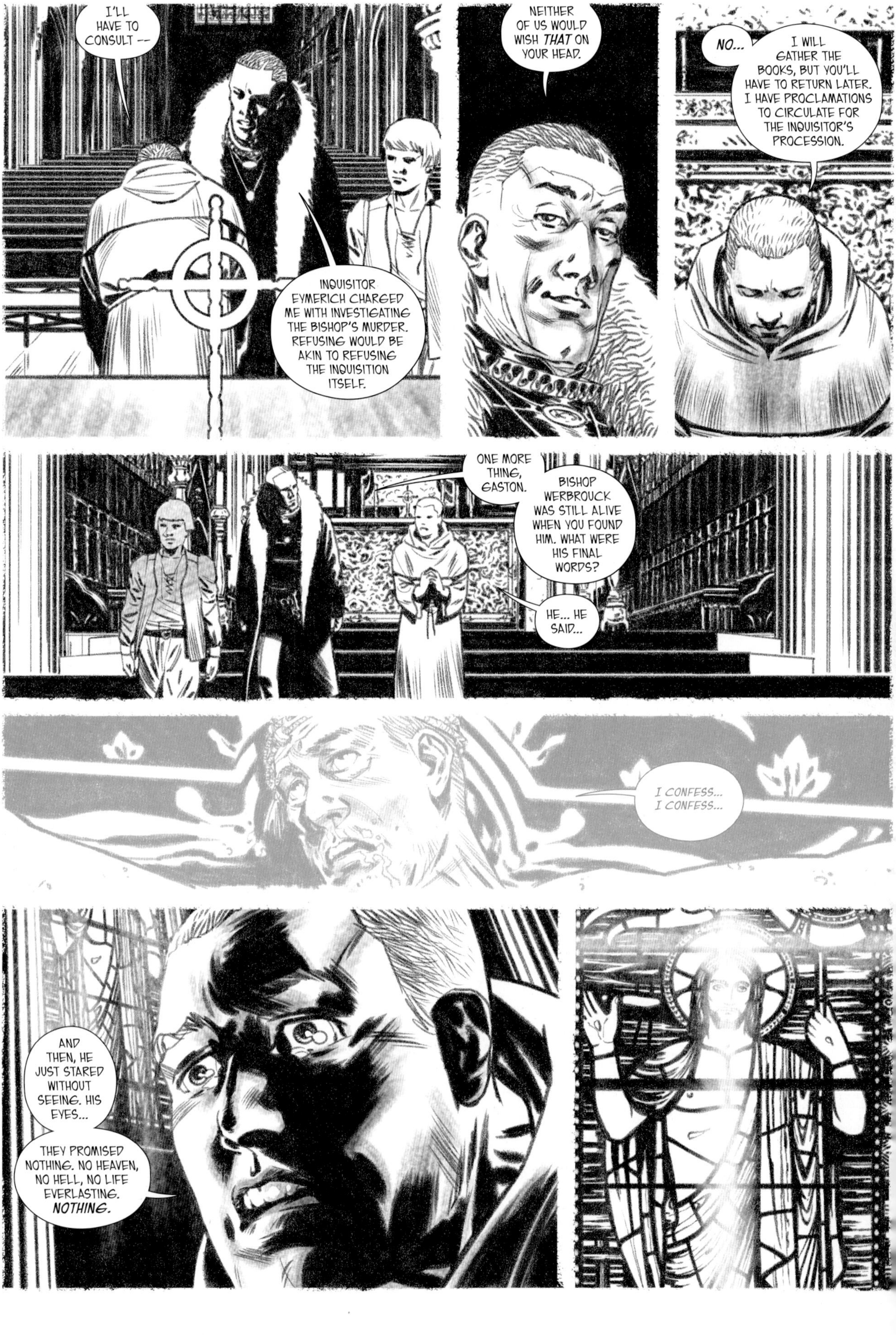
I'LL HAVE TO CONSULT --
INQUISITOR EYMERICH CHARGED ME WITH INVESTIGATING THE BISHOP'S MURDER. REFUSING WOULD BE AKIN TO REFUSING THE INQUISITION ITSELF.
NEITHER OF US WOULD WISH *THAT* ON YOUR HEAD.
NO...
I WILL GATHER THE BOOKS, BUT YOU'LL HAVE TO RETURN LATER. I HAVE PROCLAMATIONS TO CIRCULATE FOR THE INQUISITOR'S PROCESSION.
ONE MORE THING, GASTON.
BISHOP WERBROUCK WAS STILL ALIVE WHEN YOU FOUND HIM. WHAT WERE HIS FINAL WORDS?
HE... HE SAID...
I CONFESS... I CONFESS...
AND THEN, HE JUST STARED WITHOUT SEEING. HIS EYES...
THEY PROMISED NOTHING. NO HEAVEN, NO HELL, NO LIFE EVERLASTING. ***NOTHING.***

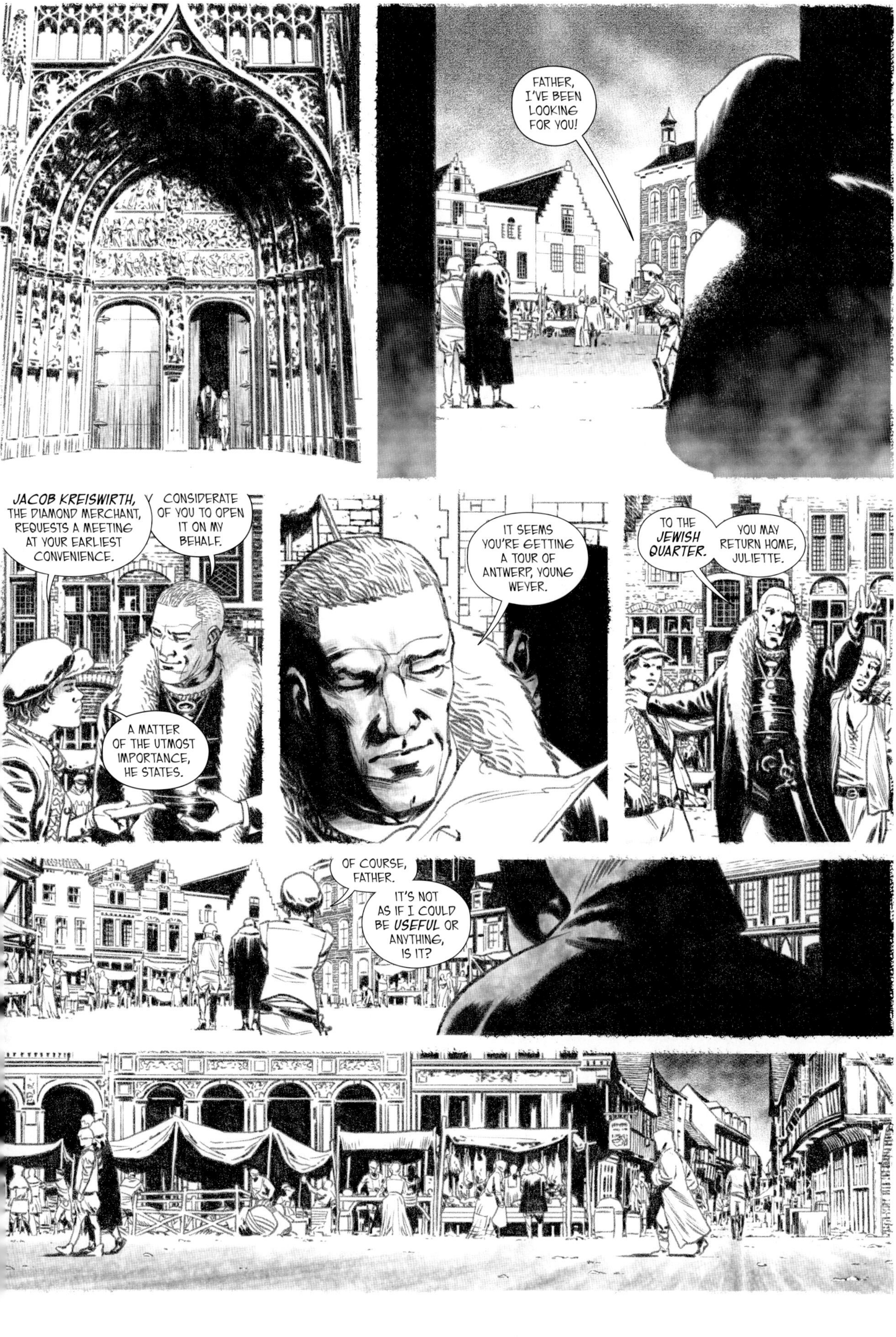
FATHER, I'VE BEEN LOOKING FOR YOU!
JACOB KREISWIRTH, THE DIAMOND MERCHANT, REQUESTS A MEETING AT YOUR EARLIEST CONVENIENCE.
CONSIDERATE OF YOU TO OPEN IT ON MY BEHALF.
A MATTER OF THE UTMOST IMPORTANCE, HE STATES.
IT SEEMS YOU'RE GETTING A TOUR OF ANTWERP, YOUNG WEYER.
TO THE JEWISH QUARTER.
YOU MAY RETURN HOME, JULIETTE.
OF COURSE, FATHER.
IT'S NOT AS IF I COULD BE USEFUL OR ANYTHING, IS IT?

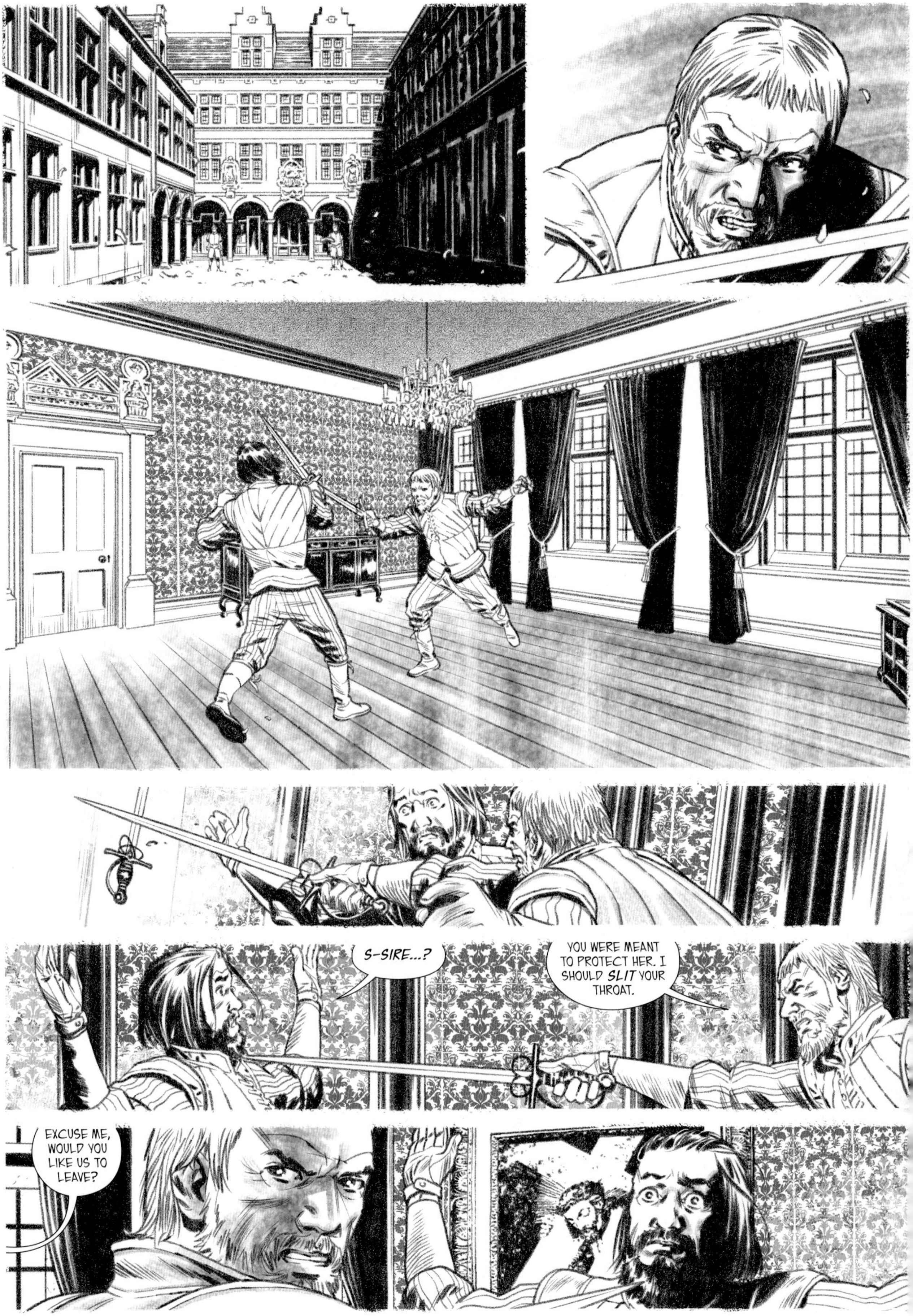
S-SIRE...?
YOU WERE MEANT TO PROTECT HER. I SHOULD SLIT YOUR THROAT.
EXCUSE ME, WOULD YOU LIKE US TO LEAVE?

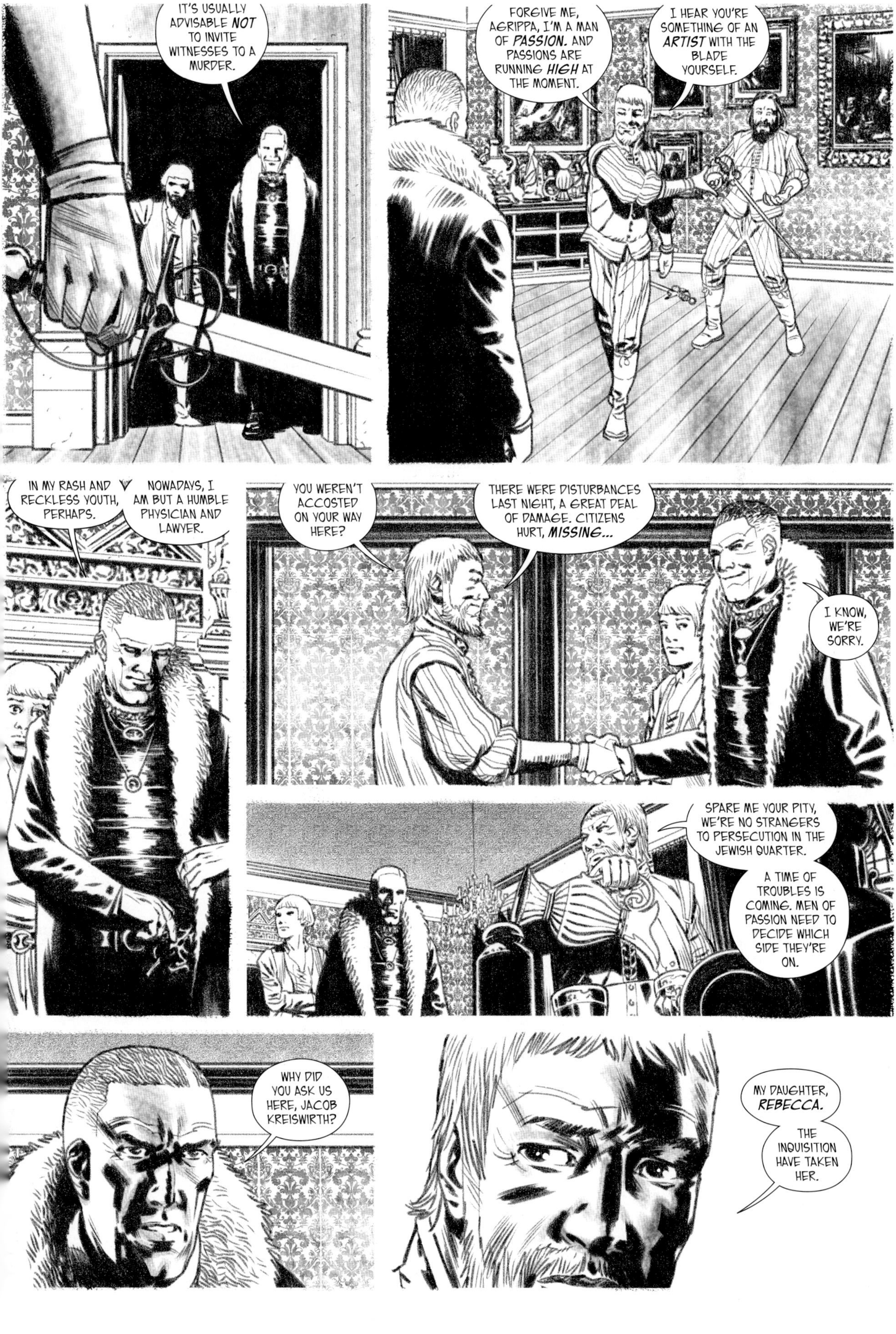
IT'S USUALLY ADVISABLE NOT TO INVITE WITNESSES TO A MURDER.
FORGIVE ME, AGRIPPA, I'M A MAN OF PASSION. AND PASSIONS ARE RUNNING HIGH AT THE MOMENT.
I HEAR YOU'RE SOMETHING OF AN ARTIST WITH THE BLADE YOURSELF.
IN MY RASH AND RECKLESS YOUTH, PERHAPS.
NOWADAYS, I AM BUT A HUMBLE PHYSICIAN AND LAWYER.
YOU WEREN'T ACCOSTED ON YOUR WAY HERE?
THERE WERE DISTURBANCES LAST NIGHT, A GREAT DEAL OF DAMAGE. CITIZENS HURT, MISSING...
I KNOW, WE'RE SORRY.
SPARE ME YOUR PITY, WE'RE NO STRANGERS TO PERSECUTION IN THE JEWISH QUARTER.
A TIME OF TROUBLES IS COMING. MEN OF PASSION NEED TO DECIDE WHICH SIDE THEY'RE ON.
WHY DID YOU ASK US HERE, JACOB KREISWIRTH?
MY DAUGHTER, REBECCA.
THE INQUISITION HAVE TAKEN HER.

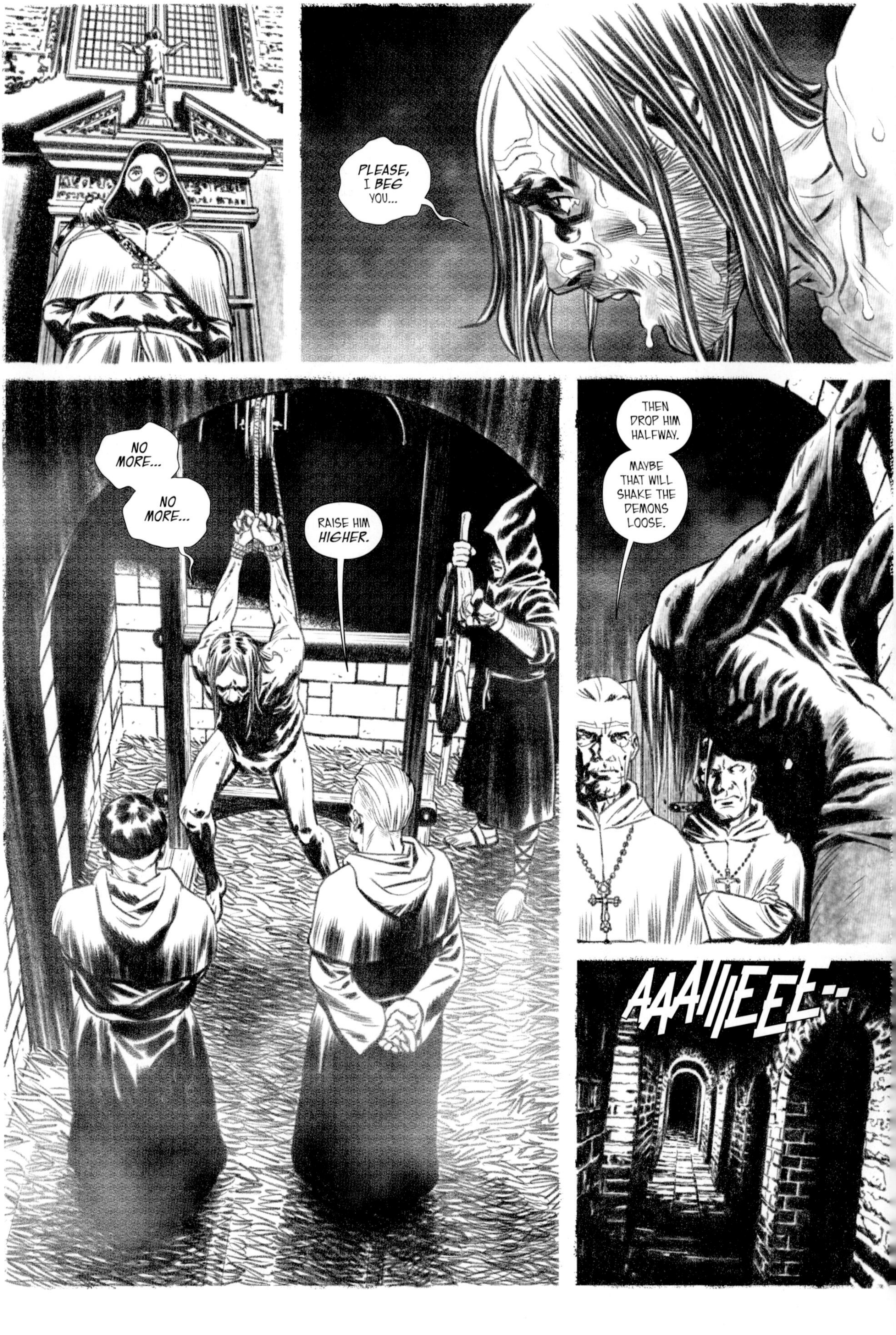
PLEASE, I BEG YOU...
NO MORE...
NO MORE...
RAISE HIM HIGHER.
THEN DROP HIM HALFWAY.
MAYBE THAT WILL SHAKE THE DEMONS LOOSE.
AAAIIIIEEE--

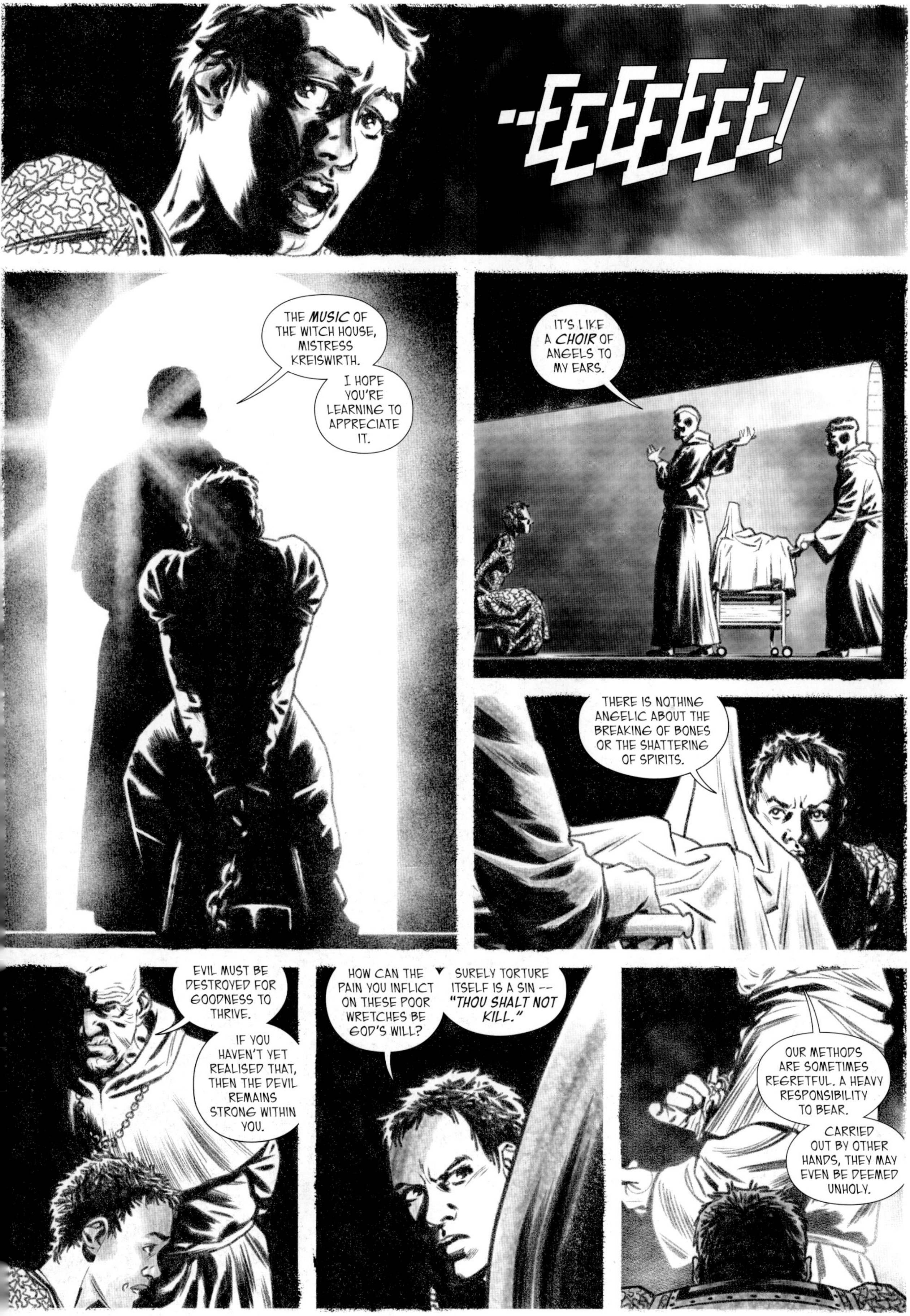
--EEEEEEE!
THE MUSIC OF THE WITCH HOUSE, MISTRESS KREISWIRTH.
I HOPE YOU'RE LEARNING TO APPRECIATE IT.
IT'S LIKE A CHOIR OF ANGELS TO MY EARS.
THERE IS NOTHING ANGELIC ABOUT THE BREAKING OF BONES OR THE SHATTERING OF SPIRITS.
EVIL MUST BE DESTROYED FOR GOODNESS TO THRIVE.
IF YOU HAVEN'T YET REALISED THAT, THEN THE DEVIL REMAINS STRONG WITHIN YOU.
HOW CAN THE PAIN YOU INFLICT ON THESE POOR WRETCHES BE GOD'S WILL?
SURELY TORTURE ITSELF IS A SIN -- "THOU SHALT NOT KILL."
OUR METHODS ARE SOMETIMES REGRETFUL. A HEAVY RESPONSIBILITY TO BEAR.
CARRIED OUT BY OTHER HANDS, THEY MAY EVEN BE DEEMED UNHOLY.

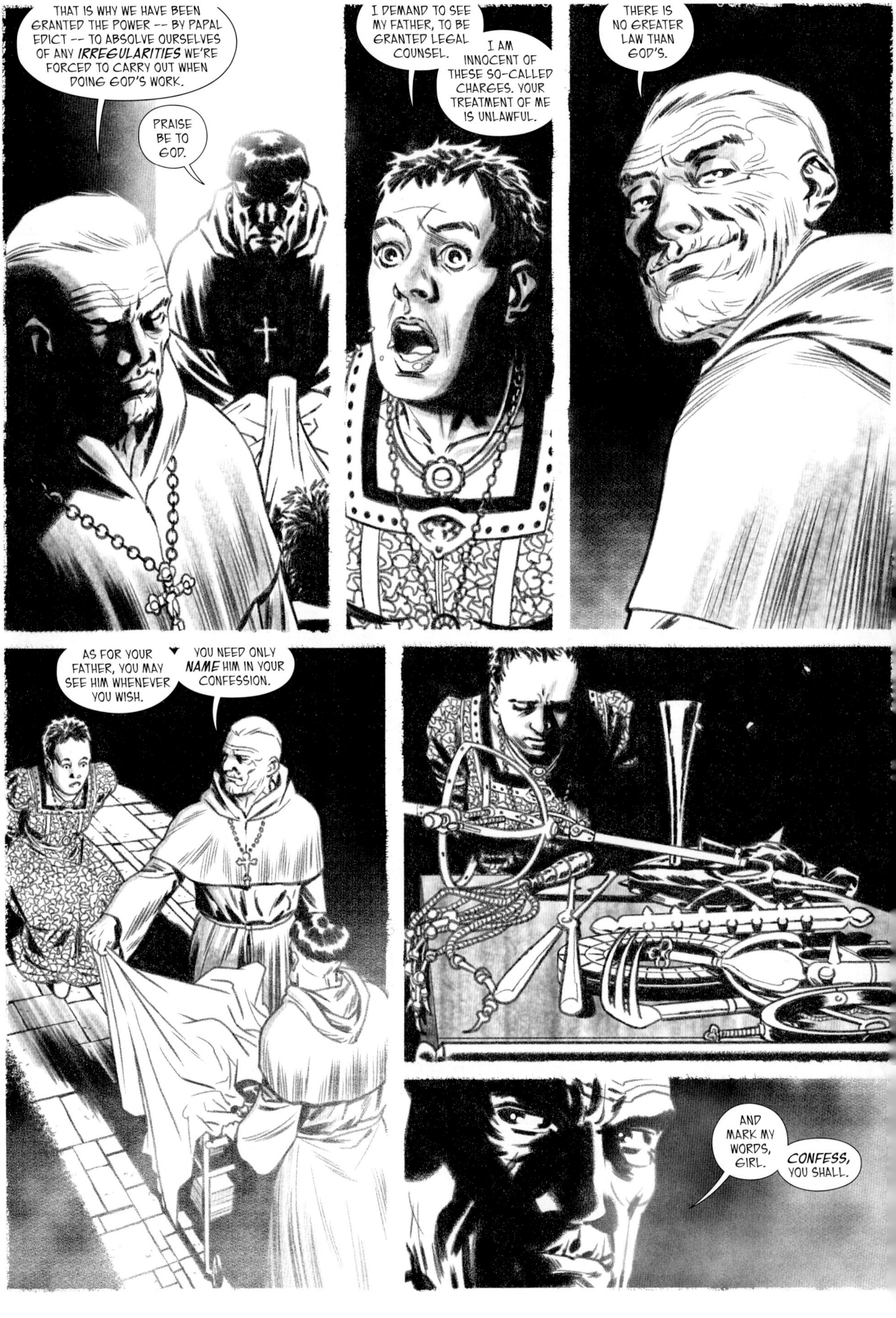
THAT IS WHY WE HAVE BEEN GRANTED THE POWER -- BY PAPAL EDICT -- TO ABSOLVE OURSELVES OF ANY IRREGULARITIES WE'RE FORCED TO CARRY OUT WHEN DOING GOD'S WORK.
PRAISE BE TO GOD.
I DEMAND TO SEE MY FATHER, TO BE GRANTED LEGAL COUNSEL.
I AM INNOCENT OF THESE SO-CALLED CHARGES. YOUR TREATMENT OF ME IS UNLAWFUL.
THERE IS NO GREATER LAW THAN GOD'S.
AS FOR YOUR FATHER, YOU MAY SEE HIM WHENEVER YOU WISH.
YOU NEED ONLY NAME HIM IN YOUR CONFESSION.
AND MARK MY WORDS, GIRL.
CONFESS, YOU SHALL.

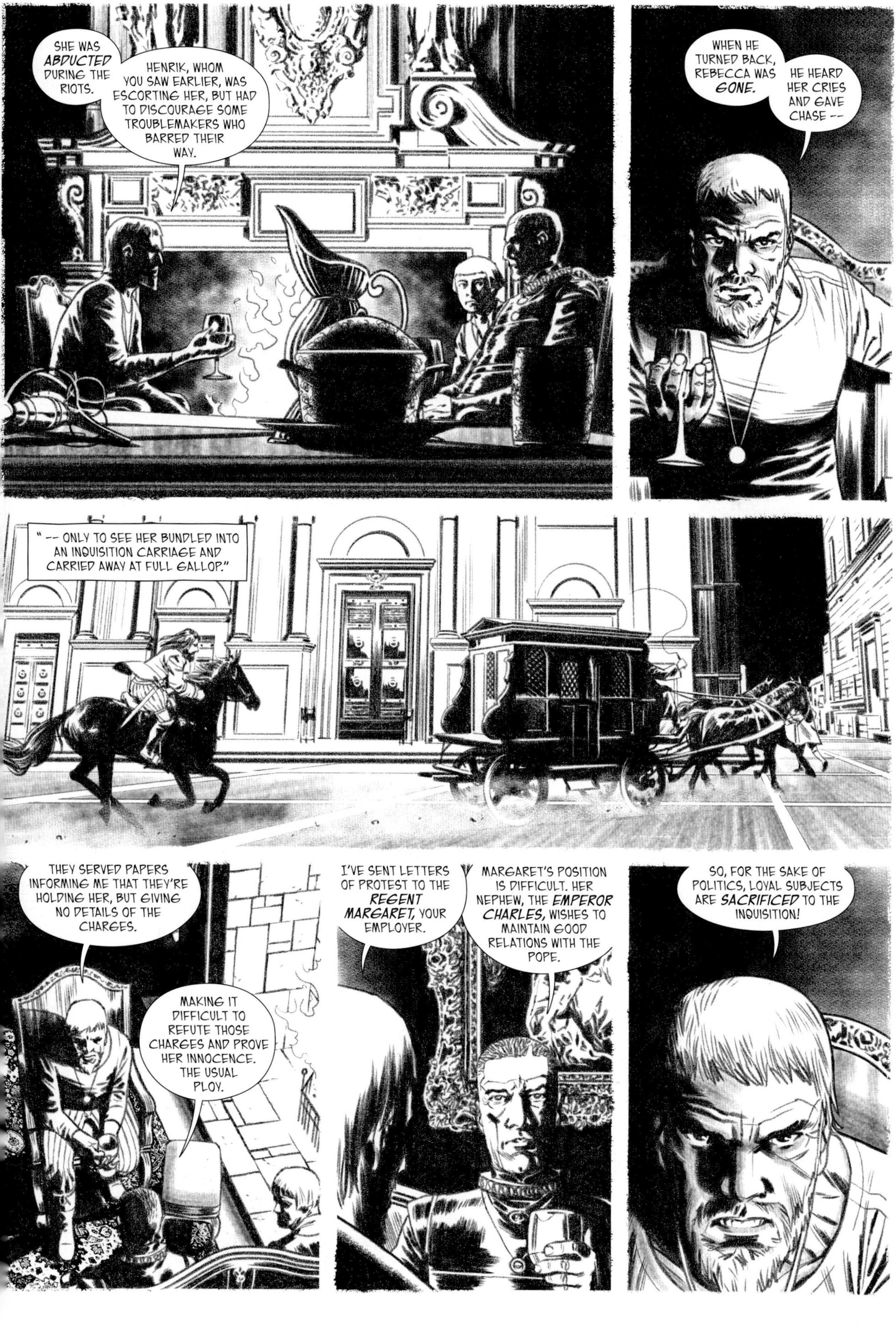
SHE WAS ABDUCTED DURING THE RIOTS.
HENRIK, WHOM YOU SAW EARLIER, WAS ESCORTING HER, BUT HAD TO DISCOURAGE SOME TROUBLEMAKERS WHO BARRED THEIR WAY.
WHEN HE TURNED BACK, REBECCA WAS GONE.
HE HEARD HER CRIES AND GAVE CHASE --
" -- ONLY TO SEE HER BUNDLED INTO AN INQUISITION CARRIAGE AND CARRIED AWAY AT FULL GALLOP."
THEY SERVED PAPERS INFORMING ME THAT THEY'RE HOLDING HER, BUT GIVING NO DETAILS OF THE CHARGES.
MAKING IT DIFFICULT TO REFUTE THOSE CHARGES AND PROVE HER INNOCENCE. THE USUAL PLOY.
I'VE SENT LETTERS OF PROTEST TO THE REGENT MARGARET, YOUR EMPLOYER.
MARGARET'S POSITION IS DIFFICULT. HER NEPHEW, THE EMPEROR CHARLES, WISHES TO MAINTAIN GOOD RELATIONS WITH THE POPE.
SO, FOR THE SAKE OF POLITICS, LOYAL SUBJECTS ARE SACRIFICED TO THE INQUISITION!

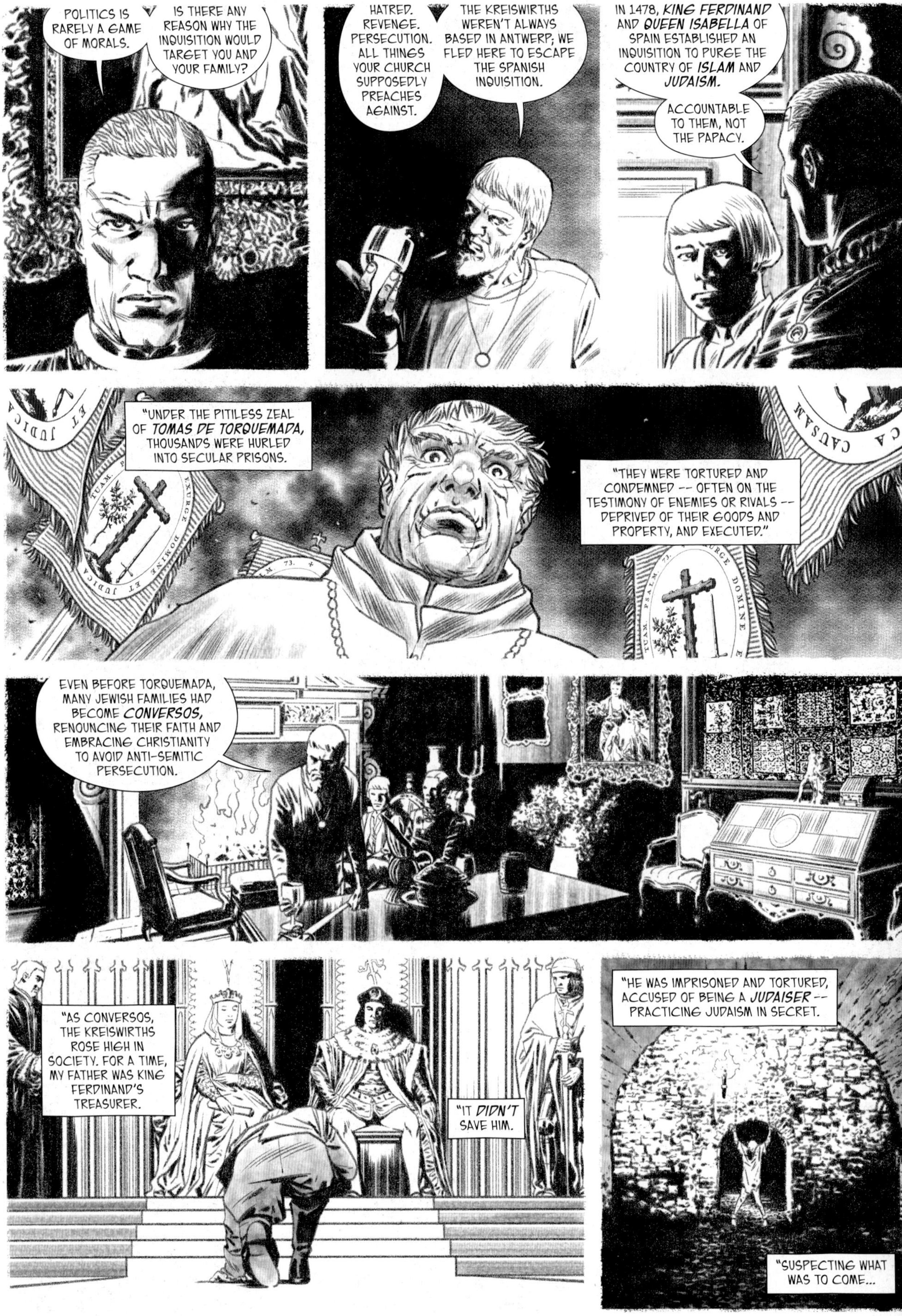
POLITICS IS RARELY A GAME OF MORALS.
IS THERE ANY REASON WHY THE INQUISITION WOULD TARGET YOU AND YOUR FAMILY?
HATRED. REVENGE. PERSECUTION. ALL THINGS YOUR CHURCH SUPPOSEDLY PREACHES AGAINST.
THE KREISWIRTHS WEREN'T ALWAYS BASED IN ANTWERP; WE FLED HERE TO ESCAPE THE SPANISH INQUISITION.
IN 1478, KING FERDINAND AND QUEEN ISABELLA OF SPAIN ESTABLISHED AN INQUISITION TO PURGE THE COUNTRY OF ISLAM AND JUDAISM.
ACCOUNTABLE TO THEM, NOT THE PAPACY.
"UNDER THE PITILESS ZEAL OF TOMAS DE TORQUEMADA, THOUSANDS WERE HURLED INTO SECULAR PRISONS.
"THEY WERE TORTURED AND CONDEMNED -- OFTEN ON THE TESTIMONY OF ENEMIES OR RIVALS -- DEPRIVED OF THEIR GOODS AND PROPERTY, AND EXECUTED."
EVEN BEFORE TORQUEMADA, MANY JEWISH FAMILIES HAD BECOME CONVERSOS, RENOUNCING THEIR FAITH AND EMBRACING CHRISTIANITY TO AVOID ANTI-SEMITIC PERSECUTION.
"AS CONVERSOS, THE KREISWIRTHS ROSE HIGH IN SOCIETY. FOR A TIME, MY FATHER WAS KING FERDINAND'S TREASURER.
"IT DIDN'T SAVE HIM.
"HE WAS IMPRISONED AND TORTURED, ACCUSED OF BEING A JUDAISER -- PRACTICING JUDAISM IN SECRET.
"SUSPECTING WHAT WAS TO COME...

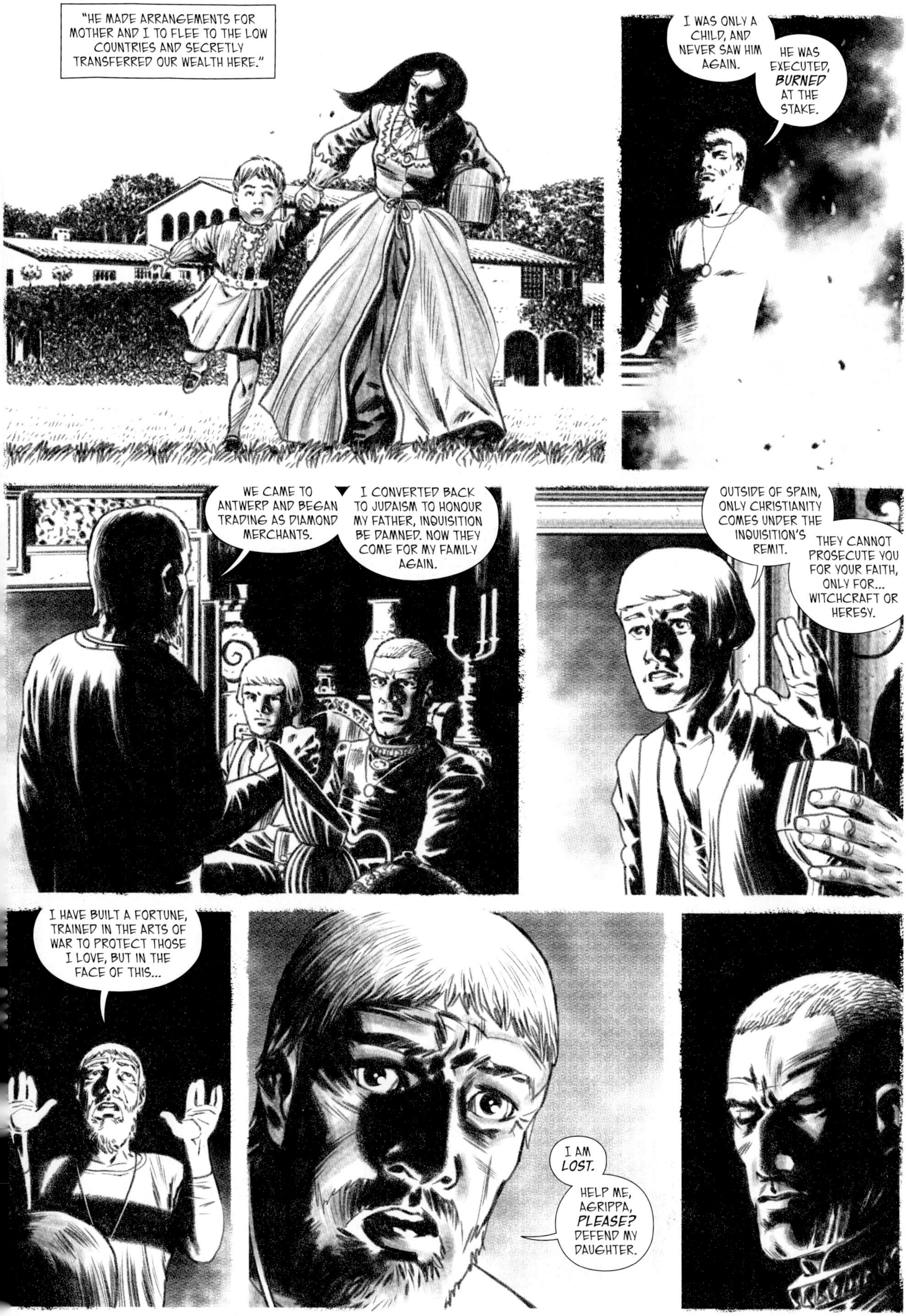
"HE MADE ARRANGEMENTS FOR MOTHER AND I TO FLEE TO THE LOW COUNTRIES AND SECRETLY TRANSFERRED OUR WEALTH HERE."
I WAS ONLY A CHILD, AND NEVER SAW HIM AGAIN.
HE WAS EXECUTED, BURNED AT THE STAKE.
WE CAME TO ANTWERP AND BEGAN TRADING AS DIAMOND MERCHANTS.
I CONVERTED BACK TO JUDAISM TO HONOUR MY FATHER, INQUISITION BE DAMNED. NOW THEY COME FOR MY FAMILY AGAIN.
OUTSIDE OF SPAIN, ONLY CHRISTIANITY COMES UNDER THE INQUISITION'S REMIT.
THEY CANNOT PROSECUTE YOU FOR YOUR FAITH, ONLY FOR... WITCHCRAFT OR HERESY.
I HAVE BUILT A FORTUNE, TRAINED IN THE ARTS OF WAR TO PROTECT THOSE I LOVE, BUT IN THE FACE OF THIS...
I AM LOST.
HELP ME, AGRIPPA, PLEASE? DEFEND MY DAUGHTER.

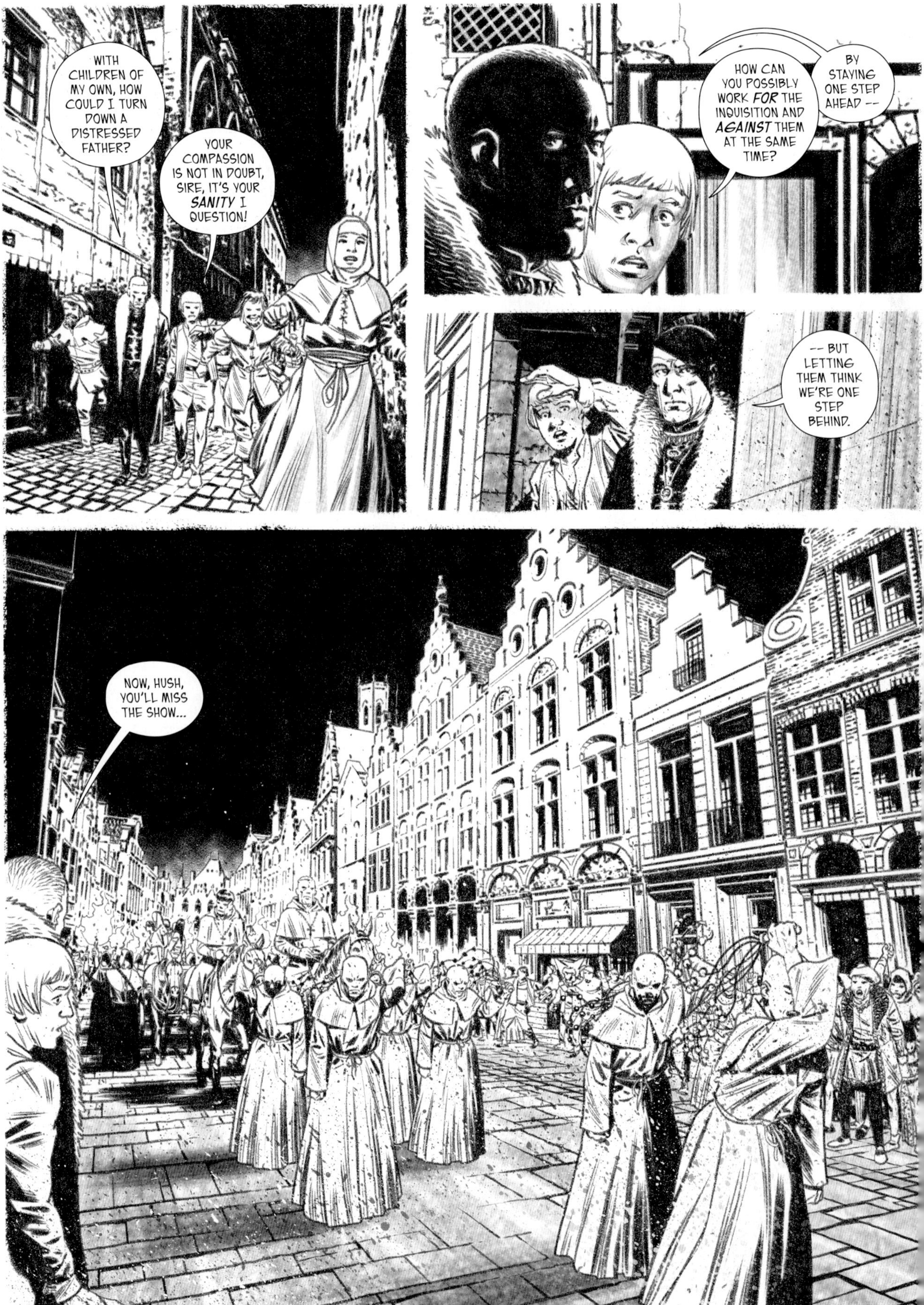
WITH CHILDREN OF MY OWN, HOW COULD I TURN DOWN A DISTRESSED FATHER?
YOUR COMPASSION IS NOT IN DOUBT, SIRE, IT'S YOUR SANITY I QUESTION!
HOW CAN YOU POSSIBLY WORK FOR THE INQUISITION AND AGAINST THEM AT THE SAME TIME?
BY STAYING ONE STEP AHEAD --
-- BUT LETTING THEM THINK WE'RE ONE STEP BEHIND.
NOW, HUSH, YOU'LL MISS THE SHOW...

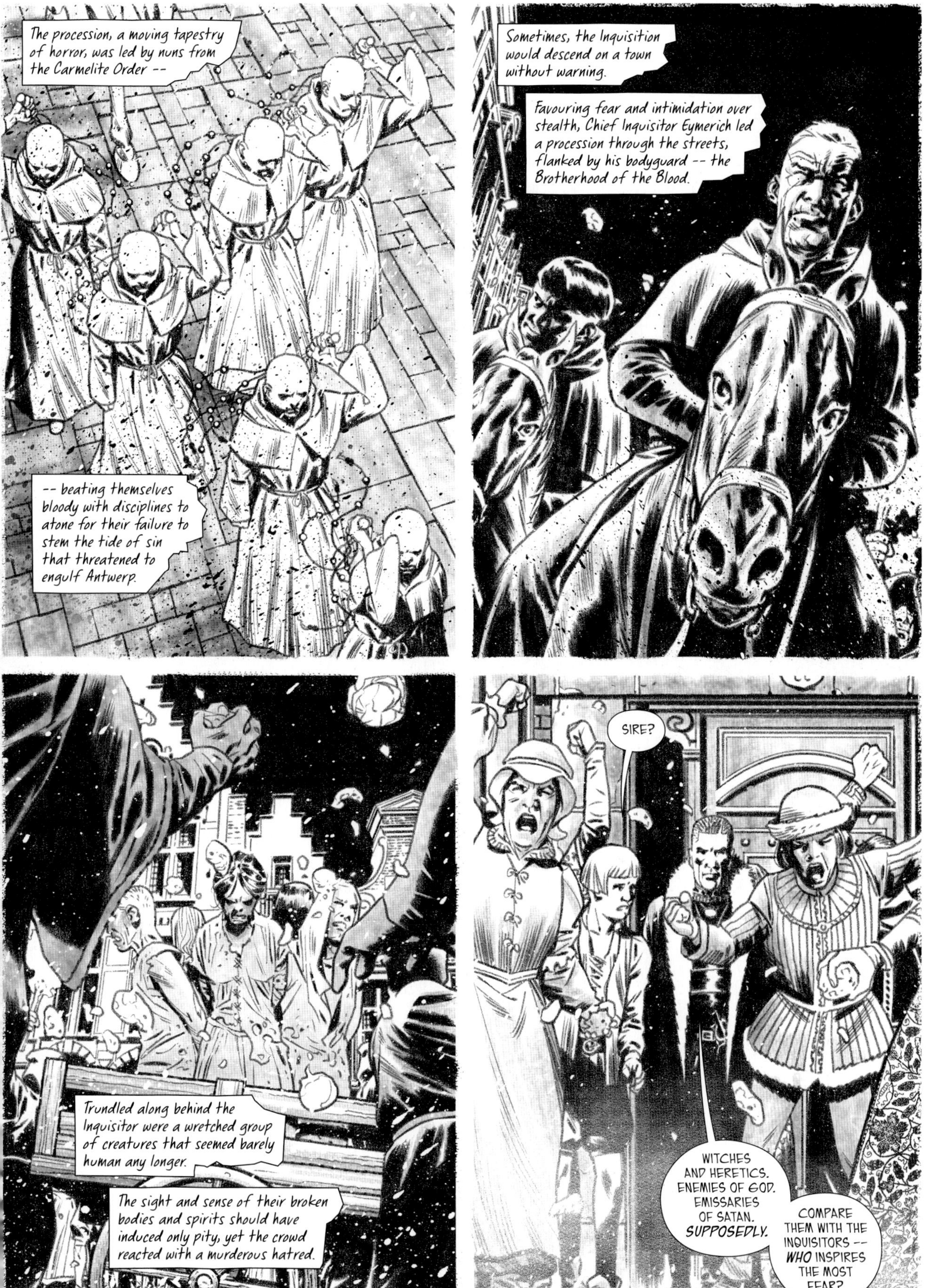
The procession, a moving tapestry of horror, was led by nuns from the Carmelite Order --
-- beating themselves bloody with disciplines to atone for their failure to stem the tide of sin that threatened to engulf Antwerp.
Sometimes, the Inquisition would descend on a town without warning.
Favouring fear and intimidation over stealth, Chief Inquisitor Eymerich led a procession through the streets, flanked by his bodyguard -- the Brotherhood of the Blood.
Trundled along behind the Inquisitor were a wretched group of creatures that seemed barely human any longer.
The sight and sense of their broken bodies and spirits should have induced only pity, yet the crowd reacted with a murderous hatred.
SIRE?
WITCHES AND HERETICS. ENEMIES OF GOD. EMISSARIES OF SATAN. SUPPOSEDLY.
COMPARE THEM WITH THE INQUISITORS -- WHO INSPIRES THE MOST FEAR?

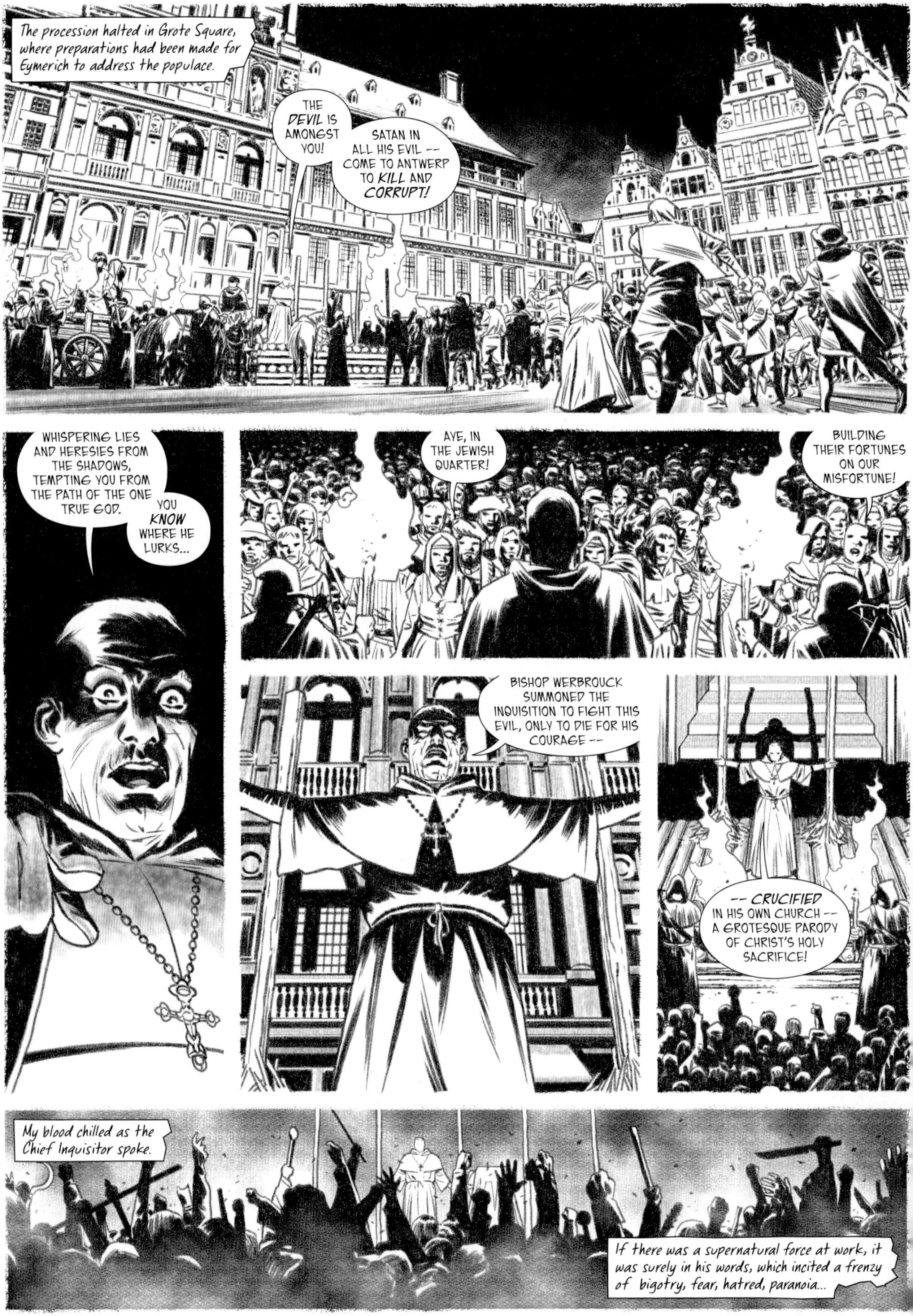

The procession halted in Grote Square, where preparations had been made for Eymerich to address the populace.
THE DEVIL IS AMONGST YOU!
SATAN IN ALL HIS EVIL -- COME TO ANTWERP TO KILL AND CORRUPT!
WHISPERING LIES AND HERESIES FROM THE SHADOWS, TEMPTING YOU FROM THE PATH OF THE ONE TRUE GOD.
YOU KNOW WHERE HE LURKS...
AYE, IN THE JEWISH QUARTER!
BUILDING THEIR FORTUNES ON OUR MISFORTUNE!
BISHOP WERBROUCK SUMMONED THE INQUISITION TO FIGHT THIS EVIL, ONLY TO DIE FOR HIS COURAGE --
-- CRUCIFIED IN HIS OWN CHURCH -- A GROTESQUE PARODY OF CHRIST'S HOLY SACRIFICE!
My blood chilled as the Chief Inquisitor spoke.
If there was a supernatural force at work, it was surely in his words, which incited a frenzy of bigotry, fear, hatred, paranoia...

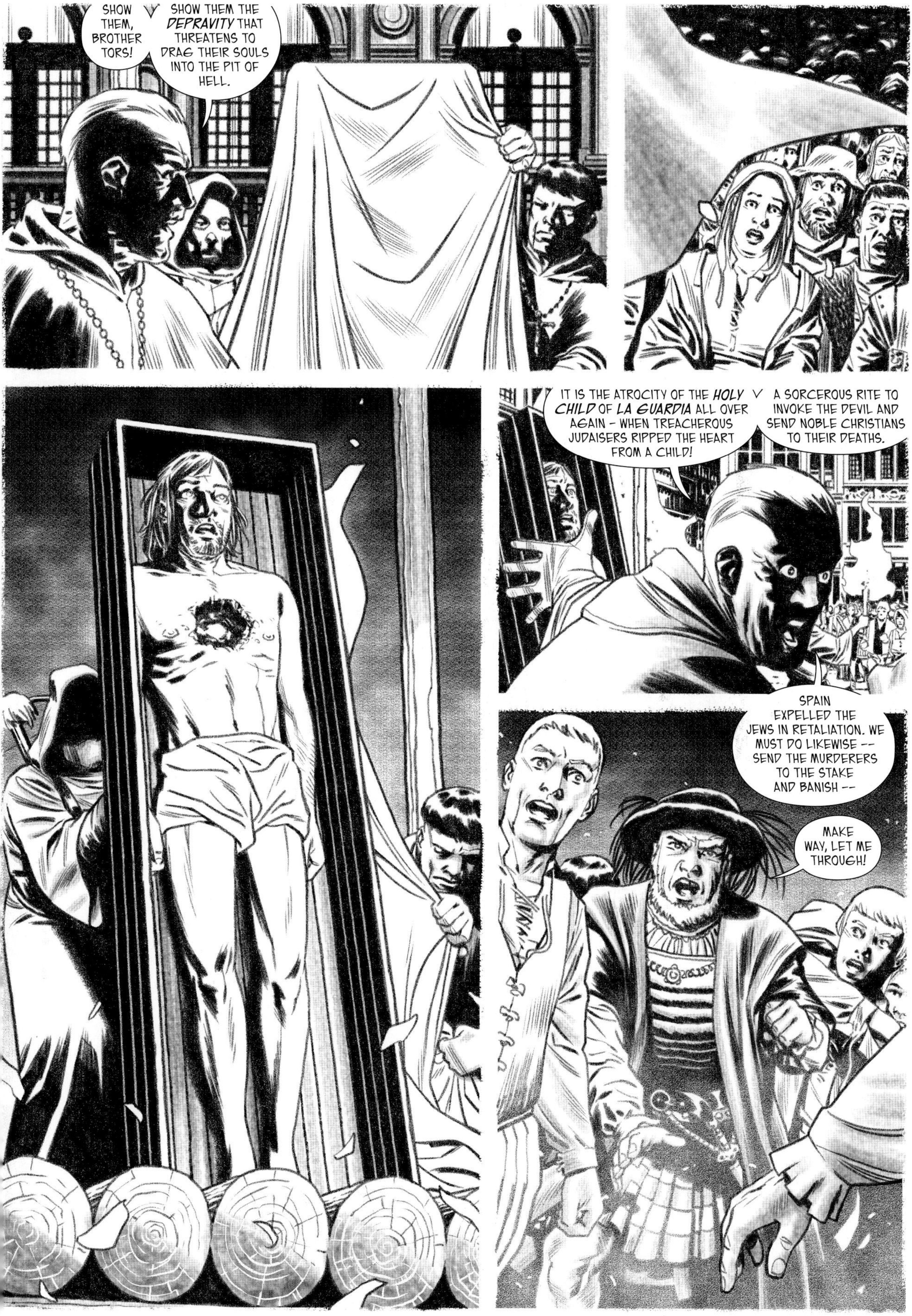
SHOW THEM, BROTHER TORS!
SHOW THEM THE DEPRAVITY THAT THREATENS TO DRAG THEIR SOULS INTO THE PIT OF HELL.
IT IS THE ATROCITY OF THE HOLY CHILD OF LA GUARDIA ALL OVER AGAIN – WHEN TREACHEROUS JUDAISERS RIPPED THE HEART FROM A CHILD!
A SORCEROUS RITE TO INVOKE THE DEVIL AND SEND NOBLE CHRISTIANS TO THEIR DEATHS.
SPAIN EXPELLED THE JEWS IN RETALIATION. WE MUST DO LIKEWISE -- SEND THE MURDERERS TO THE STAKE AND BANISH --
MAKE WAY, LET ME THROUGH!

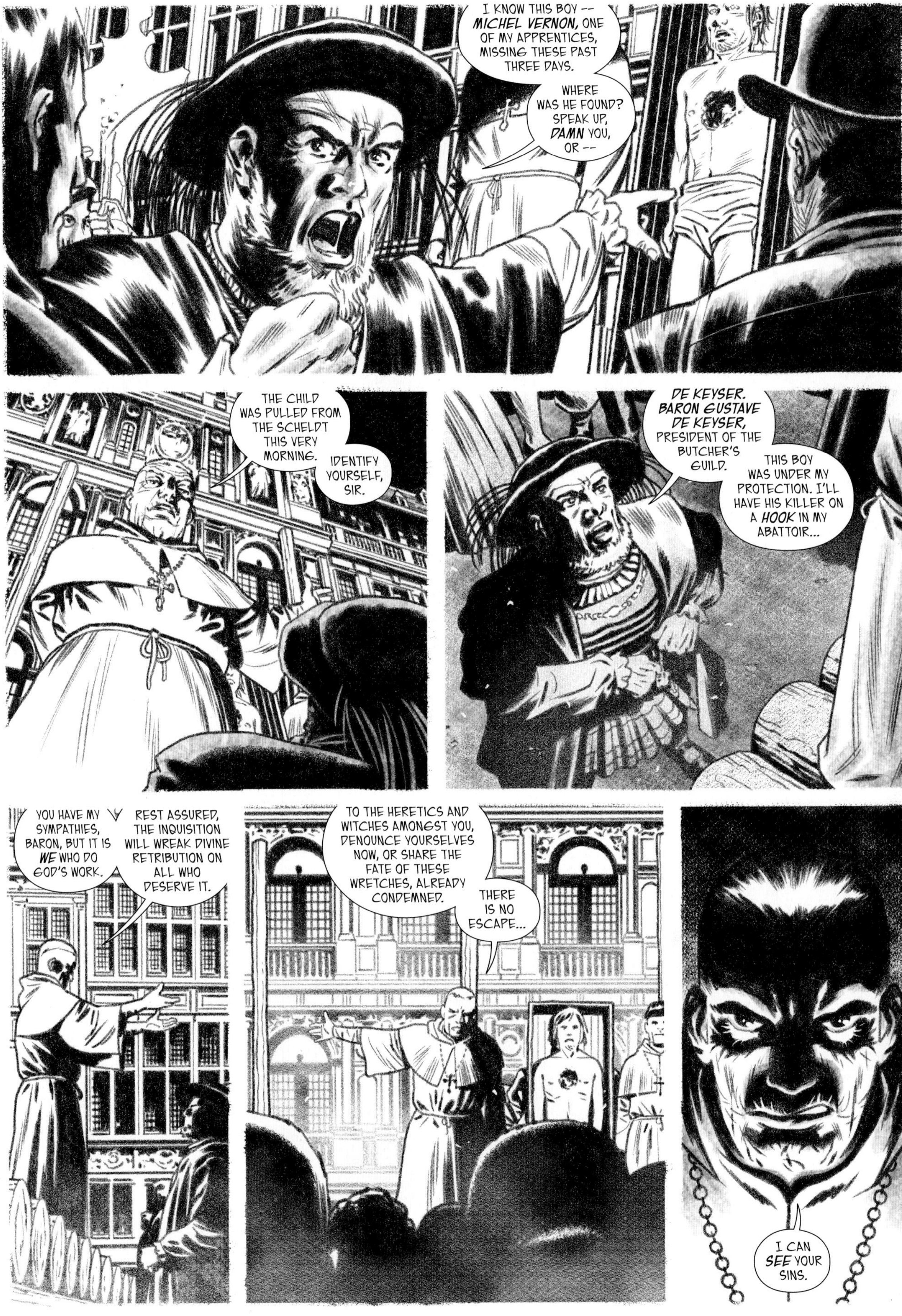
I KNOW THIS BOY -- MICHEL VERNON, ONE OF MY APPRENTICES, MISSING THESE PAST THREE DAYS.
WHERE WAS HE FOUND? SPEAK UP, DAMN YOU, OR --
THE CHILD WAS PULLED FROM THE SCHELDT THIS VERY MORNING.
IDENTIFY YOURSELF, SIR.
DE KEYSER. BARON GUSTAVE DE KEYSER, PRESIDENT OF THE BUTCHER'S GUILD.
THIS BOY WAS UNDER MY PROTECTION. I'LL HAVE HIS KILLER ON A HOOK IN MY ABATTOIR...
YOU HAVE MY SYMPATHIES, BARON, BUT IT IS WE WHO DO GOD'S WORK.
REST ASSURED, THE INQUISITION WILL WREAK DIVINE RETRIBUTION ON ALL WHO DESERVE IT.
TO THE HERETICS AND WITCHES AMONGST YOU, DENOUNCE YOURSELVES NOW, OR SHARE THE FATE OF THESE WRETCHES, ALREADY CONDEMNED.
THERE IS NO ESCAPE...
I CAN SEE YOUR SINS.

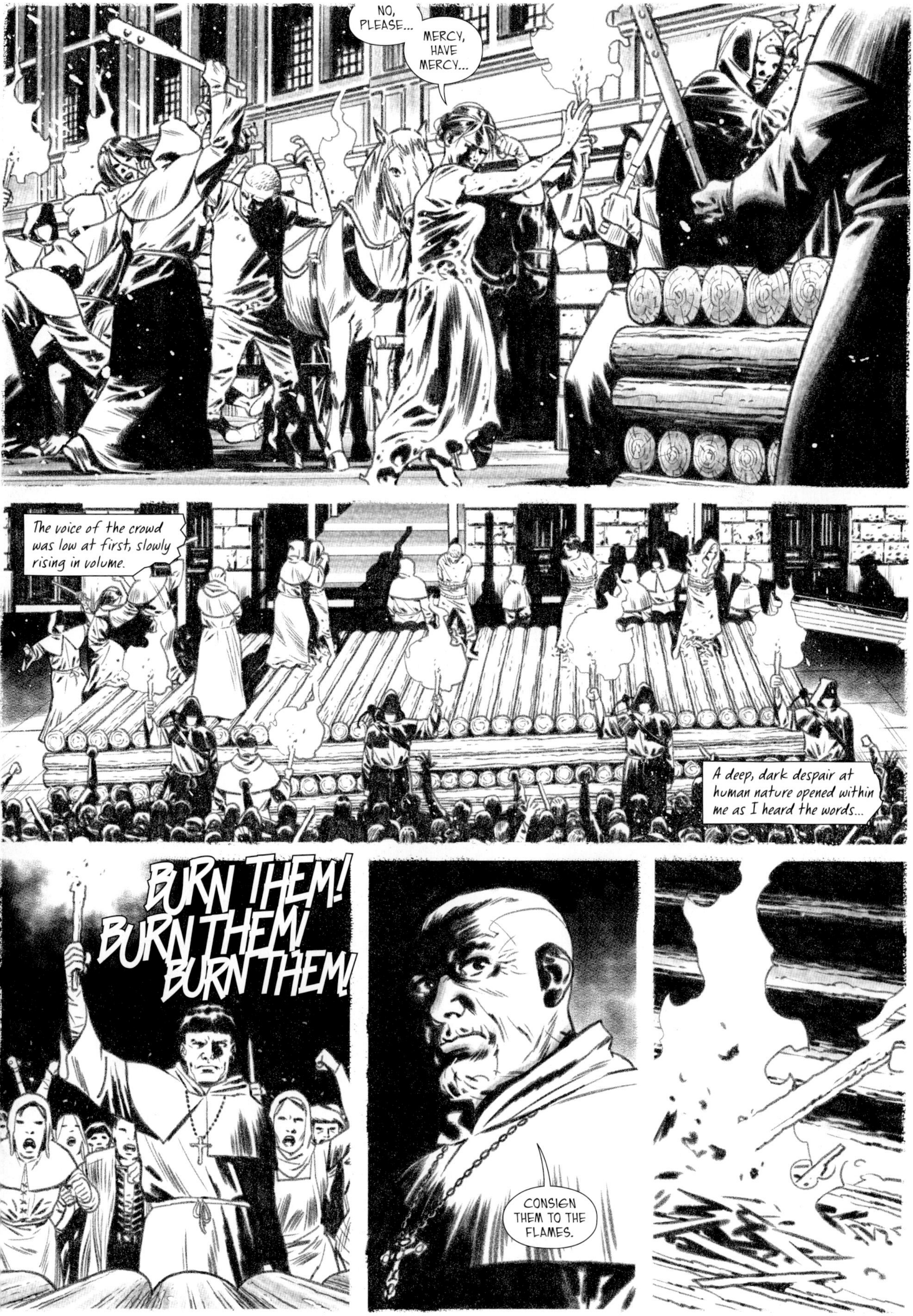
NO, PLEASE...
MERCY, HAVE MERCY...
The voice of the crowd was low at first, slowly rising in volume.
A deep, dark despair at human nature opened within me as I heard the words...
BURN THEM! BURN THEM! BURN THEM!
CONSIGN THEM TO THE FLAMES.

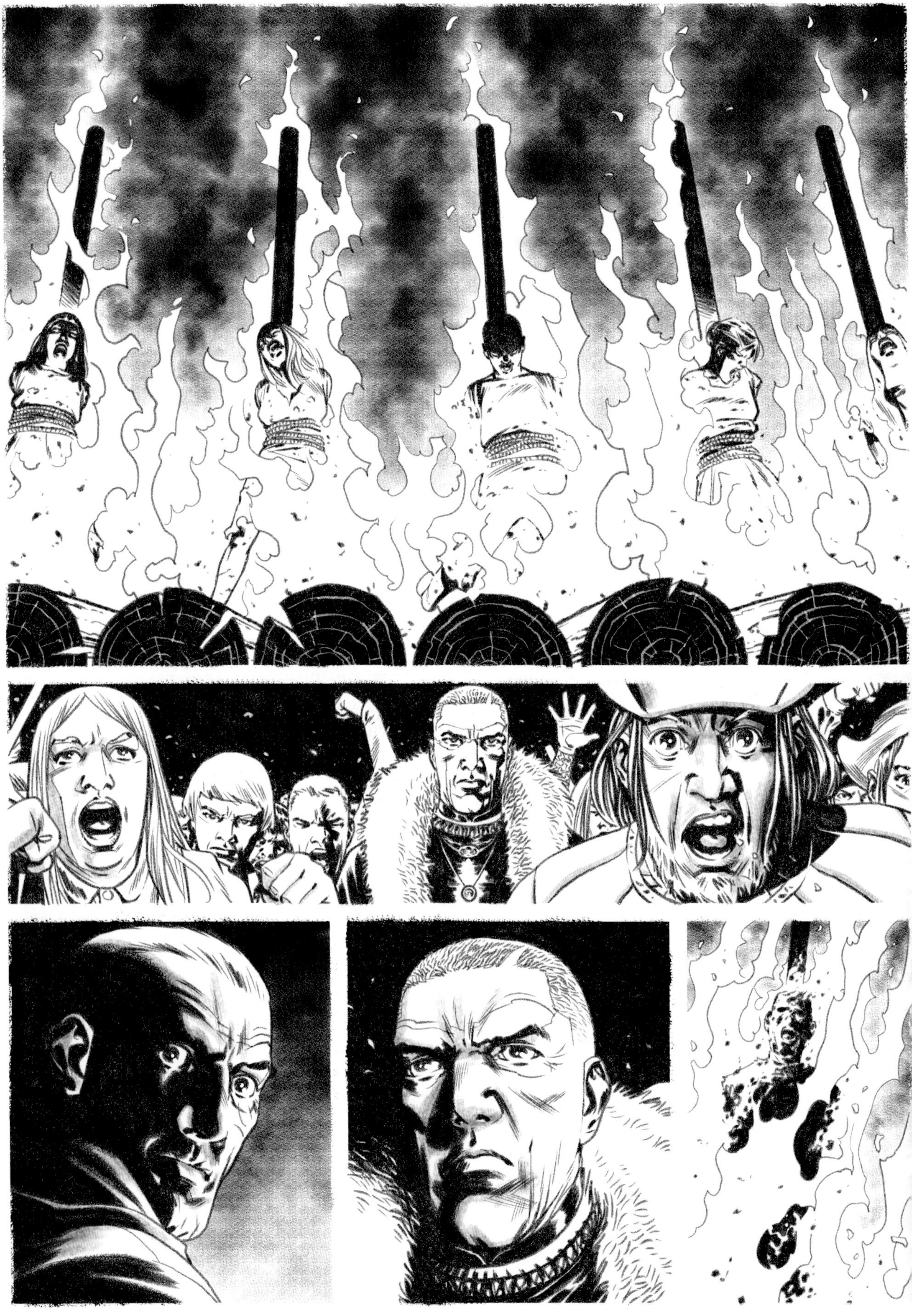

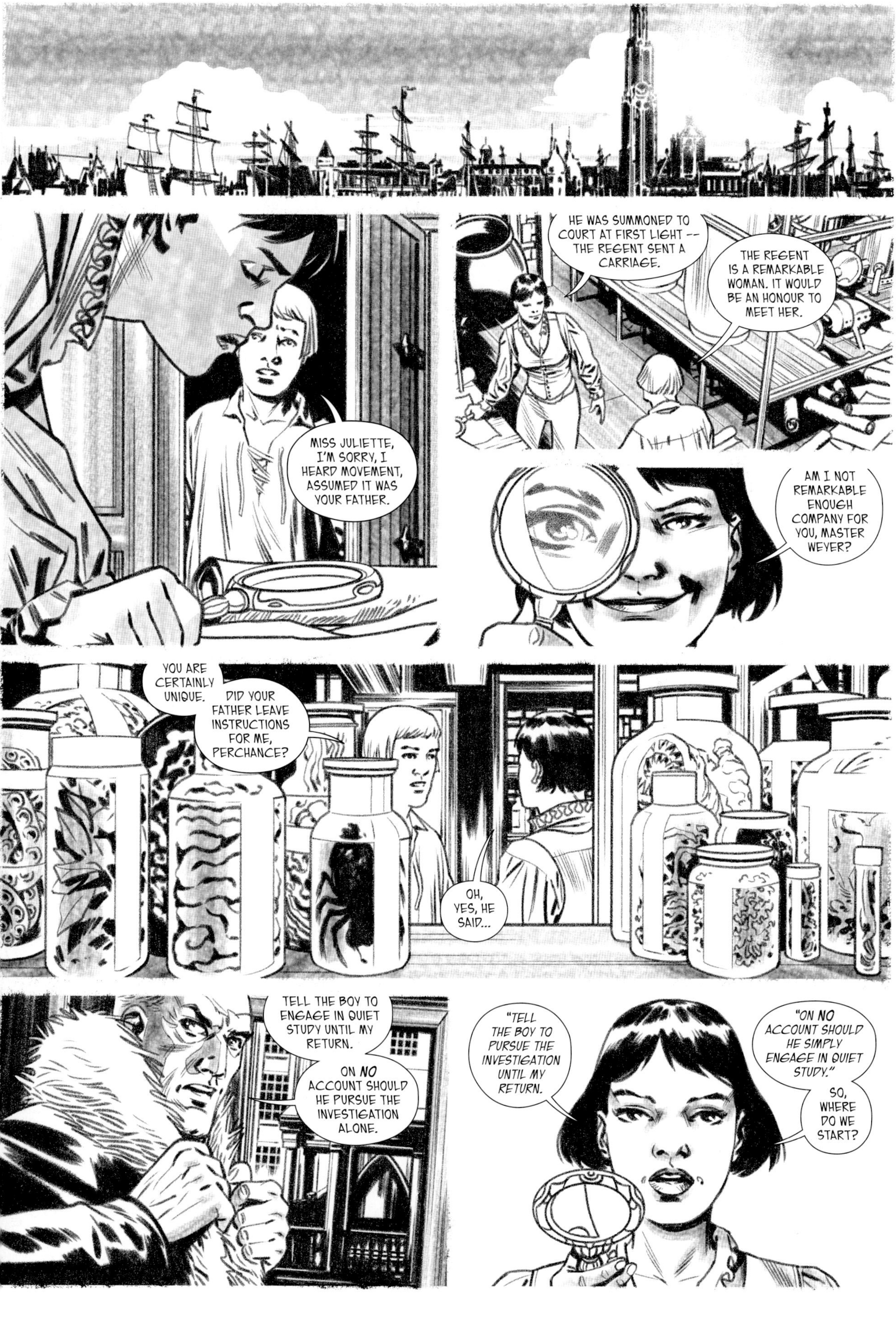

MISS JULIETTE, I'M SORRY, I HEARD MOVEMENT, ASSUMED IT WAS YOUR FATHER.
HE WAS SUMMONED TO COURT AT FIRST LIGHT -- THE REGENT SENT A CARRIAGE.
THE REGENT IS A REMARKABLE WOMAN. IT WOULD BE AN HONOUR TO MEET HER.
AM I NOT REMARKABLE ENOUGH COMPANY FOR YOU, MASTER WEYER?
YOU ARE CERTAINLY UNIQUE.
DID YOUR FATHER LEAVE INSTRUCTIONS FOR ME, PERCHANCE?
OH, YES, HE SAID...
TELL THE BOY TO ENGAGE IN QUIET STUDY UNTIL MY RETURN.
ON NO ACCOUNT SHOULD HE PURSUE THE INVESTIGATION ALONE.
"TELL THE BOY TO PURSUE THE INVESTIGATION UNTIL MY RETURN.
"ON NO ACCOUNT SHOULD HE SIMPLY ENGAGE IN QUIET STUDY."
SO, WHERE DO WE START?

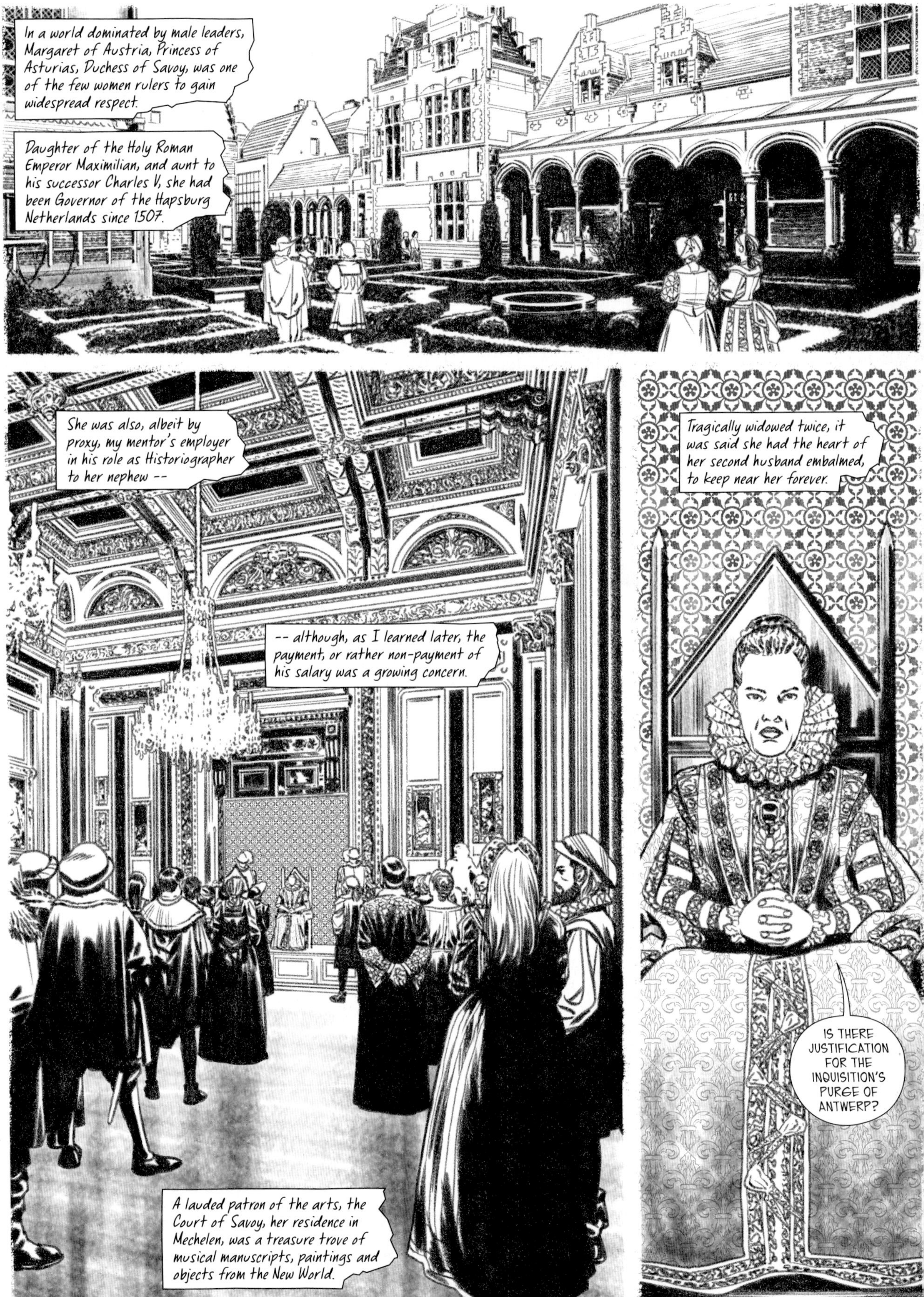
In a world dominated by male leaders, Margaret of Austria, Princess of Asturias, Duchess of Savoy, was one of the few women rulers to gain widespread respect.
Daughter of the Holy Roman Emperor Maximilian, and aunt to his successor Charles V, she had been Governor of the Hapsburg Netherlands since 1507.
She was also, albeit by proxy, my mentor's employer in his role as Historiographer to her nephew --
-- although, as I learned later, the payment, or rather non-payment of his salary was a growing concern.
A lauded patron of the arts, the Court of Savoy, her residence in Mechelen, was a treasure trove of musical manuscripts, paintings and objects from the New World.
Tragically widowed twice, it was said she had the heart of her second husband embalmed, to keep near her forever.
IS THERE JUSTIFICATION FOR THE INQUISITION'S PURGE OF ANTWERP?

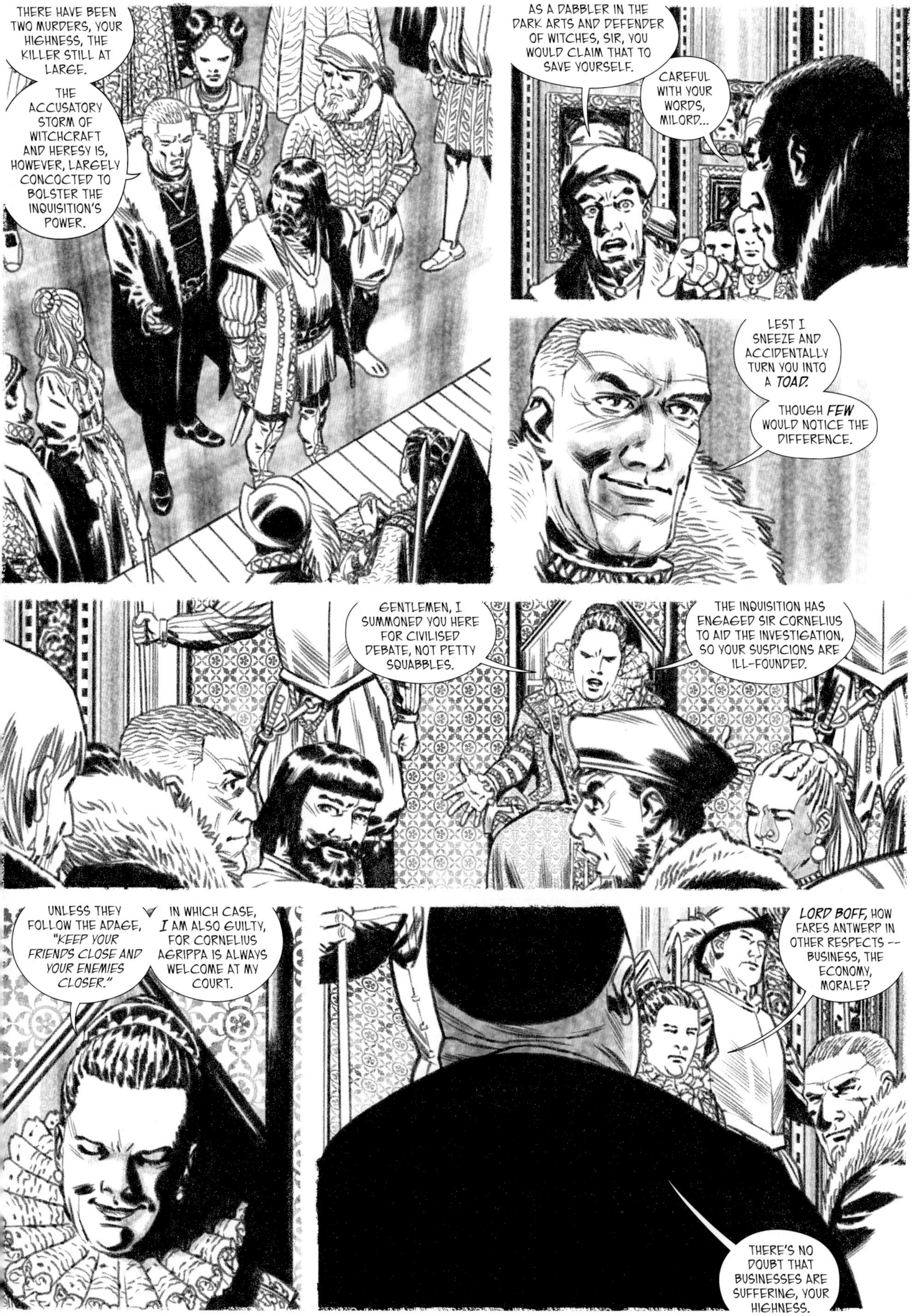
THERE HAVE BEEN TWO MURDERS, YOUR HIGHNESS, THE KILLER STILL AT LARGE.
THE ACCUSATORY STORM OF WITCHCRAFT AND HERESY IS, HOWEVER, LARGELY CONCOCTED TO BOLSTER THE INQUISITION'S POWER.
AS A DABBLER IN THE DARK ARTS AND DEFENDER OF WITCHES, SIR, YOU WOULD CLAIM THAT TO SAVE YOURSELF.
CAREFUL WITH YOUR WORDS, MILORD...
LEST I SNEEZE AND ACCIDENTALLY TURN YOU INTO A *TOAD.*
THOUGH *FEW* WOULD NOTICE THE DIFFERENCE.
GENTLEMEN, I SUMMONED YOU HERE FOR CIVILISED DEBATE, NOT PETTY SQUABBLES.
THE INQUISITION HAS ENGAGED SIR CORNELIUS TO AID THE INVESTIGATION, SO YOUR SUSPICIONS ARE ILL-FOUNDED.
UNLESS THEY FOLLOW THE ADAGE, *"KEEP YOUR FRIENDS CLOSE AND YOUR ENEMIES CLOSER."*
IN WHICH CASE, *I* AM ALSO GUILTY, FOR CORNELIUS AGRIPPA IS ALWAYS WELCOME AT MY COURT.
LORD BOFF, HOW FARES ANTWERP IN OTHER RESPECTS -- BUSINESS, THE ECONOMY, MORALE?
THERE'S NO DOUBT THAT BUSINESSES ARE SUFFERING, YOUR HIGHNESS.

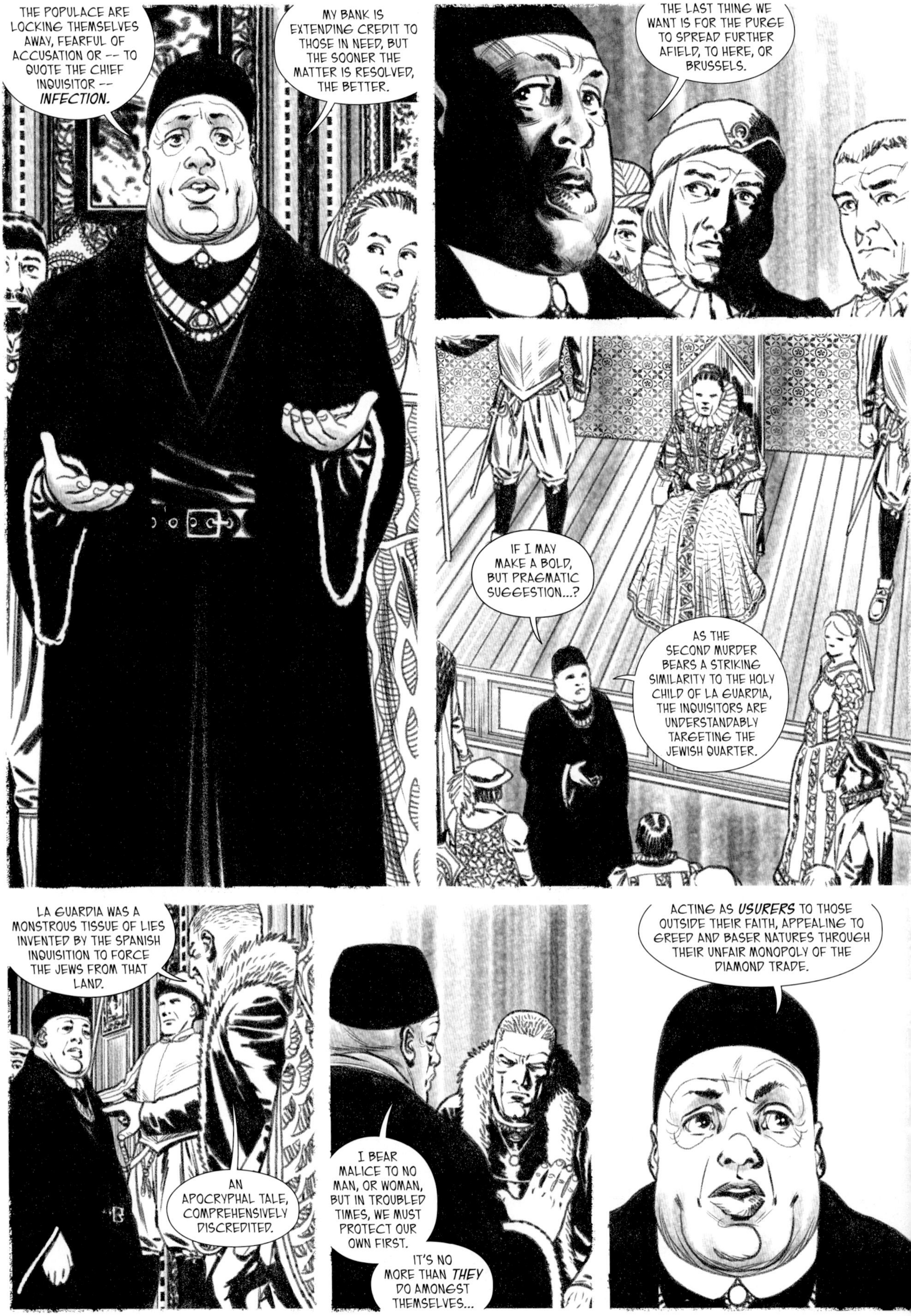
THE POPULACE ARE LOCKING THEMSELVES AWAY, FEARFUL OF ACCUSATION OR -- TO QUOTE THE CHIEF INQUISITOR -- INFECTION.
MY BANK IS EXTENDING CREDIT TO THOSE IN NEED, BUT THE SOONER THE MATTER IS RESOLVED, THE BETTER.
THE LAST THING WE WANT IS FOR THE PURGE TO SPREAD FURTHER AFIELD, TO HERE, OR BRUSSELS.
IF I MAY MAKE A BOLD, BUT PRAGMATIC SUGGESTION...?
AS THE SECOND MURDER BEARS A STRIKING SIMILARITY TO THE HOLY CHILD OF LA GUARDIA, THE INQUISITORS ARE UNDERSTANDABLY TARGETING THE JEWISH QUARTER.
LA GUARDIA WAS A MONSTROUS TISSUE OF LIES INVENTED BY THE SPANISH INQUISITION TO FORCE THE JEWS FROM THAT LAND.
AN APOCRYPHAL TALE, COMPREHENSIVELY DISCREDITED.
I BEAR MALICE TO NO MAN, OR WOMAN, BUT IN TROUBLED TIMES, WE MUST PROTECT OUR OWN FIRST.
IT'S NO MORE THAN THEY DO AMONGST THEMSELVES...
ACTING AS USURERS TO THOSE OUTSIDE THEIR FAITH, APPEALING TO GREED AND BASER NATURES THROUGH THEIR UNFAIR MONOPOLY OF THE DIAMOND TRADE.

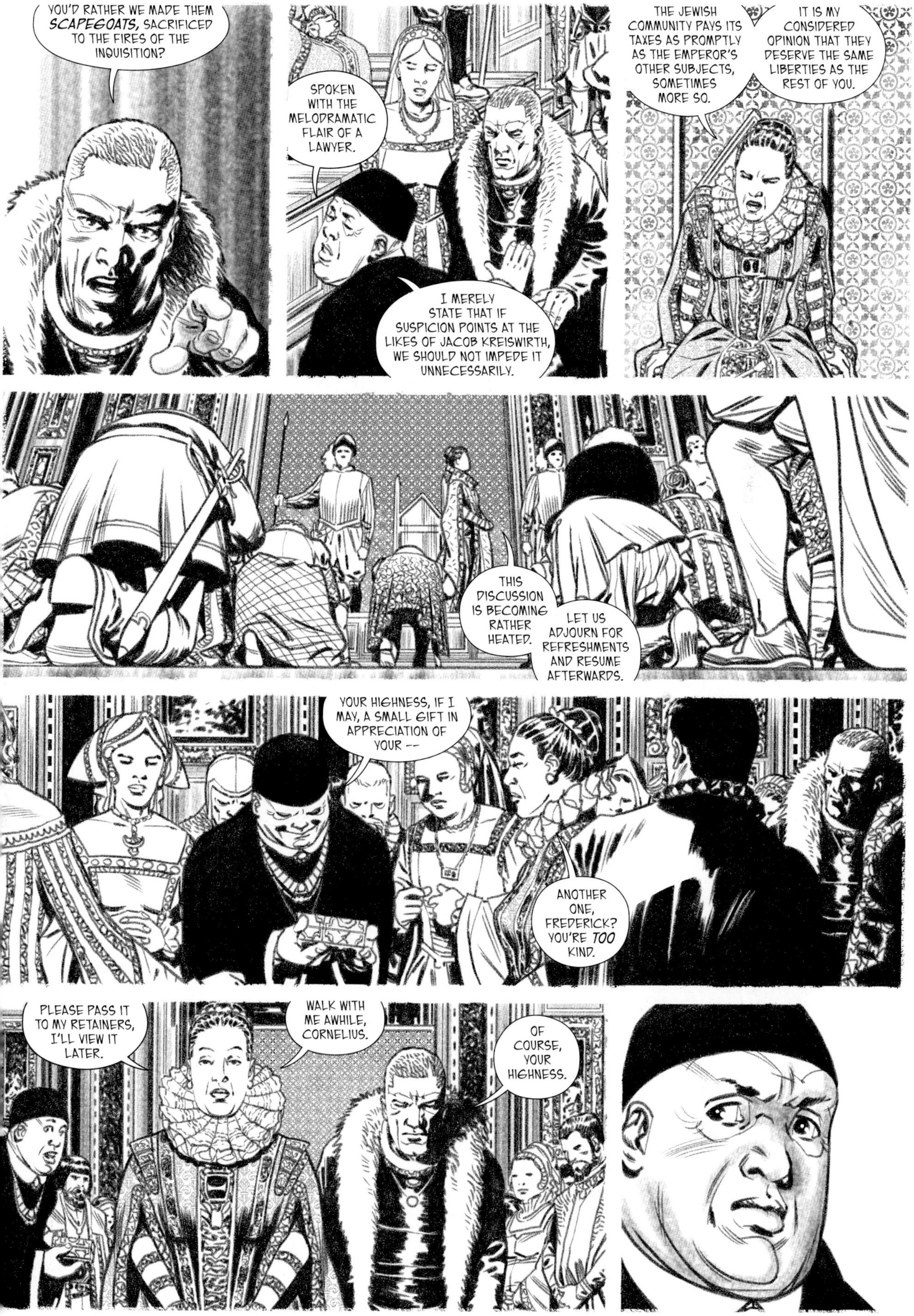
YOU'D RATHER WE MADE THEM SCAPEGOATS, SACRIFICED TO THE FIRES OF THE INQUISITION?
SPOKEN WITH THE MELODRAMATIC FLAIR OF A LAWYER.
I MERELY STATE THAT IF SUSPICION POINTS AT THE LIKES OF JACOB KREISWIRTH, WE SHOULD NOT IMPEDE IT UNNECESSARILY.
THE JEWISH COMMUNITY PAYS ITS TAXES AS PROMPTLY AS THE EMPEROR'S OTHER SUBJECTS, SOMETIMES MORE SO.
IT IS MY CONSIDERED OPINION THAT THEY DESERVE THE SAME LIBERTIES AS THE REST OF YOU.
THIS DISCUSSION IS BECOMING RATHER HEATED.
LET US ADJOURN FOR REFRESHMENTS AND RESUME AFTERWARDS.
YOUR HIGHNESS, IF I MAY, A SMALL GIFT IN APPRECIATION OF YOUR --
ANOTHER ONE, FREDERICK? YOU'RE TOO KIND.
PLEASE PASS IT TO MY RETAINERS, I'LL VIEW IT LATER.
WALK WITH ME AWHILE, CORNELIUS.
OF COURSE, YOUR HIGHNESS.

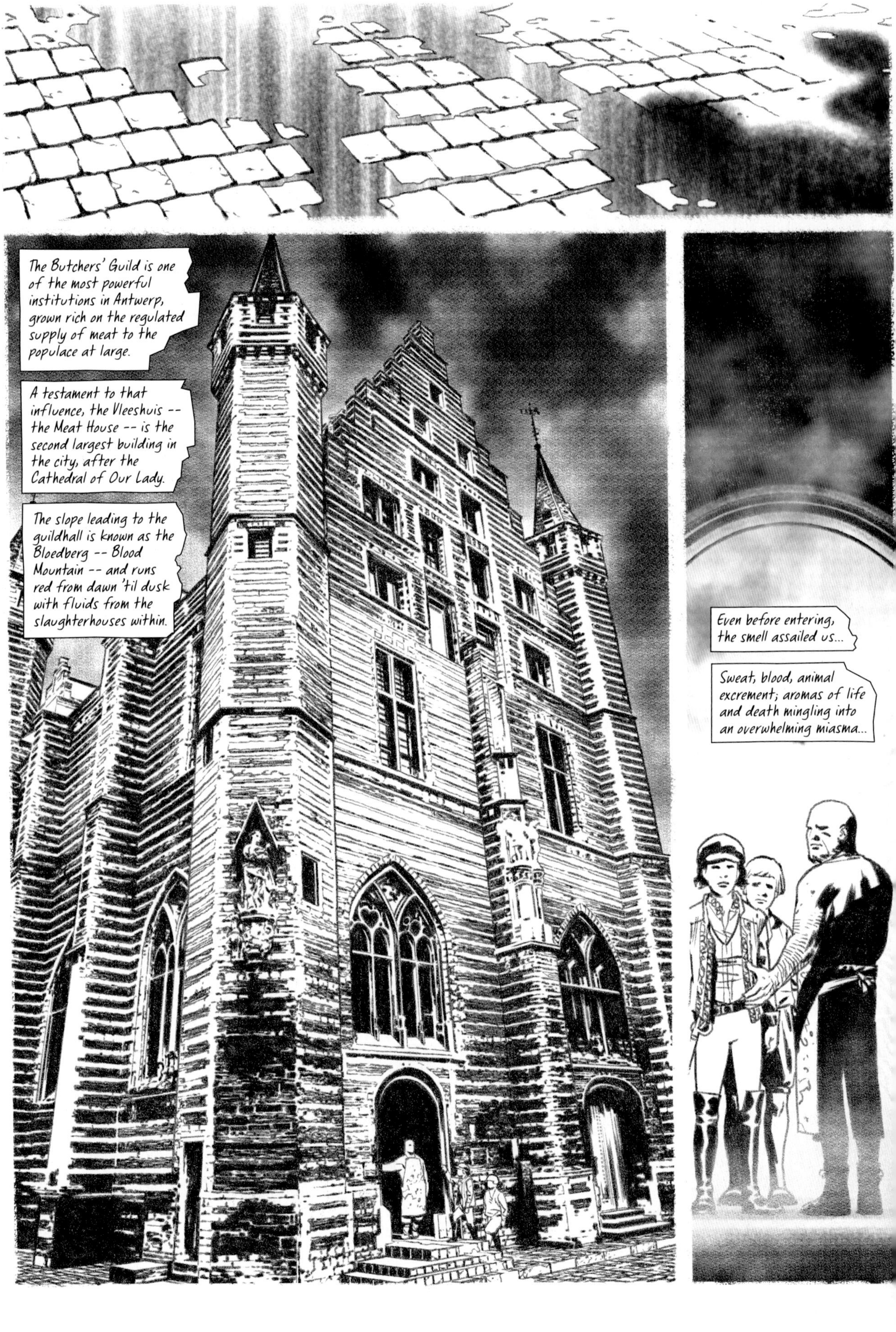
The Butchers' Guild is one of the most powerful institutions in Antwerp, grown rich on the regulated supply of meat to the populace at large.
A testament to that influence, the Vleeshuis -- the Meat House -- is the second largest building in the city, after the Cathedral of Our Lady.
The slope leading to the guildhall is known as the Bloedberg -- Blood Mountain -- and runs red from dawn 'til dusk with fluids from the slaughterhouses within.
Even before entering, the smell assailed us...
Sweat, blood, animal excrement; aromas of life and death mingling into an overwhelming miasma...

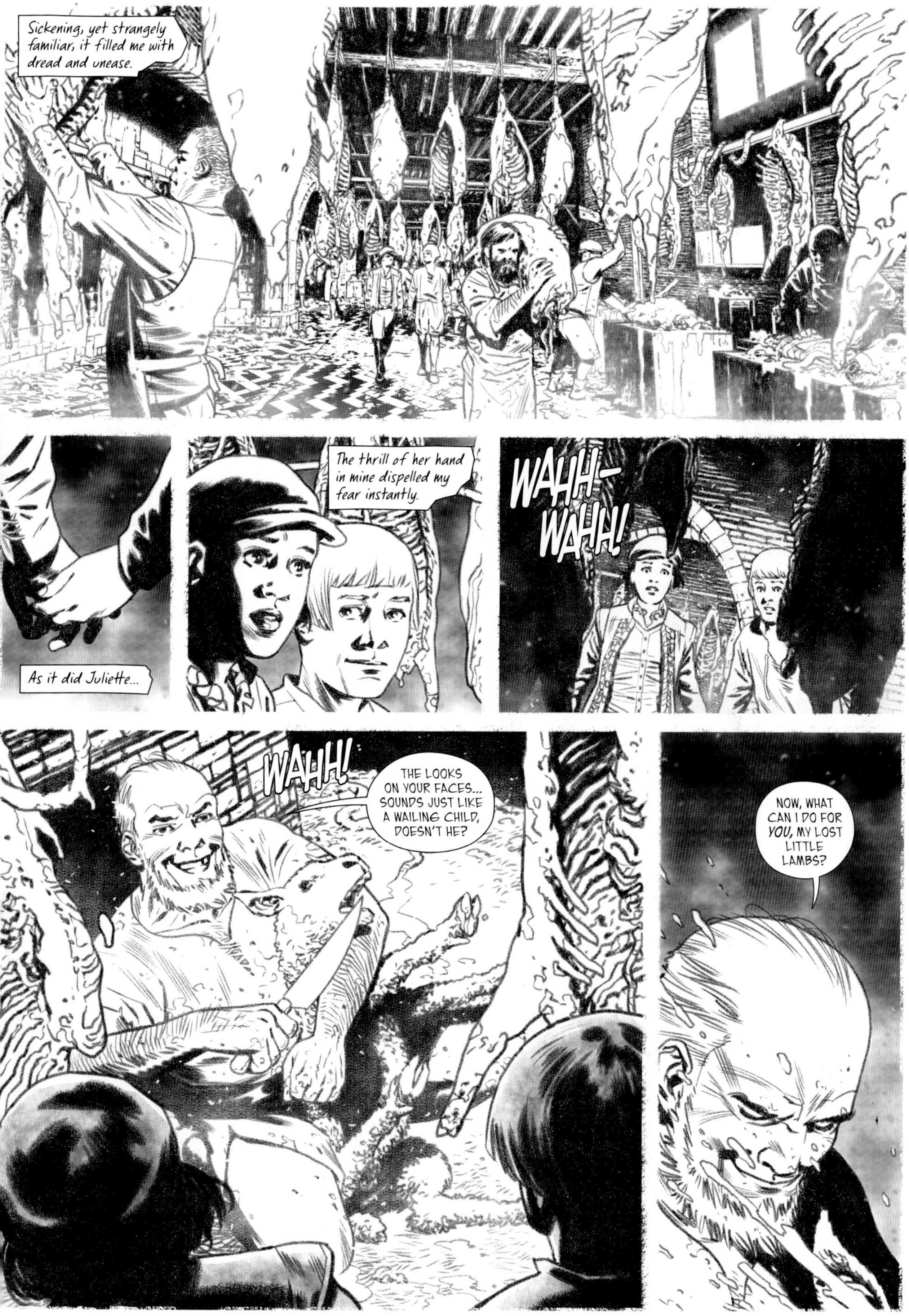
Sickening, yet strangely familiar, it filled me with dread and unease.
As it did Juliette...
The thrill of her hand in mine dispelled my fear instantly.
WAHH-WAHH!
WAHH!
THE LOOKS ON YOUR FACES... SOUNDS JUST LIKE A WAILING CHILD, DOESN'T HE?
NOW, WHAT CAN I DO FOR *YOU*, MY LOST LITTLE LAMBS?

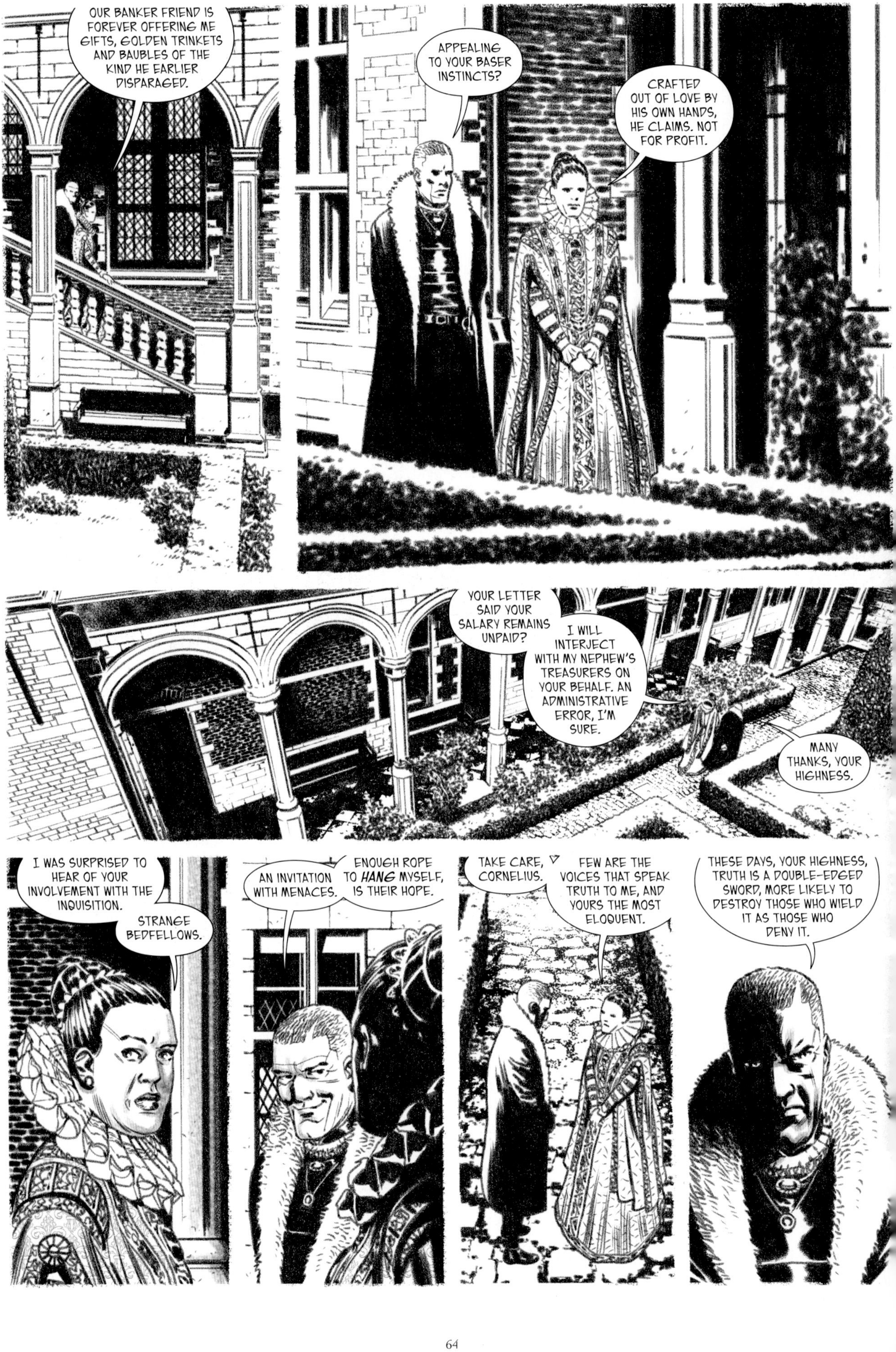
OUR BANKER FRIEND IS FOREVER OFFERING ME GIFTS, GOLDEN TRINKETS AND BAUBLES OF THE KIND HE EARLIER DISPARAGED.
APPEALING TO YOUR BASER INSTINCTS?
CRAFTED OUT OF LOVE BY HIS OWN HANDS, HE CLAIMS. NOT FOR PROFIT.
YOUR LETTER SAID YOUR SALARY REMAINS UNPAID?
I WILL INTERJECT WITH MY NEPHEW'S TREASURERS ON YOUR BEHALF. AN ADMINISTRATIVE ERROR, I'M SURE.
MANY THANKS, YOUR HIGHNESS.
I WAS SURPRISED TO HEAR OF YOUR INVOLVEMENT WITH THE INQUISITION.
STRANGE BEDFELLOWS.
AN INVITATION WITH MENACES.
ENOUGH ROPE TO *HANG* MYSELF, IS THEIR HOPE.
TAKE CARE, CORNELIUS.
FEW ARE THE VOICES THAT SPEAK TRUTH TO ME, AND YOURS THE MOST ELOQUENT.
THESE DAYS, YOUR HIGHNESS, TRUTH IS A DOUBLE-EDGED SWORD, MORE LIKELY TO DESTROY THOSE WHO WIELD IT AS THOSE WHO DENY IT.

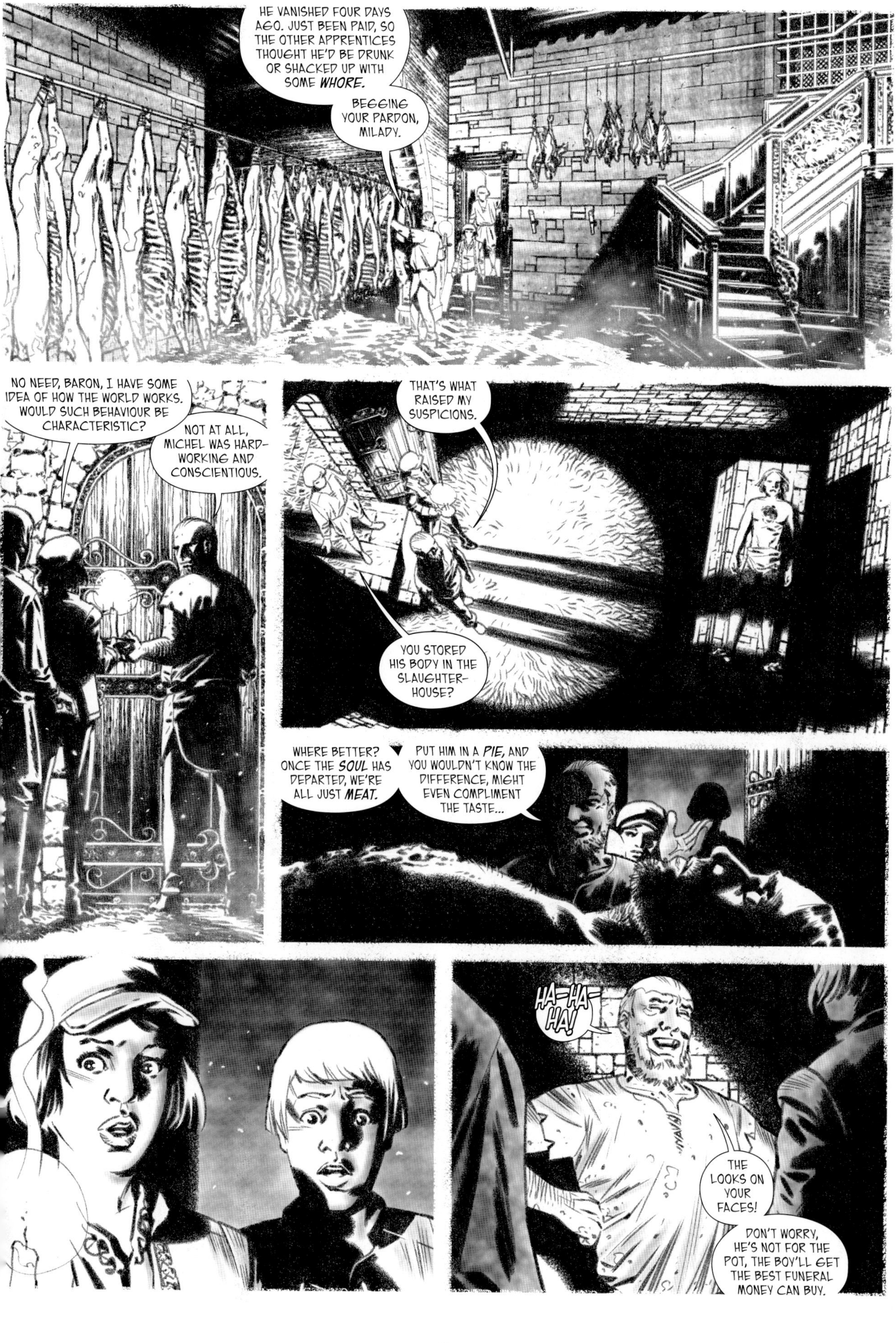
HE VANISHED FOUR DAYS AGO. JUST BEEN PAID, SO THE OTHER APPRENTICES THOUGHT HE'D BE DRUNK OR SHACKED UP WITH SOME WHORE.
BEGGING YOUR PARDON, MILADY.
NO NEED, BARON, I HAVE SOME IDEA OF HOW THE WORLD WORKS. WOULD SUCH BEHAVIOUR BE CHARACTERISTIC?
NOT AT ALL, MICHEL WAS HARD-WORKING AND CONSCIENTIOUS.
THAT'S WHAT RAISED MY SUSPICIONS.
YOU STORED HIS BODY IN THE SLAUGHTER-HOUSE?
WHERE BETTER? ONCE THE SOUL HAS DEPARTED, WE'RE ALL JUST MEAT.
PUT HIM IN A PIE, AND YOU WOULDN'T KNOW THE DIFFERENCE, MIGHT EVEN COMPLIMENT THE TASTE...
HA-HA-HA!
THE LOOKS ON YOUR FACES!
DON'T WORRY, HE'S NOT FOR THE POT, THE BOY'LL GET THE BEST FUNERAL MONEY CAN BUY.

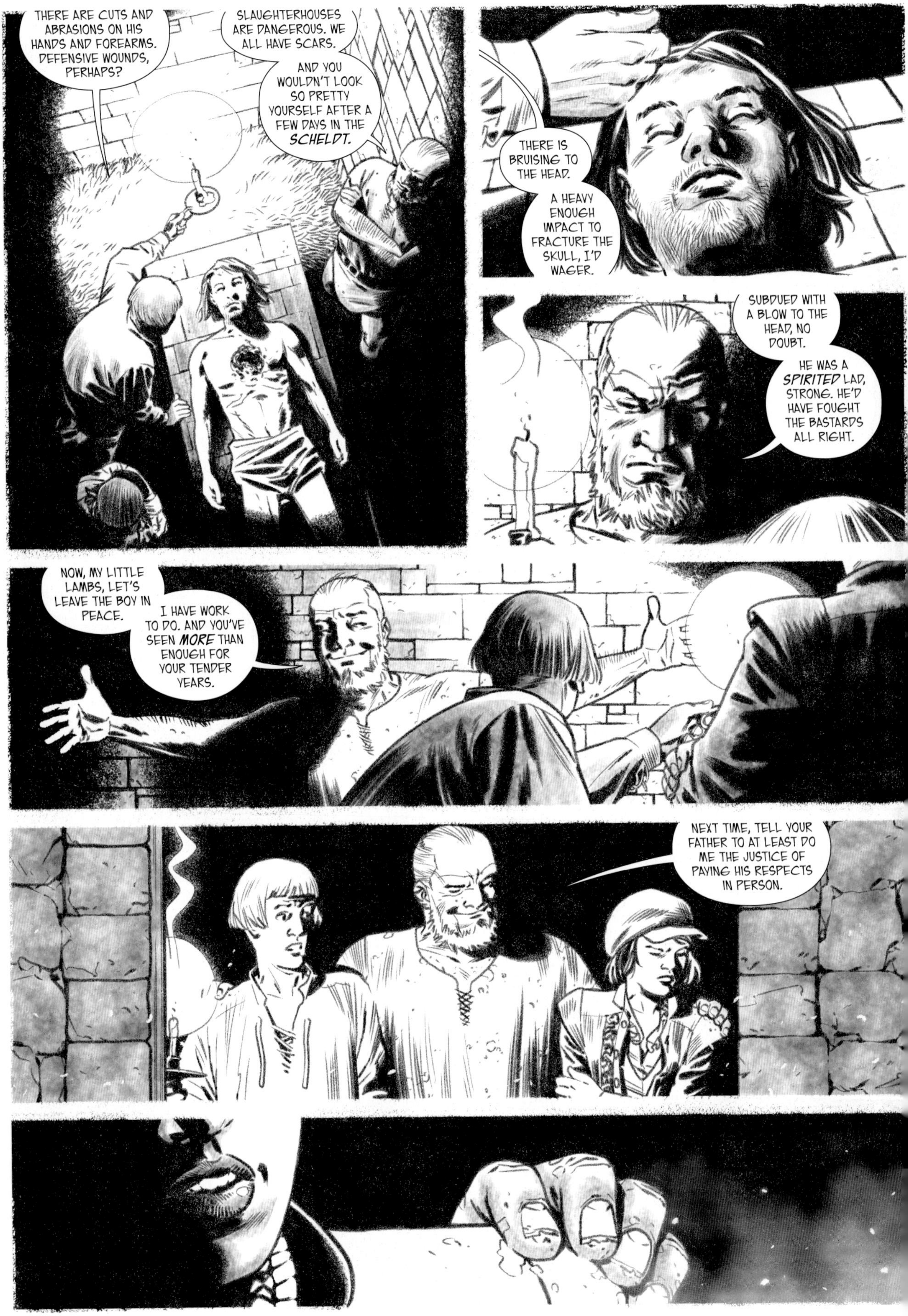
THERE ARE CUTS AND ABRASIONS ON HIS HANDS AND FOREARMS. DEFENSIVE WOUNDS, PERHAPS?
SLAUGHTERHOUSES ARE DANGEROUS. WE ALL HAVE SCARS.
AND YOU WOULDN'T LOOK SO PRETTY YOURSELF AFTER A FEW DAYS IN THE SCHELDT.
THERE IS BRUISING TO THE HEAD.
A HEAVY ENOUGH IMPACT TO FRACTURE THE SKULL, I'D WAGER.
SUBDUED WITH A BLOW TO THE HEAD, NO DOUBT.
HE WAS A SPIRITED LAD, STRONG. HE'D HAVE FOUGHT THE BASTARDS ALL RIGHT.
NOW, MY LITTLE LAMBS, LET'S LEAVE THE BOY IN PEACE.
I HAVE WORK TO DO. AND YOU'VE SEEN MORE THAN ENOUGH FOR YOUR TENDER YEARS.
NEXT TIME, TELL YOUR FATHER TO AT LEAST DO ME THE JUSTICE OF PAYING HIS RESPECTS IN PERSON.

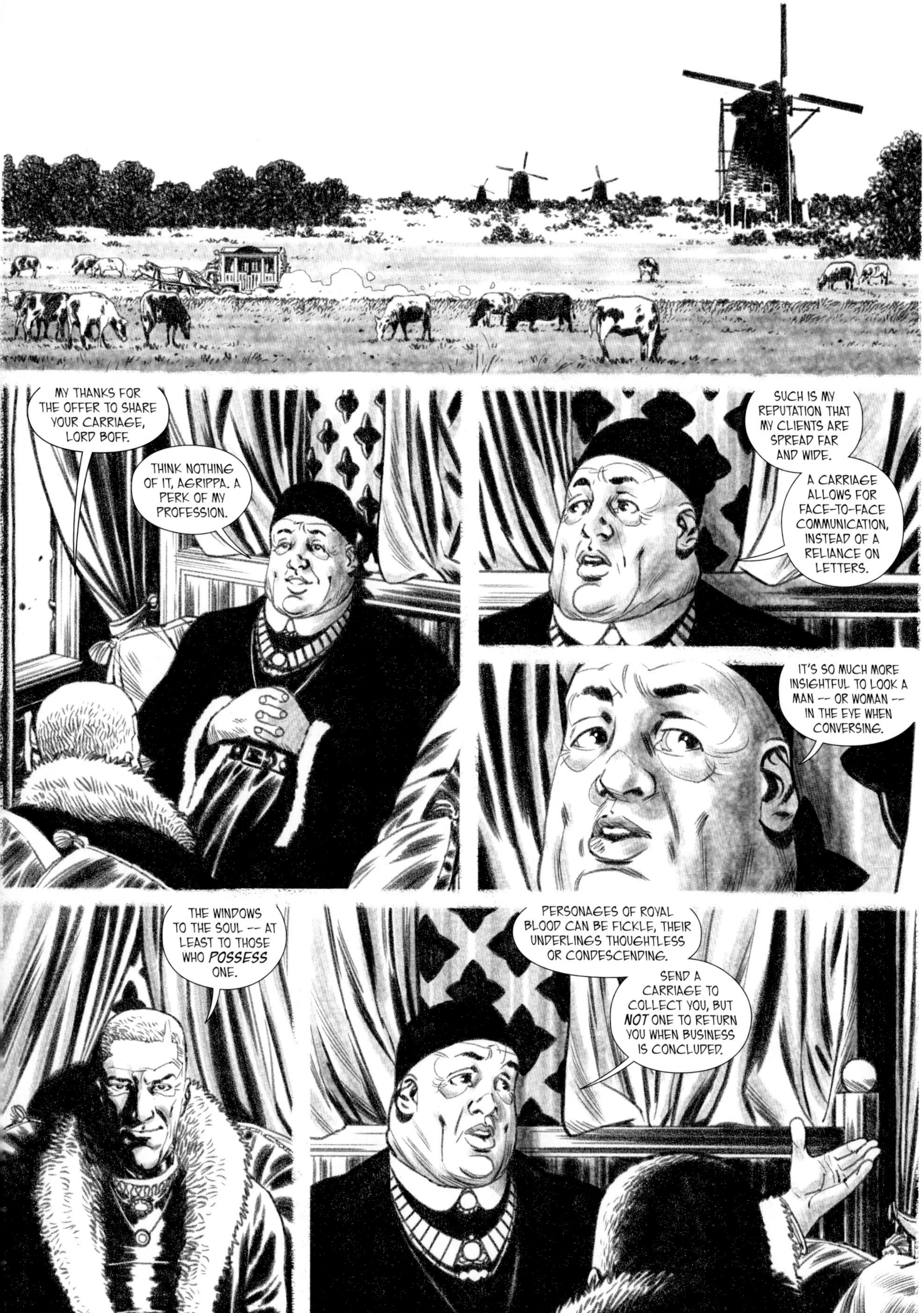
MY THANKS FOR THE OFFER TO SHARE YOUR CARRIAGE, LORD BOFF.
THINK NOTHING OF IT, AGRIPPA. A PERK OF MY PROFESSION.
SUCH IS MY REPUTATION THAT MY CLIENTS ARE SPREAD FAR AND WIDE.
A CARRIAGE ALLOWS FOR FACE-TO-FACE COMMUNICATION, INSTEAD OF A RELIANCE ON LETTERS.
IT'S SO MUCH MORE INSIGHTFUL TO LOOK A MAN -- OR WOMAN -- IN THE EYE WHEN CONVERSING.
THE WINDOWS TO THE SOUL -- AT LEAST TO THOSE WHO *POSSESS* ONE.
PERSONAGES OF ROYAL BLOOD CAN BE FICKLE, THEIR UNDERLINGS THOUGHTLESS OR CONDESCENDING.
SEND A CARRIAGE TO COLLECT YOU, BUT *NOT* ONE TO RETURN YOU WHEN BUSINESS IS CONCLUDED.

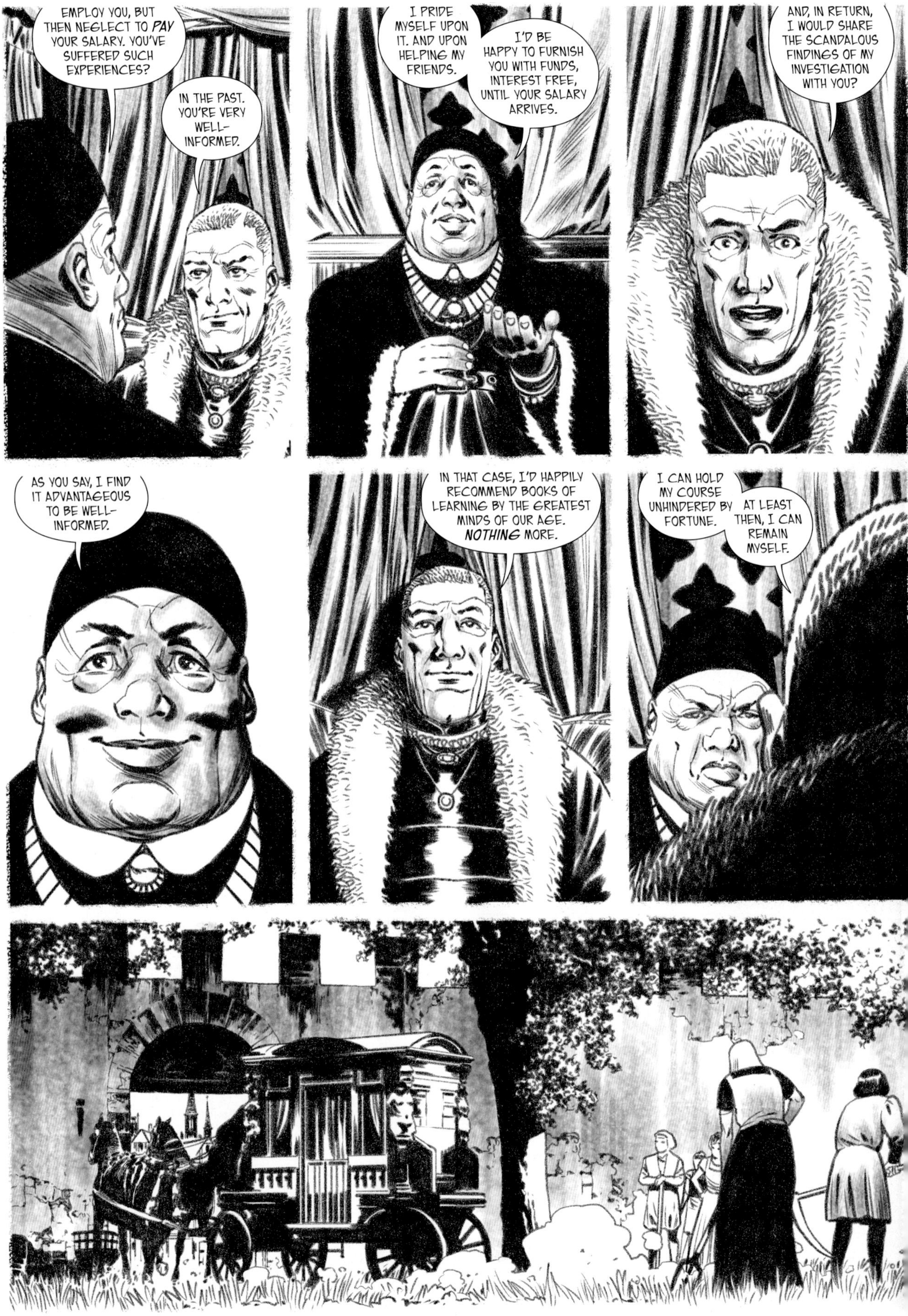
EMPLOY YOU, BUT THEN NEGLECT TO *PAY* YOUR SALARY. YOU'VE SUFFERED SUCH EXPERIENCES?
IN THE PAST. YOU'RE VERY WELL-INFORMED.
I PRIDE MYSELF UPON IT. AND UPON HELPING MY FRIENDS.
I'D BE HAPPY TO FURNISH YOU WITH FUNDS, INTEREST FREE, UNTIL YOUR SALARY ARRIVES.
AND, IN RETURN, I WOULD SHARE THE SCANDALOUS FINDINGS OF MY INVESTIGATION WITH YOU?
AS YOU SAY, I FIND IT ADVANTAGEOUS TO BE WELL-INFORMED.
IN THAT CASE, I'D HAPPILY RECOMMEND BOOKS OF LEARNING BY THE GREATEST MINDS OF OUR AGE. *NOTHING* MORE.
I CAN HOLD MY COURSE UNHINDERED BY FORTUNE.
AT LEAST THEN, I CAN REMAIN MYSELF.

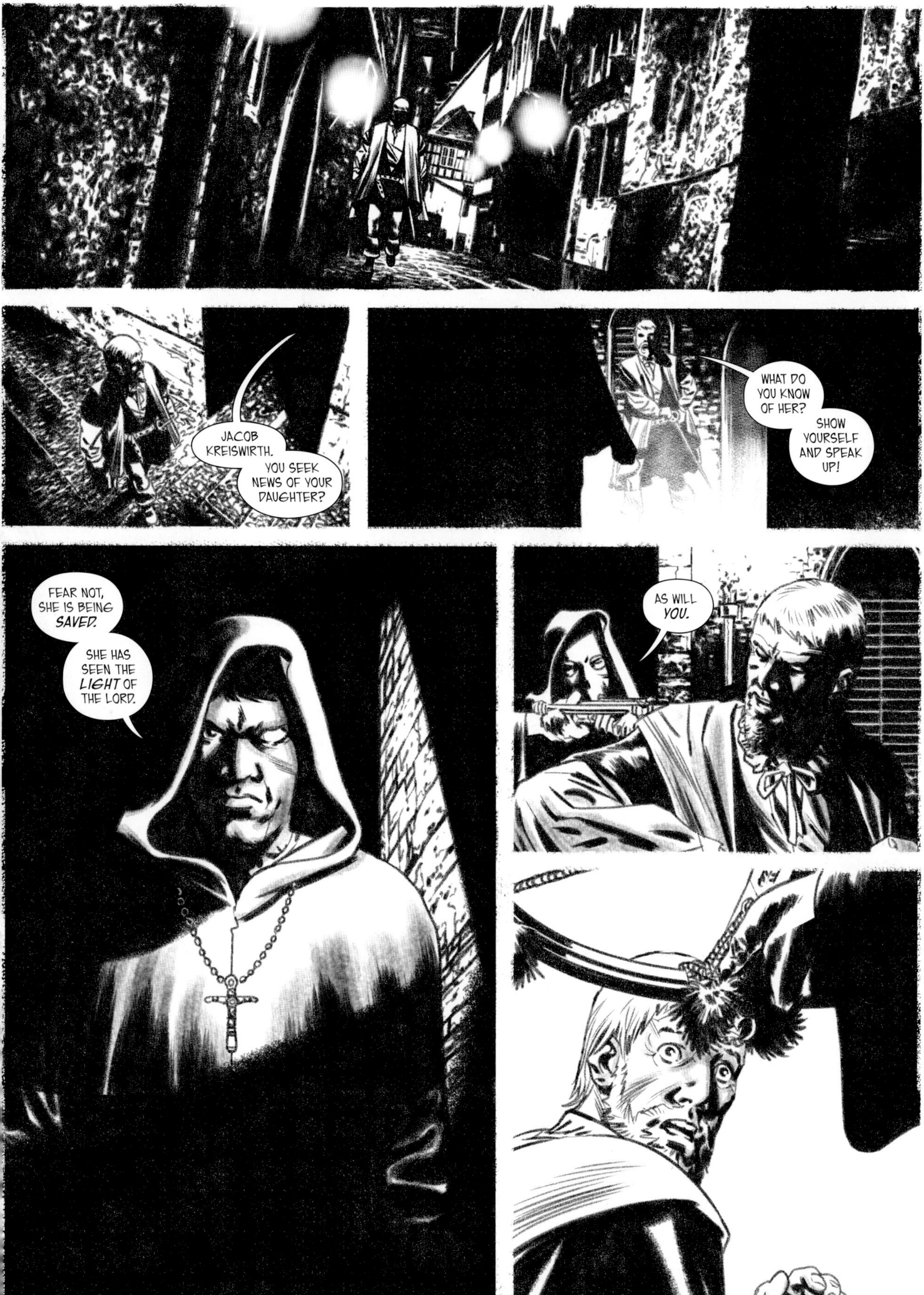
JACOB KREISWIRTH.
YOU SEEK NEWS OF YOUR DAUGHTER?
WHAT DO YOU KNOW OF HER?
SHOW YOURSELF AND SPEAK UP!
FEAR NOT, SHE IS BEING SAVED.
SHE HAS SEEN THE LIGHT OF THE LORD.
AS WILL YOU.

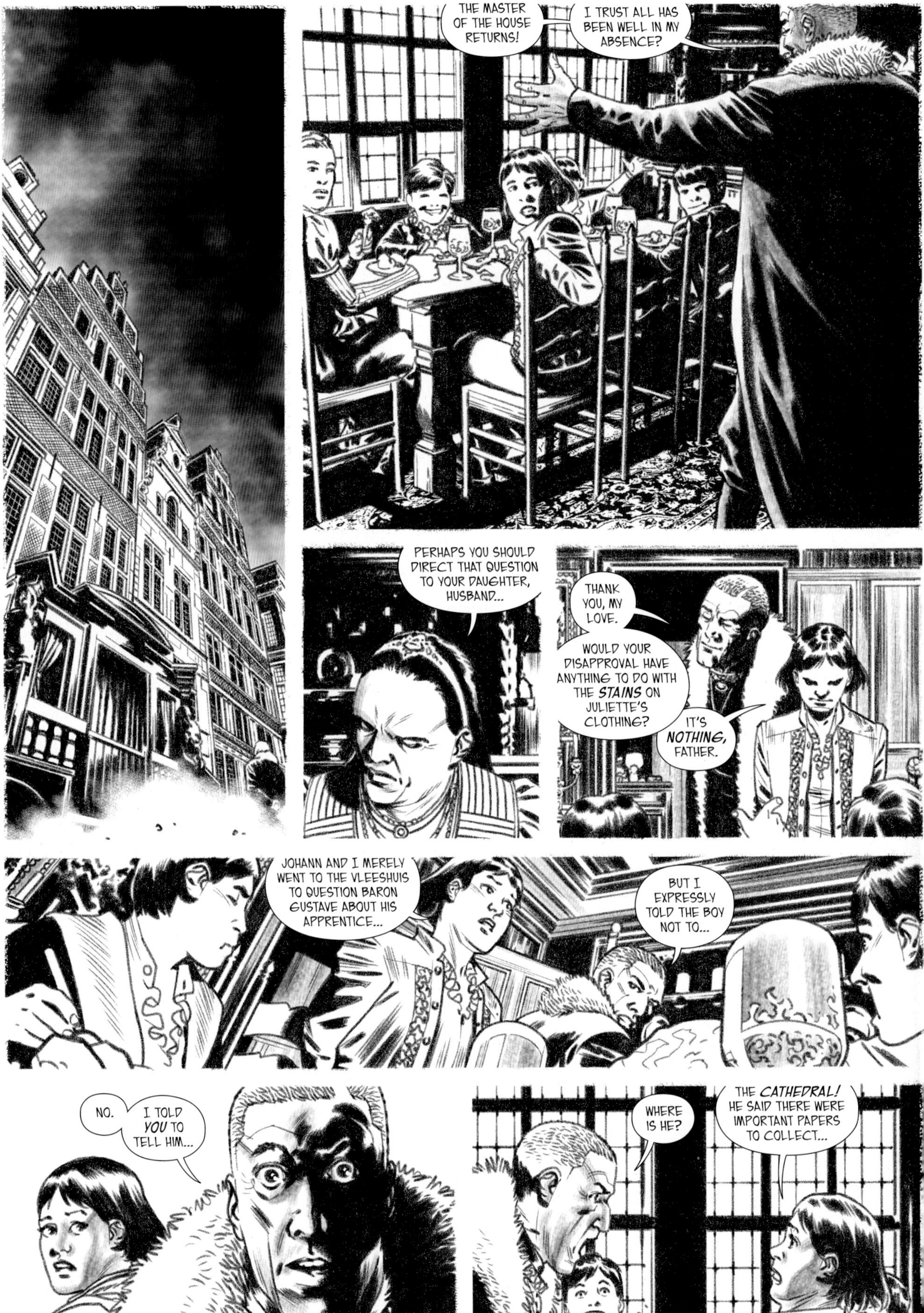

THE MASTER OF THE HOUSE RETURNS!
I TRUST ALL HAS BEEN WELL IN MY ABSENCE?
PERHAPS YOU SHOULD DIRECT THAT QUESTION TO YOUR DAUGHTER, HUSBAND...
THANK YOU, MY LOVE.
WOULD YOUR DISAPPROVAL HAVE ANYTHING TO DO WITH THE STAINS ON JULIETTE'S CLOTHING?
IT'S NOTHING, FATHER.
JOHANN AND I MERELY WENT TO THE VLEESHUIS TO QUESTION BARON GUSTAVE ABOUT HIS APPRENTICE...
BUT I EXPRESSLY TOLD THE BOY NOT TO...
NO.
I TOLD YOU TO TELL HIM...
WHERE IS HE?
THE CATHEDRAL! HE SAID THERE WERE IMPORTANT PAPERS TO COLLECT...

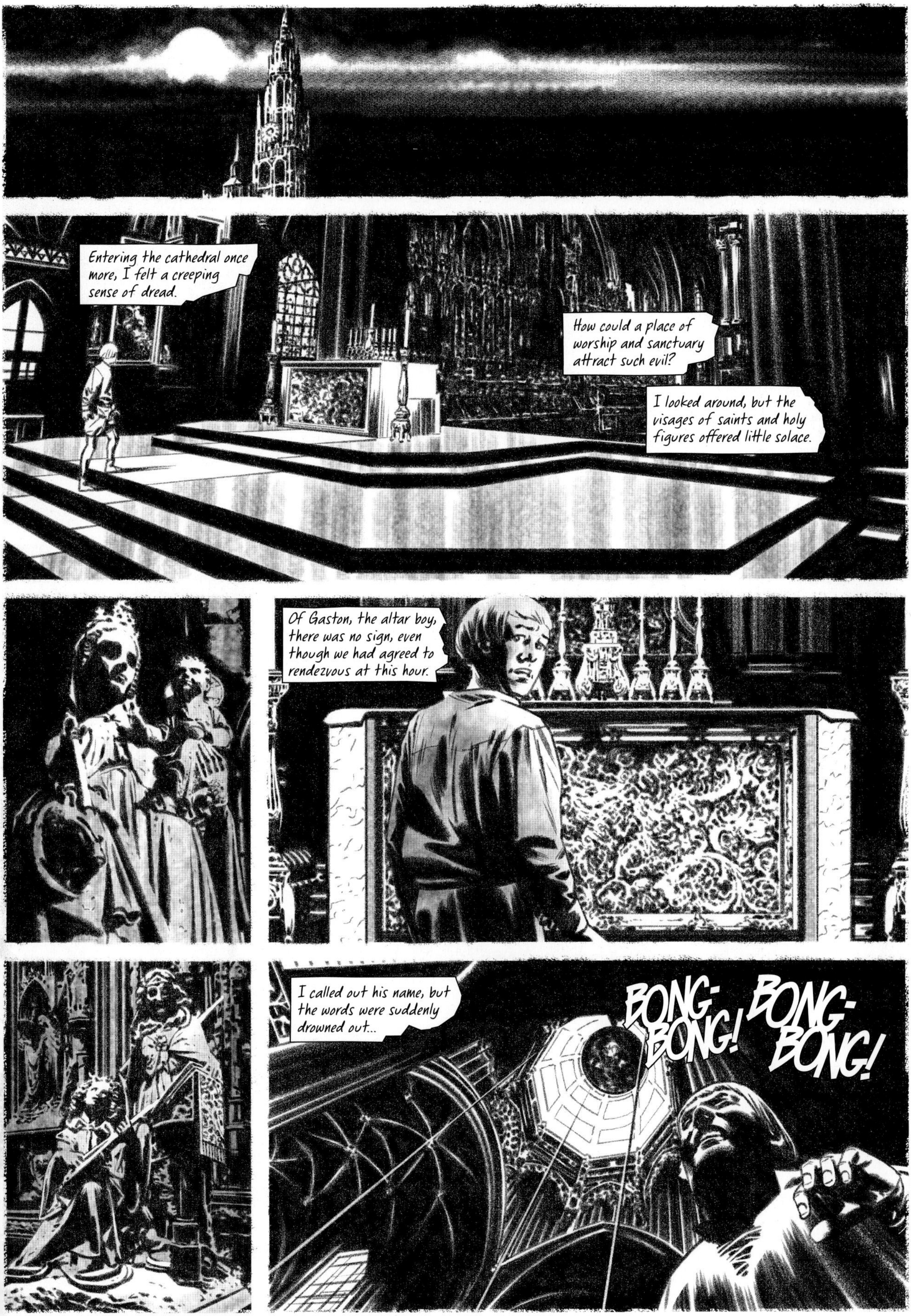
Entering the cathedral once more, I felt a creeping sense of dread.
How could a place of worship and sanctuary attract such evil?
I looked around, but the visages of saints and holy figures offered little solace.
Of Gaston, the altar boy, there was no sign, even though we had agreed to rendezvous at this hour.
I called out his name, but the words were suddenly drowned out...
BONG-BONG!
BONG-BONG!

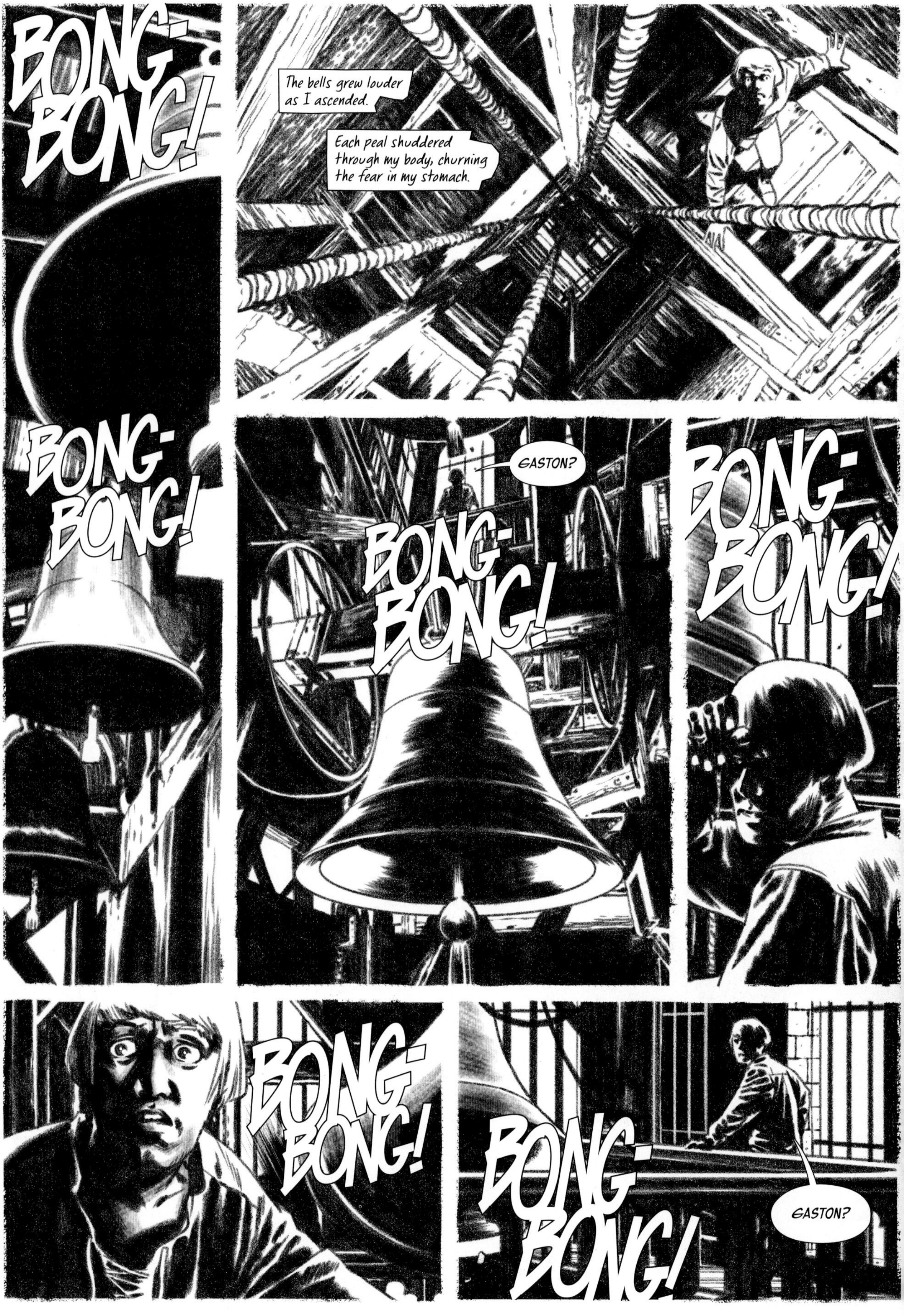

BONG-BONG!
The bells grew louder as I ascended.
Each peal shuddered through my body, churning the fear in my stomach.
BONG-BONG!
GASTON?
BONG-BONG!
BONG-BONG!
BONG-BONG!
BONG-BONG!
GASTON?

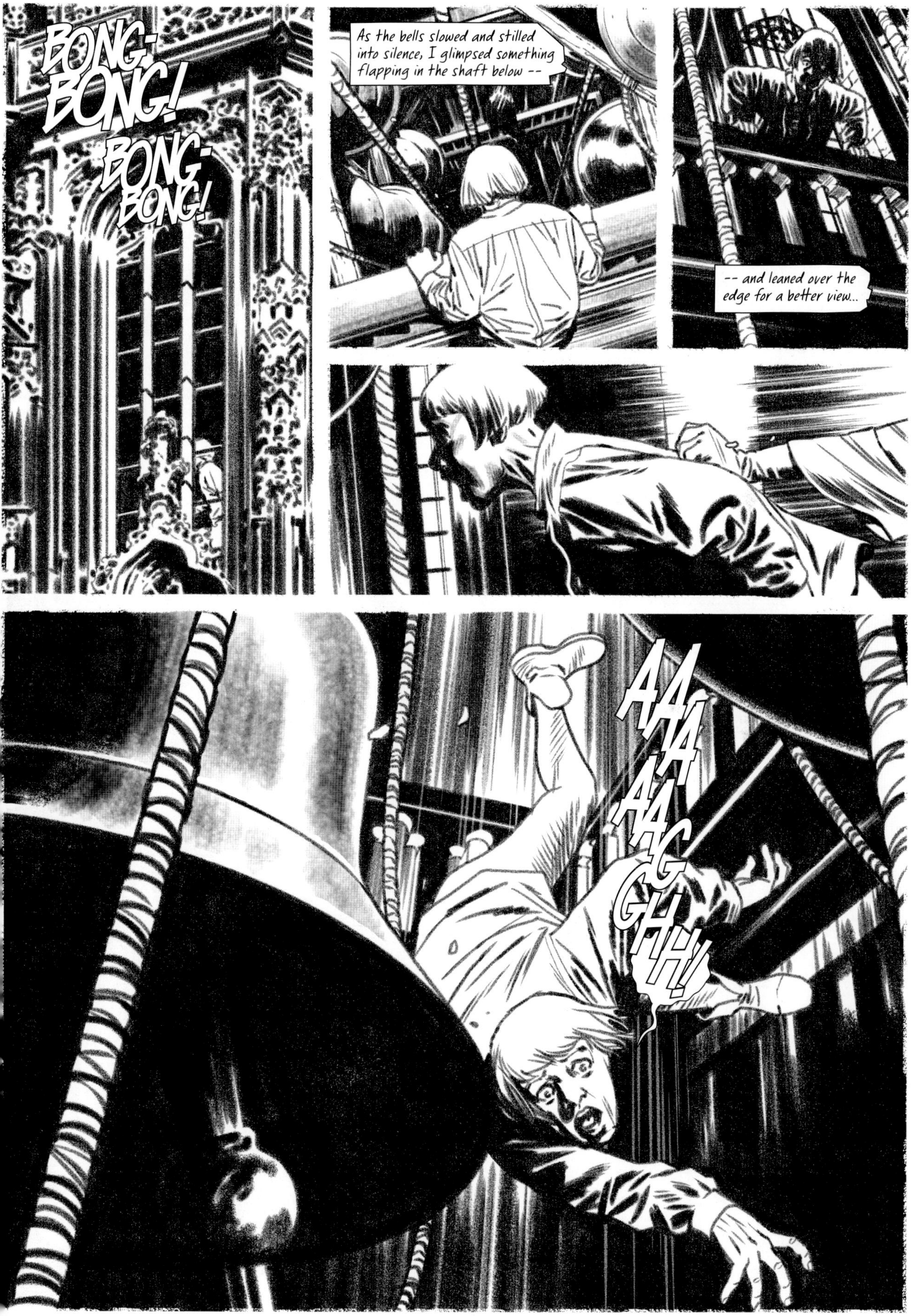
BONG-BONG!
BONG-BONG!
As the bells slowed and stilled into silence, I glimpsed something flapping in the shaft below --
-- and leaned over the edge for a better view...
AAAAAAGGHH!

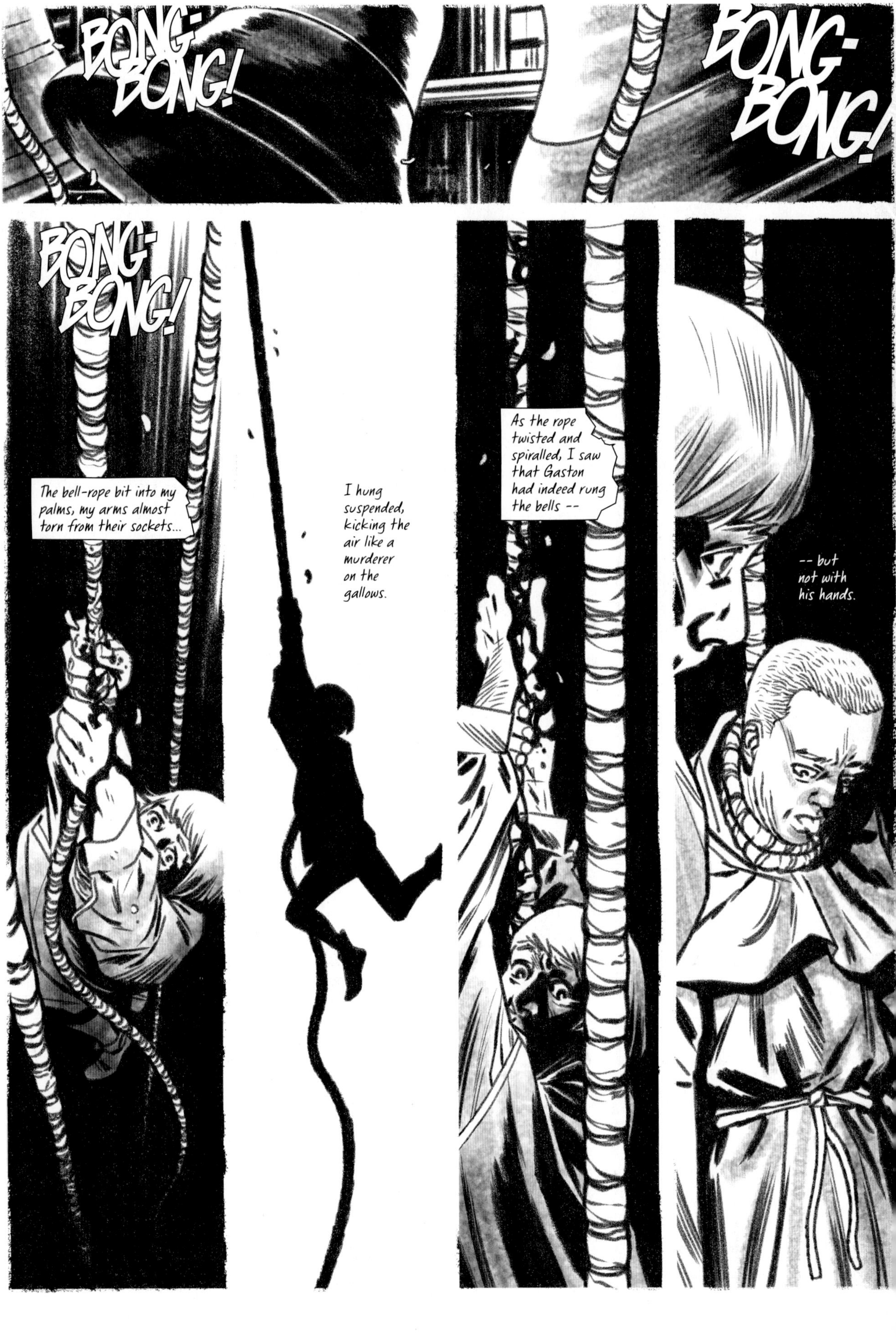
BONG-BONG!
BONG-BONG!
BONG-BONG!
The bell-rope bit into my palms, my arms almost torn from their sockets...
I hung suspended, kicking the air like a murderer on the gallows.
As the rope twisted and spiralled, I saw that Gaston had indeed rung the bells --
-- but not with his hands.

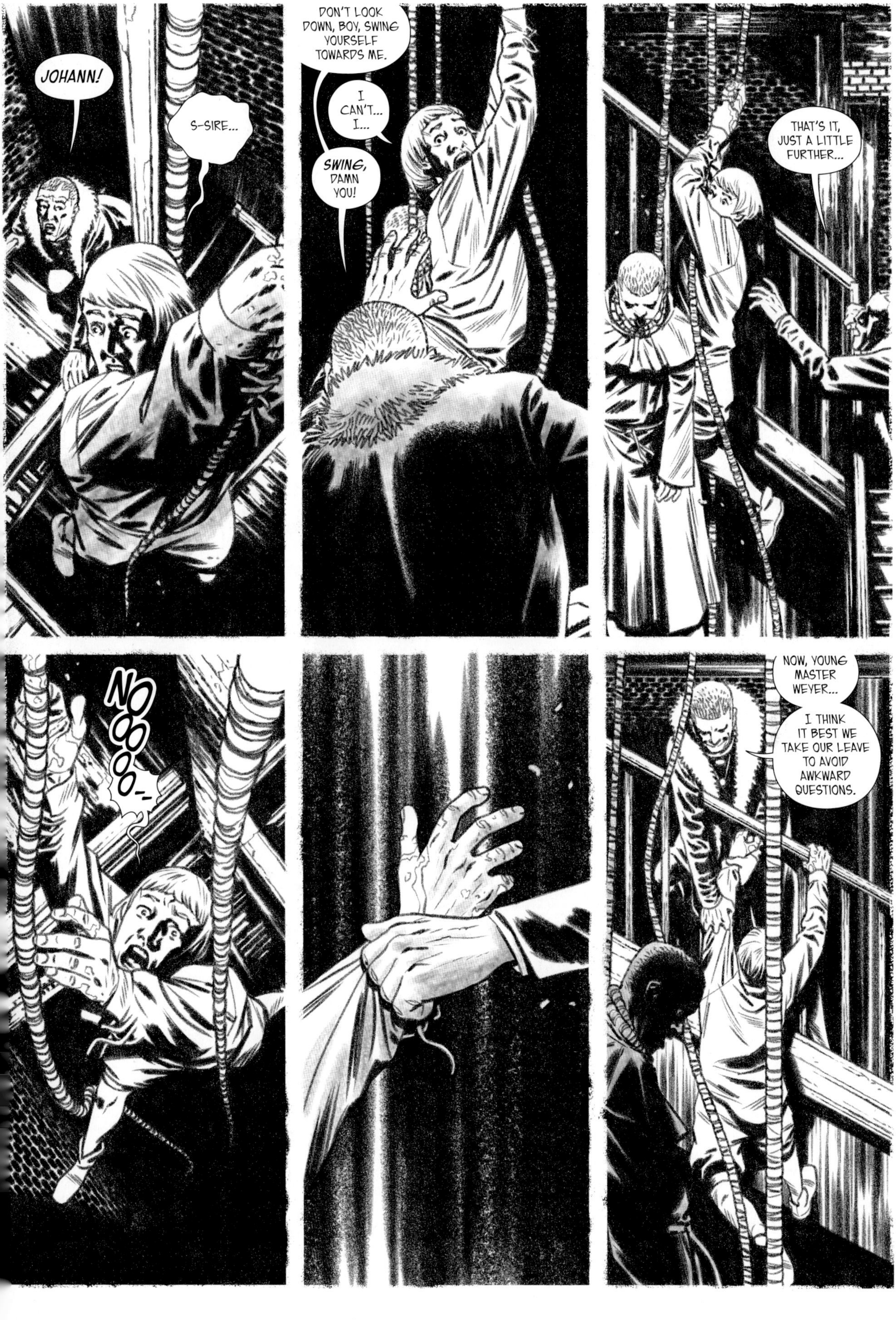

JOHANN!
S-SIRE...
DON'T LOOK DOWN, BOY, SWING YOURSELF TOWARDS ME.
I CAN'T... I...
SWING, DAMN YOU!
THAT'S IT, JUST A LITTLE FURTHER...
NOOOOO--
NOW, YOUNG MASTER WEYER...
I THINK IT BEST WE TAKE OUR LEAVE TO AVOID AWKWARD QUESTIONS.

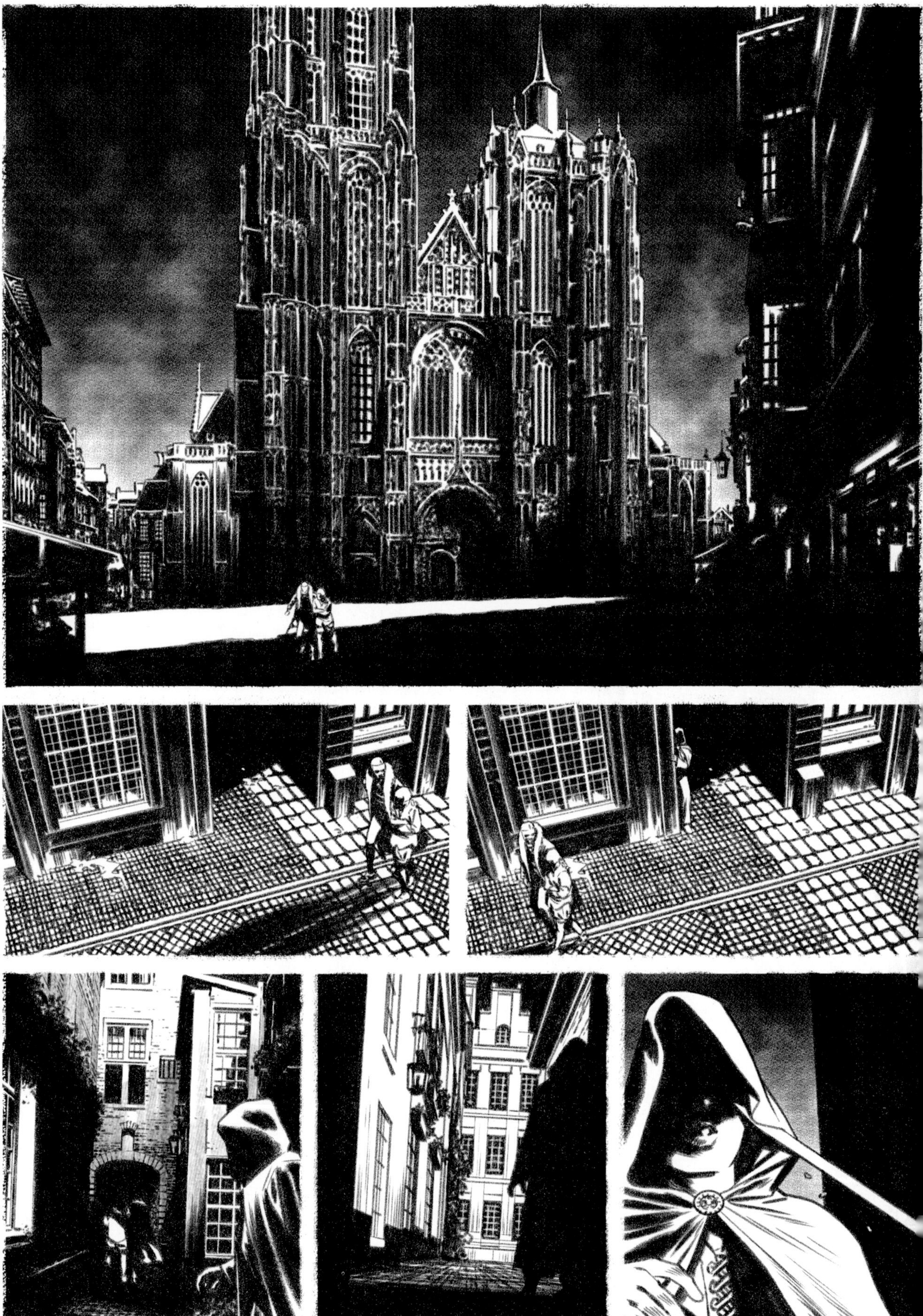

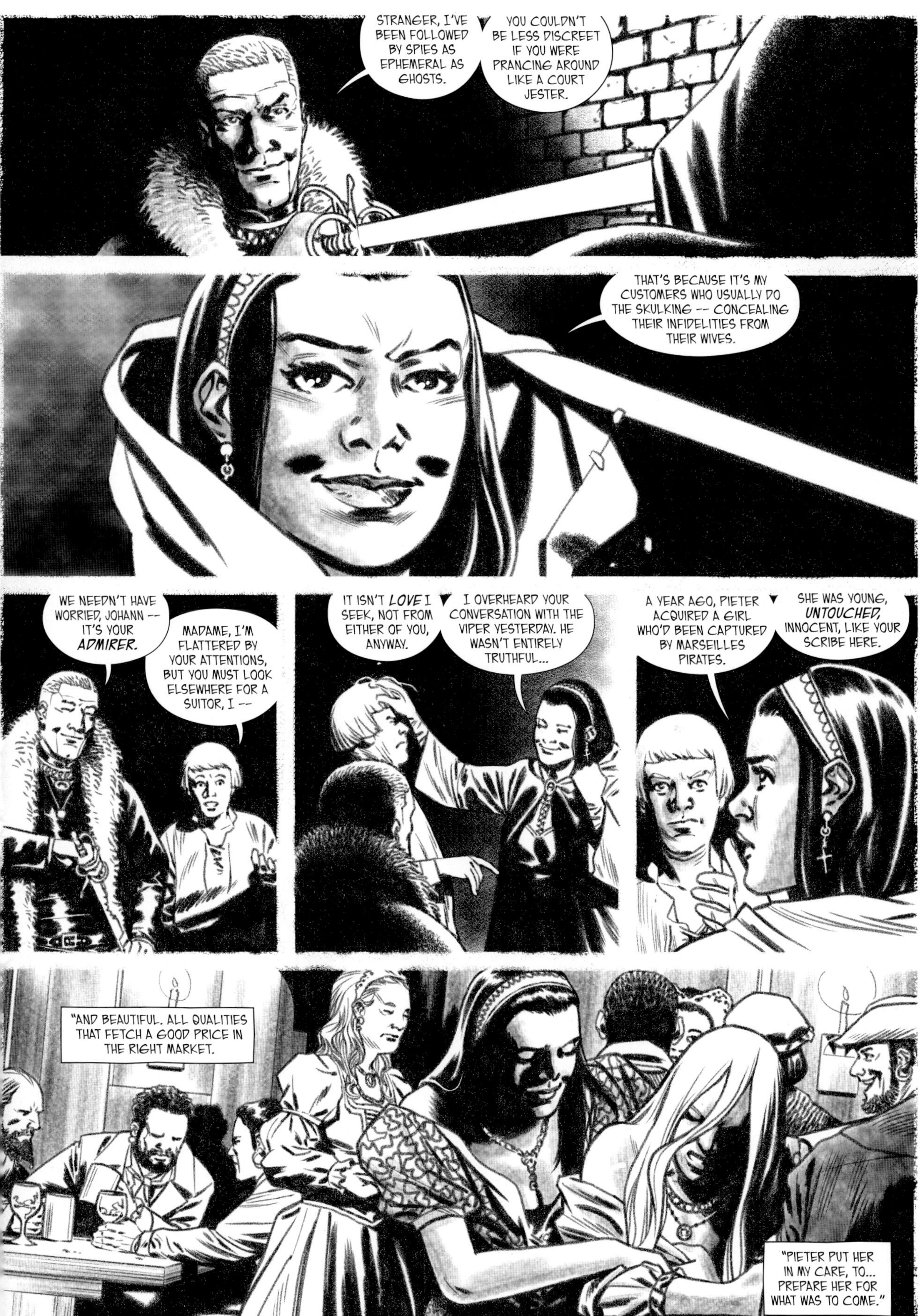
STRANGER, I'VE BEEN FOLLOWED BY SPIES AS EPHEMERAL AS GHOSTS.
YOU COULDN'T BE LESS DISCREET IF YOU WERE PRANCING AROUND LIKE A COURT JESTER.
THAT'S BECAUSE IT'S MY CUSTOMERS WHO USUALLY DO THE SKULKING -- CONCEALING THEIR INFIDELITIES FROM THEIR WIVES.
WE NEEDN'T HAVE WORRIED, JOHANN -- IT'S YOUR ADMIRER.
MADAME, I'M FLATTERED BY YOUR ATTENTIONS, BUT YOU MUST LOOK ELSEWHERE FOR A SUITOR, I --
IT ISN'T LOVE I SEEK, NOT FROM EITHER OF YOU, ANYWAY.
I OVERHEARD YOUR CONVERSATION WITH THE VIPER YESTERDAY. HE WASN'T ENTIRELY TRUTHFUL...
A YEAR AGO, PIETER ACQUIRED A GIRL WHO'D BEEN CAPTURED BY MARSEILLES PIRATES.
SHE WAS YOUNG, UNTOUCHED, INNOCENT, LIKE YOUR SCRIBE HERE.
"AND BEAUTIFUL. ALL QUALITIES THAT FETCH A GOOD PRICE IN THE RIGHT MARKET.
"PIETER PUT HER IN MY CARE, TO... PREPARE HER FOR WHAT WAS TO COME."

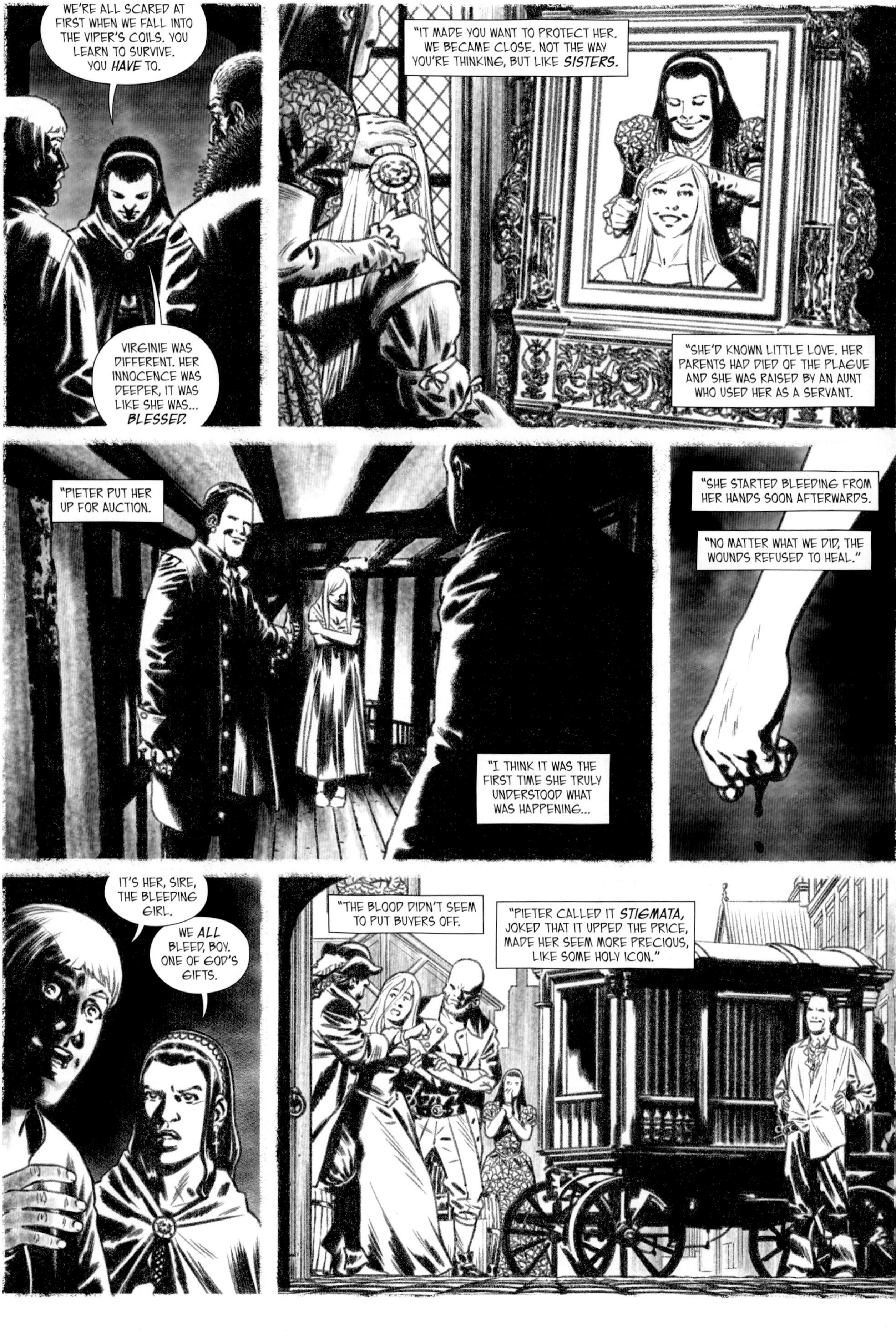
WE'RE ALL SCARED AT FIRST WHEN WE FALL INTO THE VIPER'S COILS. YOU LEARN TO SURVIVE. YOU HAVE TO.
VIRGINIE WAS DIFFERENT. HER INNOCENCE WAS DEEPER, IT WAS LIKE SHE WAS... BLESSED.
"IT MADE YOU WANT TO PROTECT HER. WE BECAME CLOSE. NOT THE WAY YOU'RE THINKING, BUT LIKE SISTERS.
"SHE'D KNOWN LITTLE LOVE. HER PARENTS HAD DIED OF THE PLAGUE AND SHE WAS RAISED BY AN AUNT WHO USED HER AS A SERVANT.
"PIETER PUT HER UP FOR AUCTION.
"I THINK IT WAS THE FIRST TIME SHE TRULY UNDERSTOOD WHAT WAS HAPPENING...
"SHE STARTED BLEEDING FROM HER HANDS SOON AFTERWARDS.
"NO MATTER WHAT WE DID, THE WOUNDS REFUSED TO HEAL."
IT'S HER, SIRE, THE BLEEDING GIRL.
WE ALL BLEED, BOY. ONE OF GOD'S GIFTS.
"THE BLOOD DIDN'T SEEM TO PUT BUYERS OFF.
"PIETER CALLED IT STIGMATA, JOKED THAT IT UPPED THE PRICE, MADE HER SEEM MORE PRECIOUS, LIKE SOME HOLY ICON."

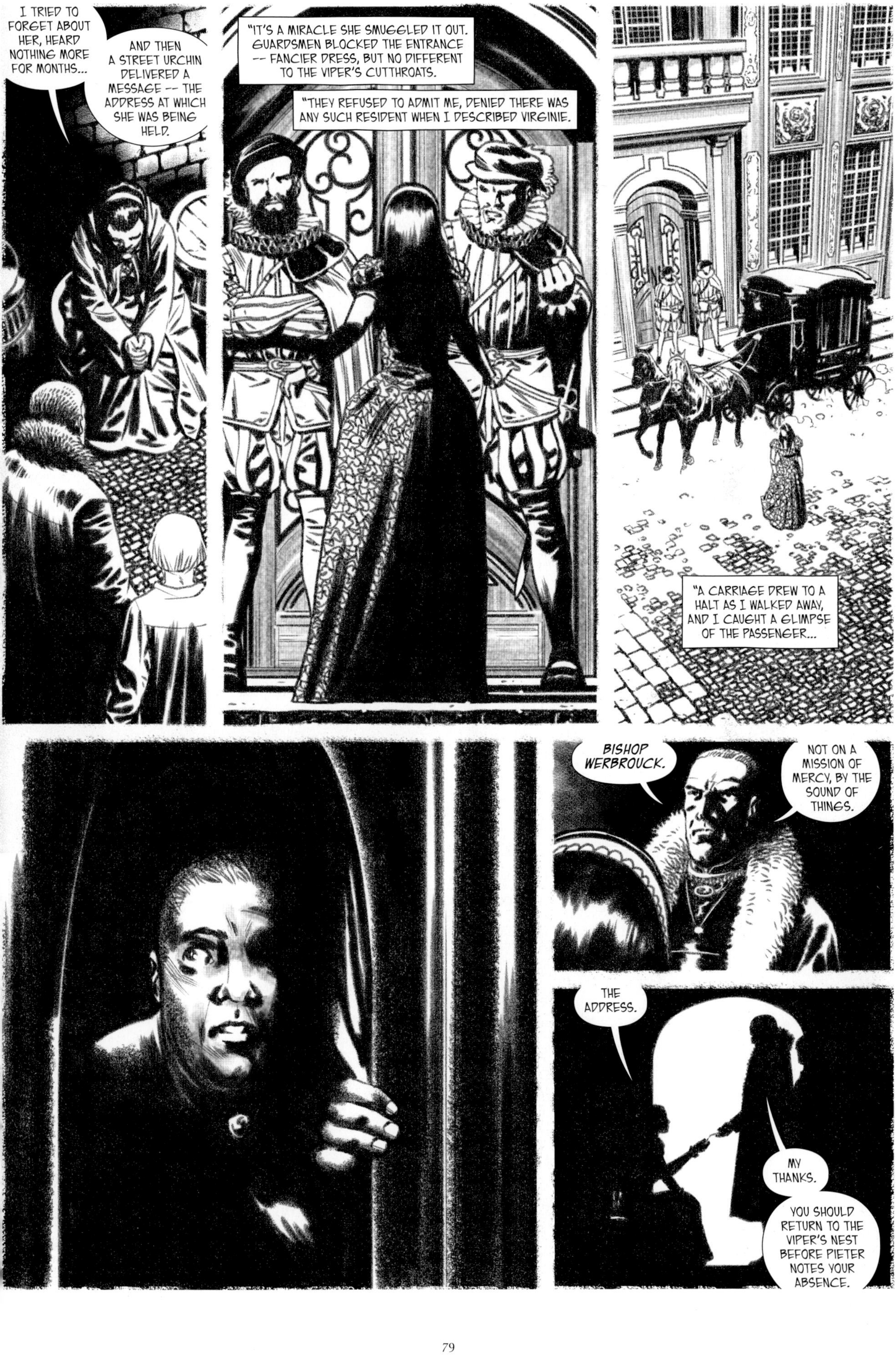

I TRIED TO FORGET ABOUT HER, HEARD NOTHING MORE FOR MONTHS...
AND THEN A STREET URCHIN DELIVERED A MESSAGE -- THE ADDRESS AT WHICH SHE WAS BEING HELD.
"IT'S A MIRACLE SHE SMUGGLED IT OUT. GUARDSMEN BLOCKED THE ENTRANCE -- FANCIER DRESS, BUT NO DIFFERENT TO THE VIPER'S CUTTHROATS.
"THEY REFUSED TO ADMIT ME, DENIED THERE WAS ANY SUCH RESIDENT WHEN I DESCRIBED VIRGINIE.
"A CARRIAGE DREW TO A HALT AS I WALKED AWAY, AND I CAUGHT A GLIMPSE OF THE PASSENGER...
BISHOP WERBROUCK.
NOT ON A MISSION OF MERCY, BY THE SOUND OF THINGS.
THE ADDRESS.
MY THANKS.
YOU SHOULD RETURN TO THE VIPER'S NEST BEFORE PIETER NOTES YOUR ABSENCE.

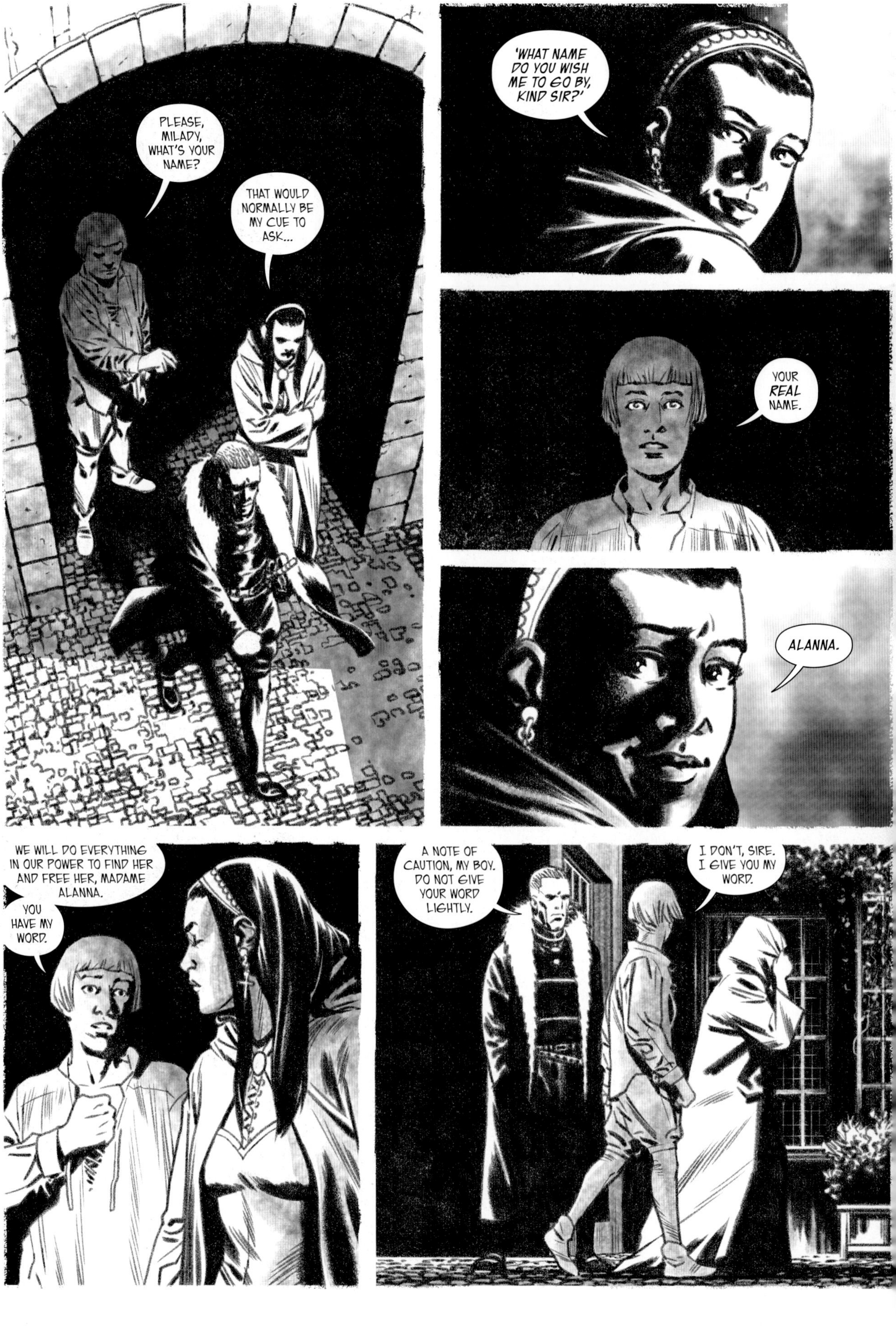
PLEASE, MILADY, WHAT'S YOUR NAME?
THAT WOULD NORMALLY BE MY CUE TO ASK...
'WHAT NAME DO YOU WISH ME TO GO BY, KIND SIR?'
YOUR REAL NAME.
ALANNA.
WE WILL DO EVERYTHING IN OUR POWER TO FIND HER AND FREE HER, MADAME ALANNA.
YOU HAVE MY WORD.
A NOTE OF CAUTION, MY BOY. DO NOT GIVE YOUR WORD LIGHTLY.
I DON'T, SIRE. I GIVE YOU MY WORD.

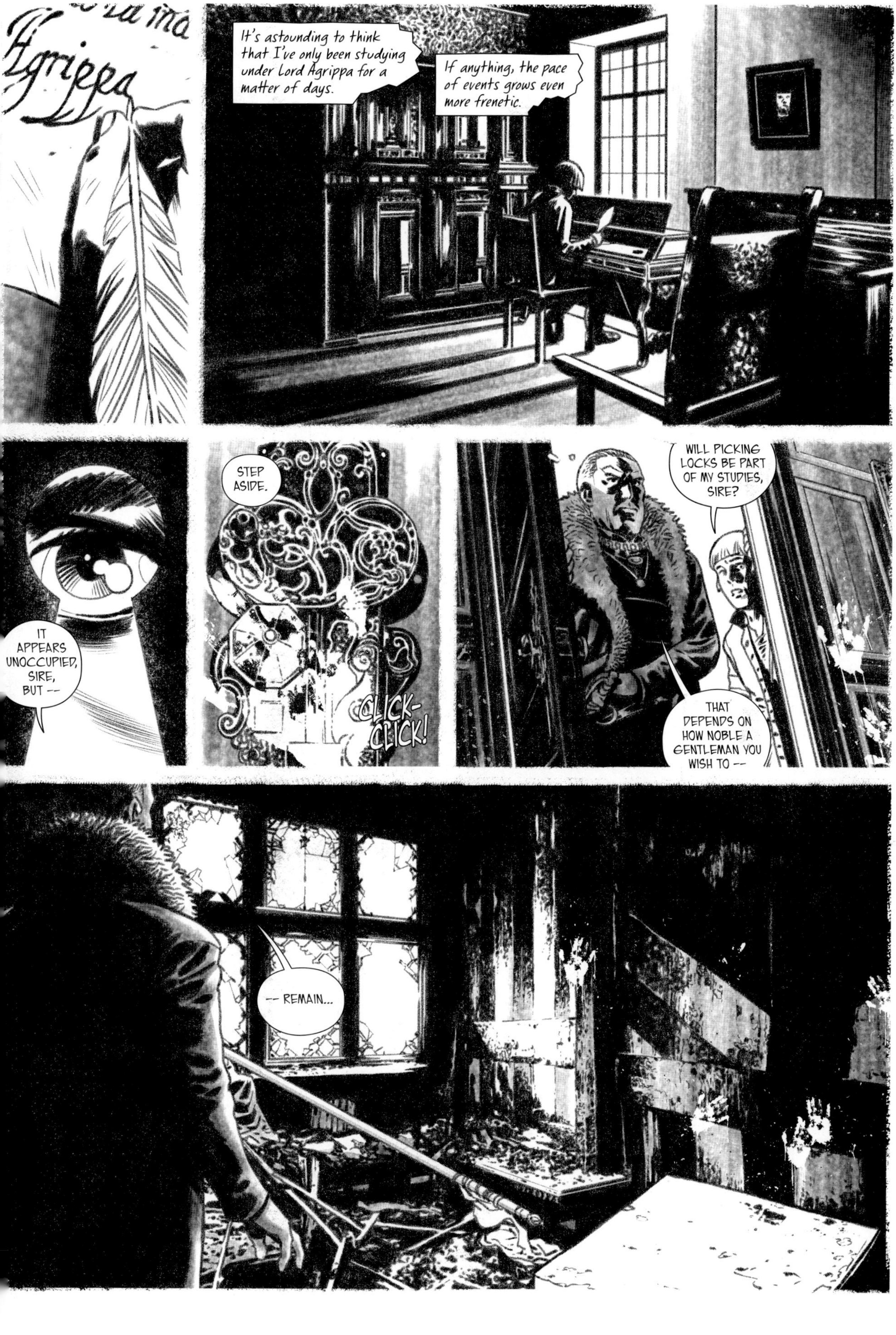
Agrippa
It's astounding to think that I've only been studying under Lord Agrippa for a matter of days.
If anything, the pace of events grows even more frenetic.
IT APPEARS UNOCCUPIED, SIRE, BUT --
STEP ASIDE.
CLICK-CLICK!
WILL PICKING LOCKS BE PART OF MY STUDIES, SIRE?
THAT DEPENDS ON HOW NOBLE A GENTLEMAN YOU WISH TO --
-- REMAIN...

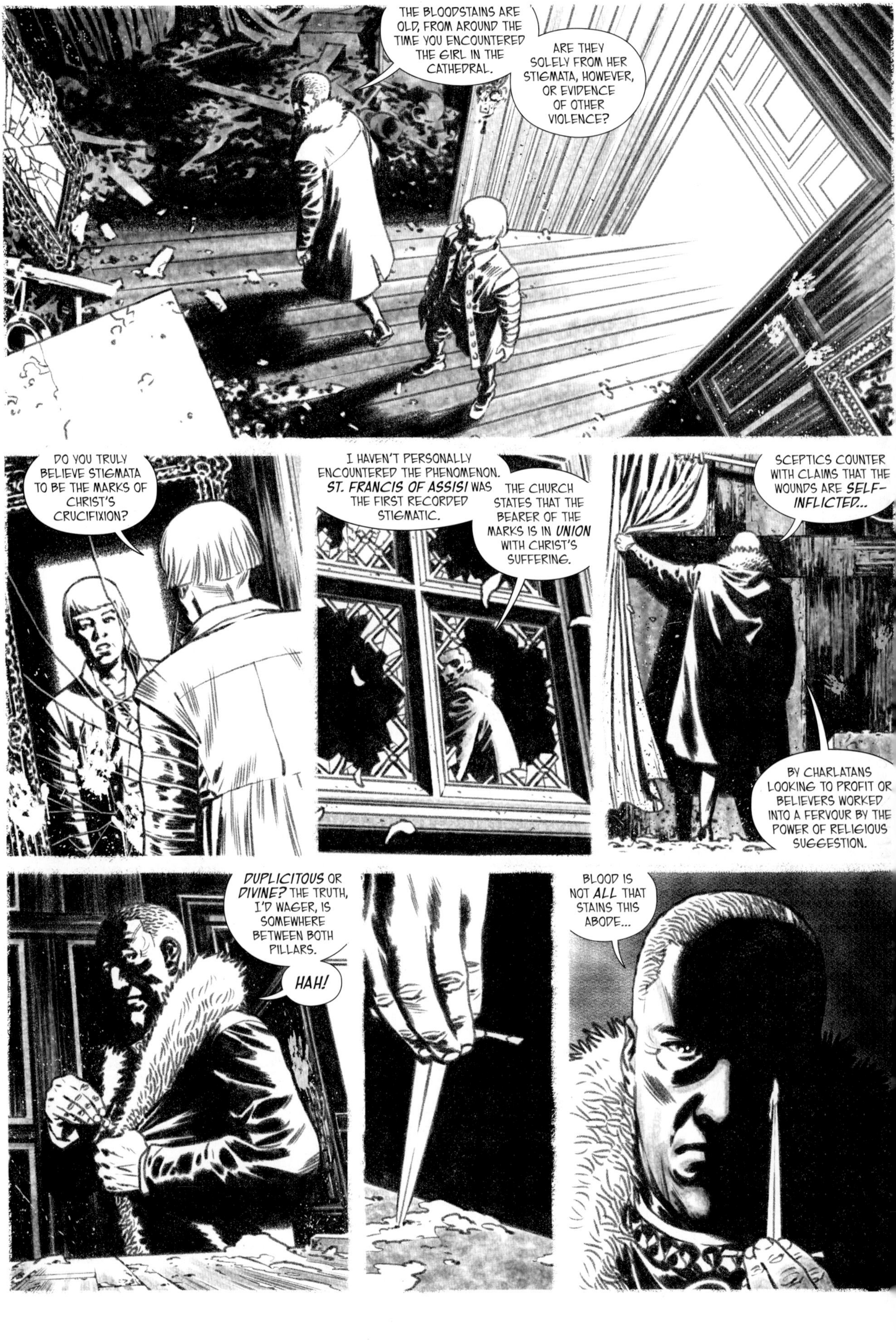
THE BLOODSTAINS ARE OLD, FROM AROUND THE TIME YOU ENCOUNTERED THE GIRL IN THE CATHEDRAL.
ARE THEY SOLELY FROM HER STIGMATA, HOWEVER, OR EVIDENCE OF OTHER VIOLENCE?
DO YOU TRULY BELIEVE STIGMATA TO BE THE MARKS OF CHRIST'S CRUCIFIXION?
I HAVEN'T PERSONALLY ENCOUNTERED THE PHENOMENON. ST. FRANCIS OF ASSISI WAS THE FIRST RECORDED STIGMATIC.
THE CHURCH STATES THAT THE BEARER OF THE MARKS IS IN UNION WITH CHRIST'S SUFFERING.
SCEPTICS COUNTER WITH CLAIMS THAT THE WOUNDS ARE SELF-INFLICTED...
BY CHARLATANS LOOKING TO PROFIT OR BELIEVERS WORKED INTO A FERVOUR BY THE POWER OF RELIGIOUS SUGGESTION.
DUPLICITOUS OR DIVINE? THE TRUTH, I'D WAGER, IS SOMEWHERE BETWEEN BOTH PILLARS.
HAH!
BLOOD IS NOT ALL THAT STAINS THIS ABODE...

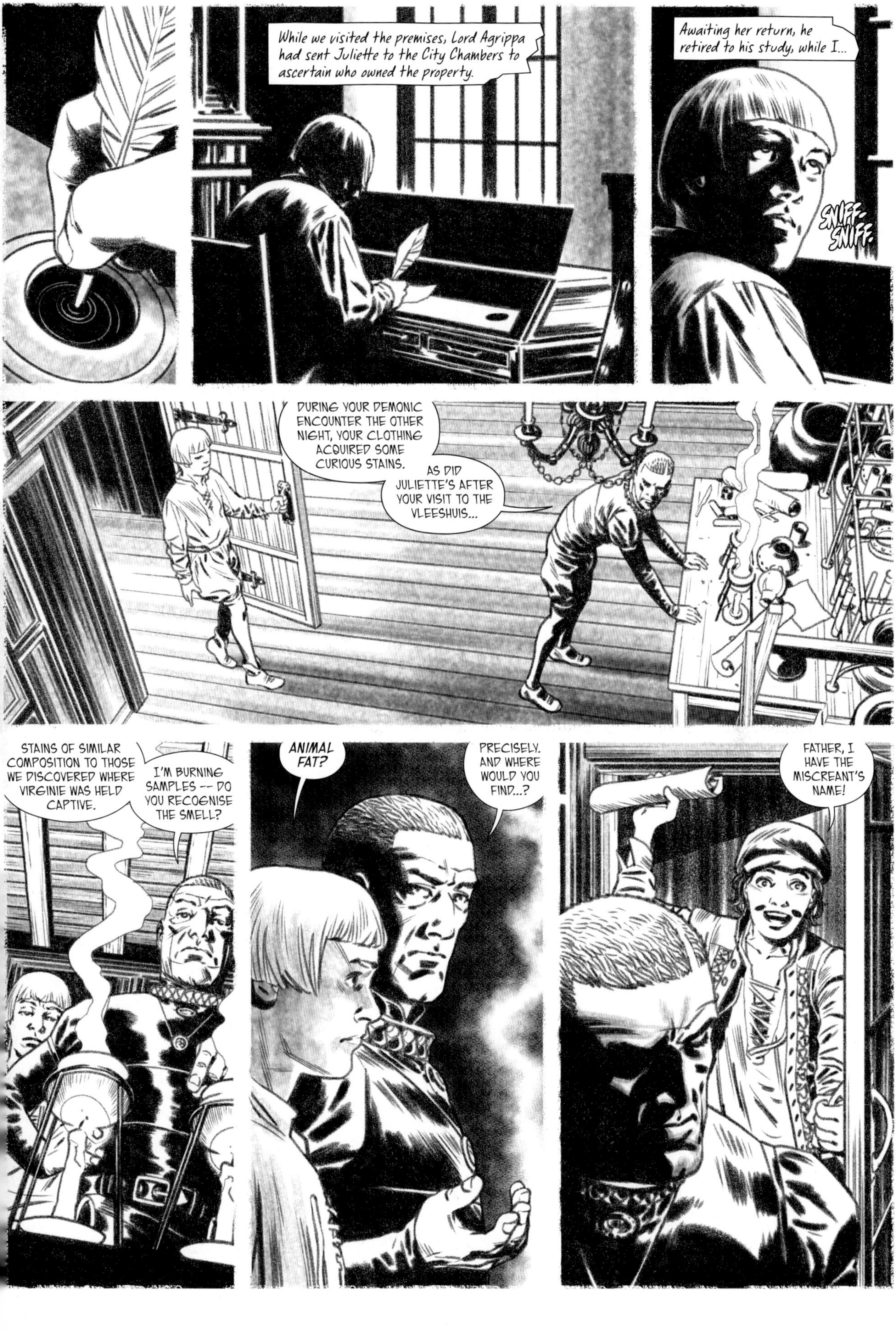

While we visited the premises, Lord Agrippa had sent Juliette to the City Chambers to ascertain who owned the property.
Awaiting her return, he retired to his study, while I...
SNIFF-SNIFF.
DURING YOUR DEMONIC ENCOUNTER THE OTHER NIGHT, YOUR CLOTHING ACQUIRED SOME CURIOUS STAINS.
AS DID JULIETTE'S AFTER YOUR VISIT TO THE VLEESHUIS...
STAINS OF SIMILAR COMPOSITION TO THOSE WE DISCOVERED WHERE VIRGINIE WAS HELD CAPTIVE.
I'M BURNING SAMPLES -- DO YOU RECOGNISE THE SMELL?
ANIMAL FAT?
PRECISELY. AND WHERE WOULD YOU FIND...?
FATHER, I HAVE THE MISCREANT'S NAME!

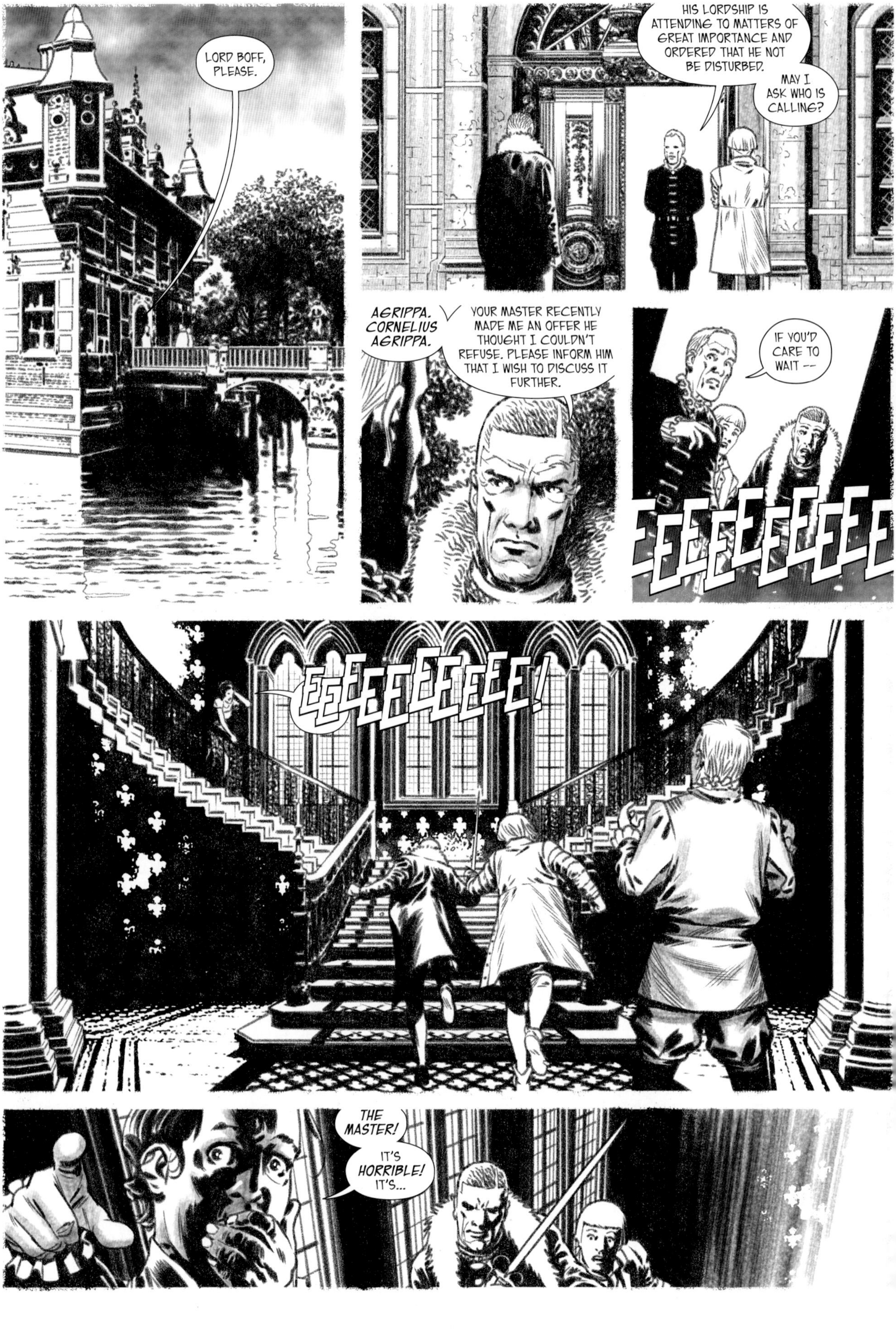

LORD BOFF, PLEASE.
HIS LORDSHIP IS ATTENDING TO MATTERS OF GREAT IMPORTANCE AND ORDERED THAT HE NOT BE DISTURBED.
MAY I ASK WHO IS CALLING?
AGRIPPA. CORNELIUS AGRIPPA.
YOUR MASTER RECENTLY MADE ME AN OFFER HE THOUGHT I COULDN'T REFUSE. PLEASE INFORM HIM THAT I WISH TO DISCUSS IT FURTHER.
IF YOU'D CARE TO WAIT --
EEEEEEEEEE
EEEEEEEEEEE!
THE MASTER!
IT'S HORRIBLE! IT'S...

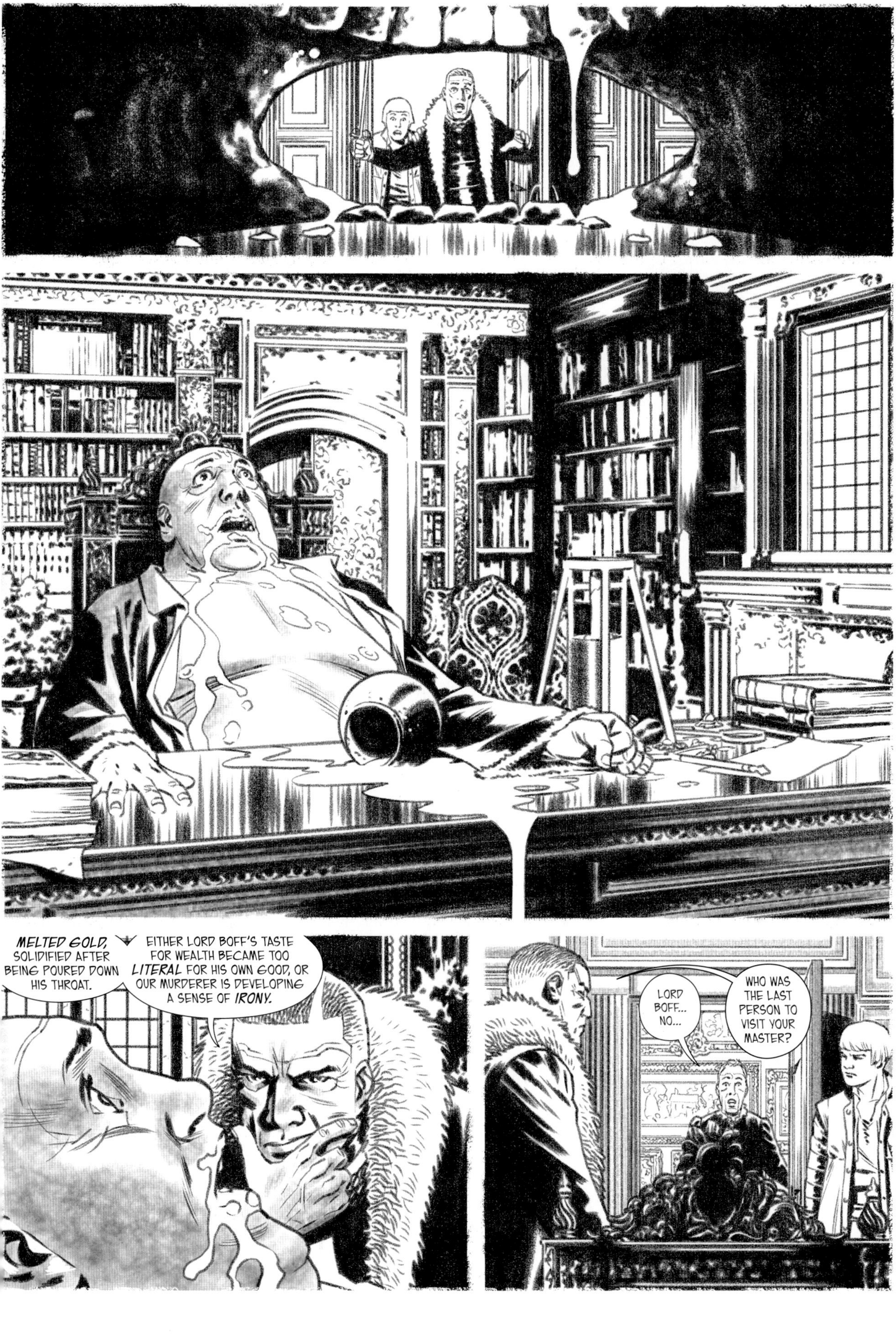
MELTED GOLD, SOLIDIFIED AFTER BEING POURED DOWN HIS THROAT.
EITHER LORD BOFF'S TASTE FOR WEALTH BECAME TOO LITERAL FOR HIS OWN GOOD, OR OUR MURDERER IS DEVELOPING A SENSE OF IRONY.
WHO WAS THE LAST PERSON TO VISIT YOUR MASTER?
LORD BOFF... NO...

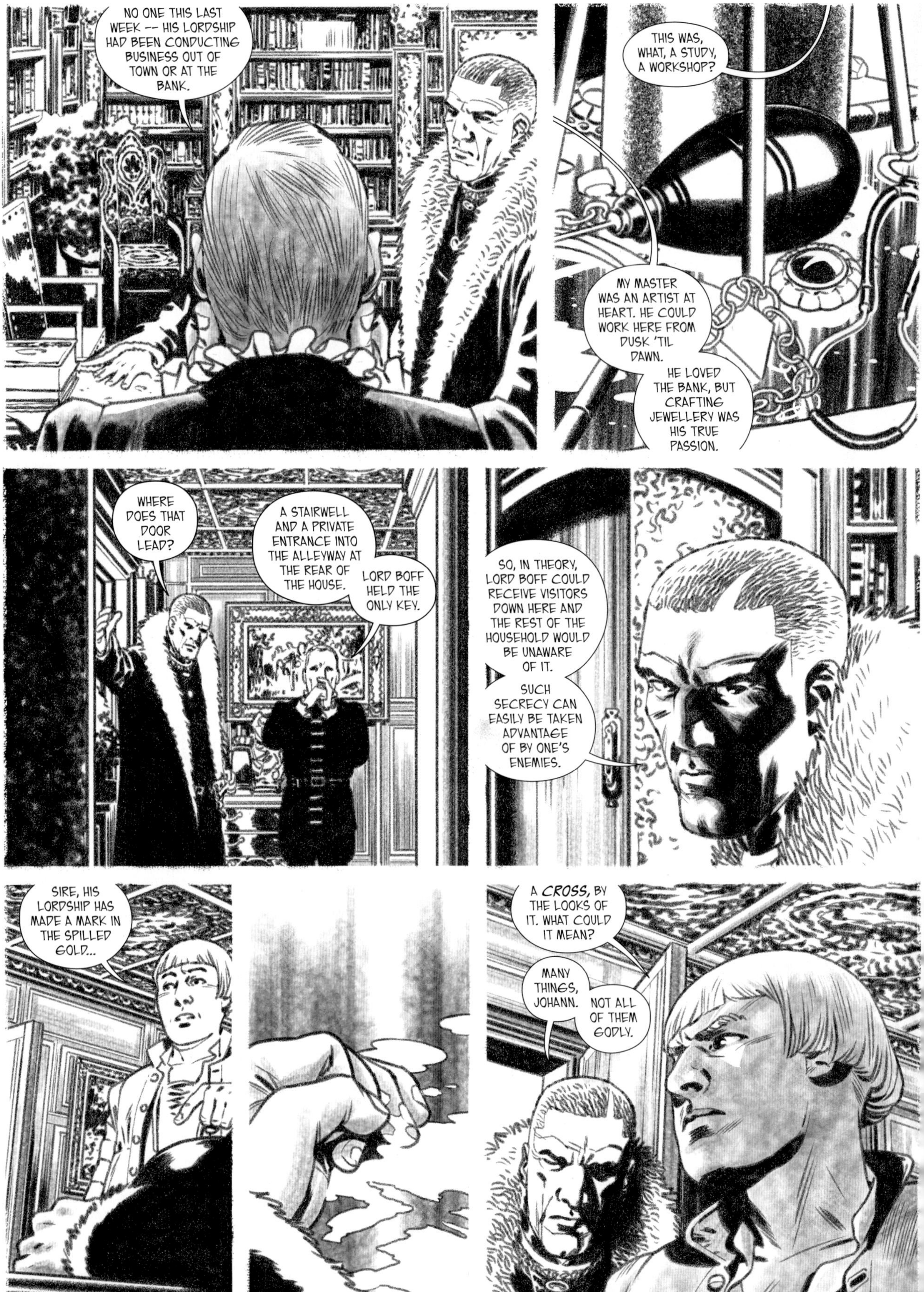
NO ONE THIS LAST WEEK -- HIS LORDSHIP HAD BEEN CONDUCTING BUSINESS OUT OF TOWN OR AT THE BANK.
THIS WAS, WHAT, A STUDY, A WORKSHOP?
MY MASTER WAS AN ARTIST AT HEART. HE COULD WORK HERE FROM DUSK 'TIL DAWN.
HE LOVED THE BANK, BUT CRAFTING JEWELLERY WAS HIS TRUE PASSION.
WHERE DOES THAT DOOR LEAD?
A STAIRWELL AND A PRIVATE ENTRANCE INTO THE ALLEYWAY AT THE REAR OF THE HOUSE.
LORD BOFF HELD THE ONLY KEY.
SO, IN THEORY, LORD BOFF COULD RECEIVE VISITORS DOWN HERE AND THE REST OF THE HOUSEHOLD WOULD BE UNAWARE OF IT.
SUCH SECRECY CAN EASILY BE TAKEN ADVANTAGE OF BY ONE'S ENEMIES.
SIRE, HIS LORDSHIP HAS MADE A MARK IN THE SPILLED GOLD...
A CROSS, BY THE LOOKS OF IT. WHAT COULD IT MEAN?
MANY THINGS, JOHANN.
NOT ALL OF THEM GODLY.

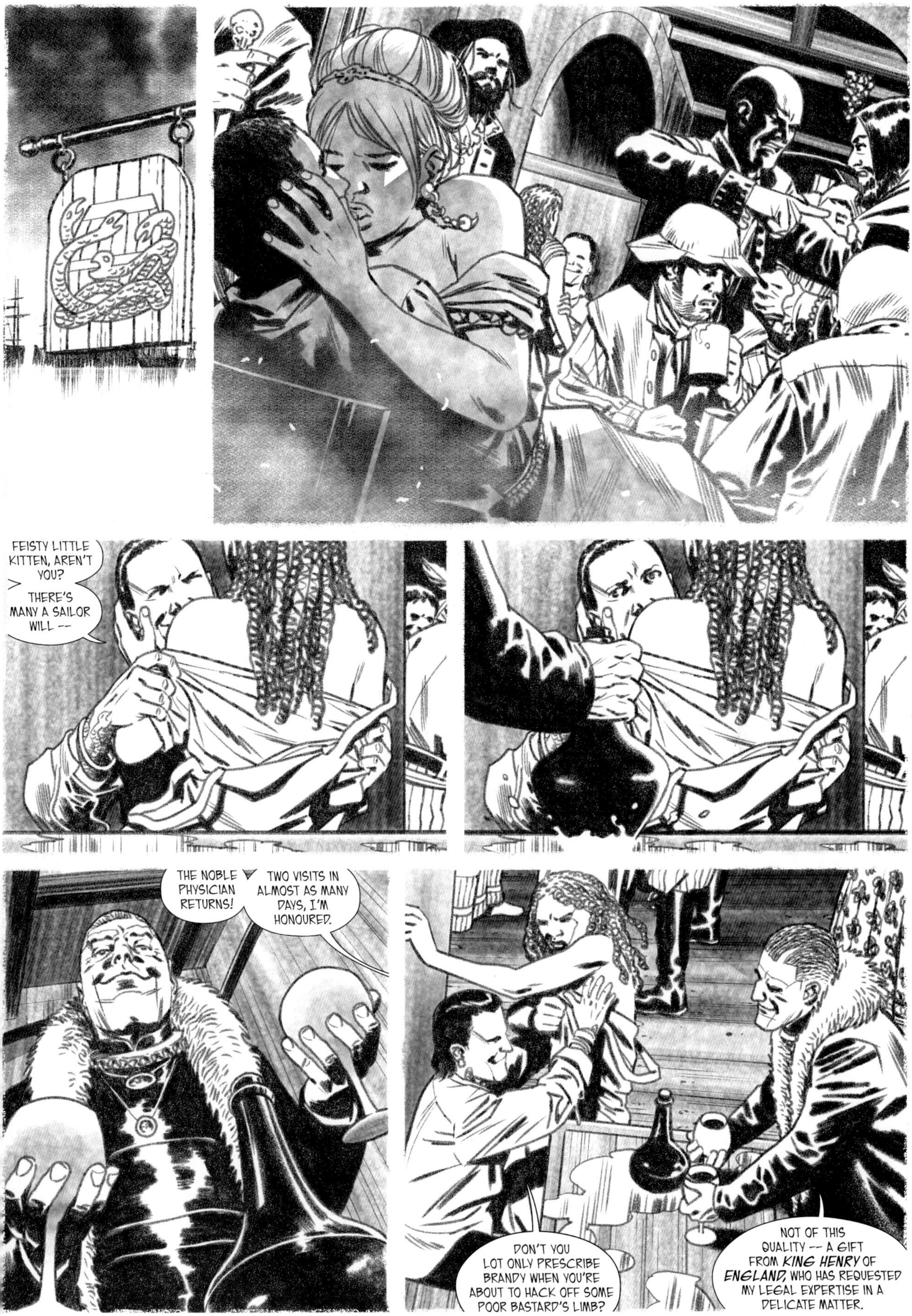

FEISTY LITTLE KITTEN, AREN'T YOU?
THERE'S MANY A SAILOR WILL --
THE NOBLE PHYSICIAN RETURNS!
TWO VISITS IN ALMOST AS MANY DAYS, I'M HONOURED.
DON'T YOU LOT ONLY PRESCRIBE BRANDY WHEN YOU'RE ABOUT TO HACK OFF SOME POOR BASTARD'S LIMB?
NOT OF THIS QUALITY -- A GIFT FROM KING HENRY OF ENGLAND, WHO HAS REQUESTED MY LEGAL EXPERTISE IN A DELICATE MATTER.

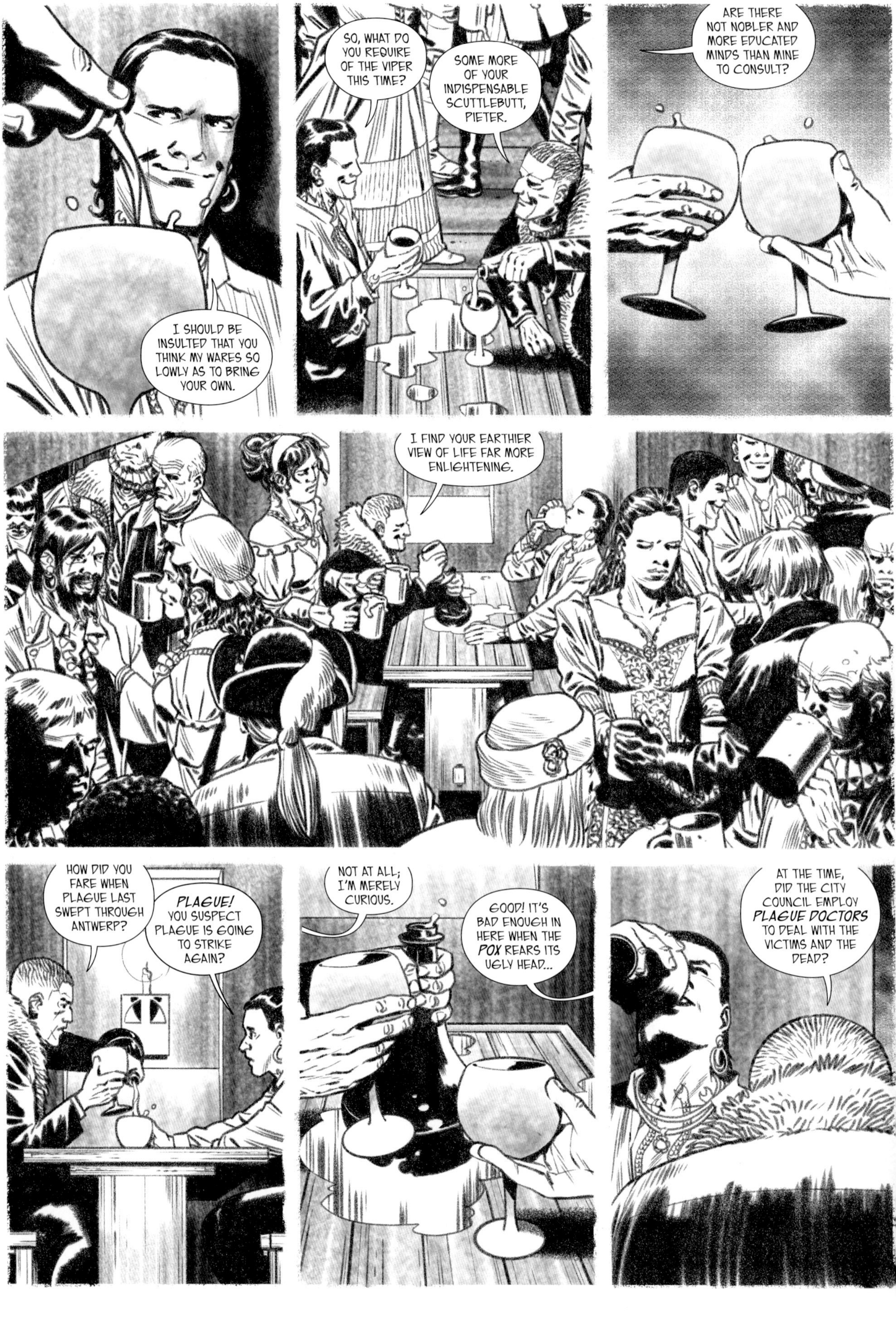
I SHOULD BE INSULTED THAT YOU THINK MY WARES SO LOWLY AS TO BRING YOUR OWN.
SO, WHAT DO YOU REQUIRE OF THE VIPER THIS TIME?
SOME MORE OF YOUR INDISPENSABLE SCUTTLEBUTT, PIETER.
ARE THERE NOT NOBLER AND MORE EDUCATED MINDS THAN MINE TO CONSULT?
I FIND YOUR EARTHIER VIEW OF LIFE FAR MORE ENLIGHTENING.
HOW DID YOU FARE WHEN PLAGUE LAST SWEPT THROUGH ANTWERP?
PLAGUE! YOU SUSPECT PLAGUE IS GOING TO STRIKE AGAIN?
NOT AT ALL; I'M MERELY CURIOUS.
GOOD! IT'S BAD ENOUGH IN HERE WHEN THE POX REARS ITS UGLY HEAD...
AT THE TIME, DID THE CITY COUNCIL EMPLOY PLAGUE DOCTORS TO DEAL WITH THE VICTIMS AND THE DEAD?

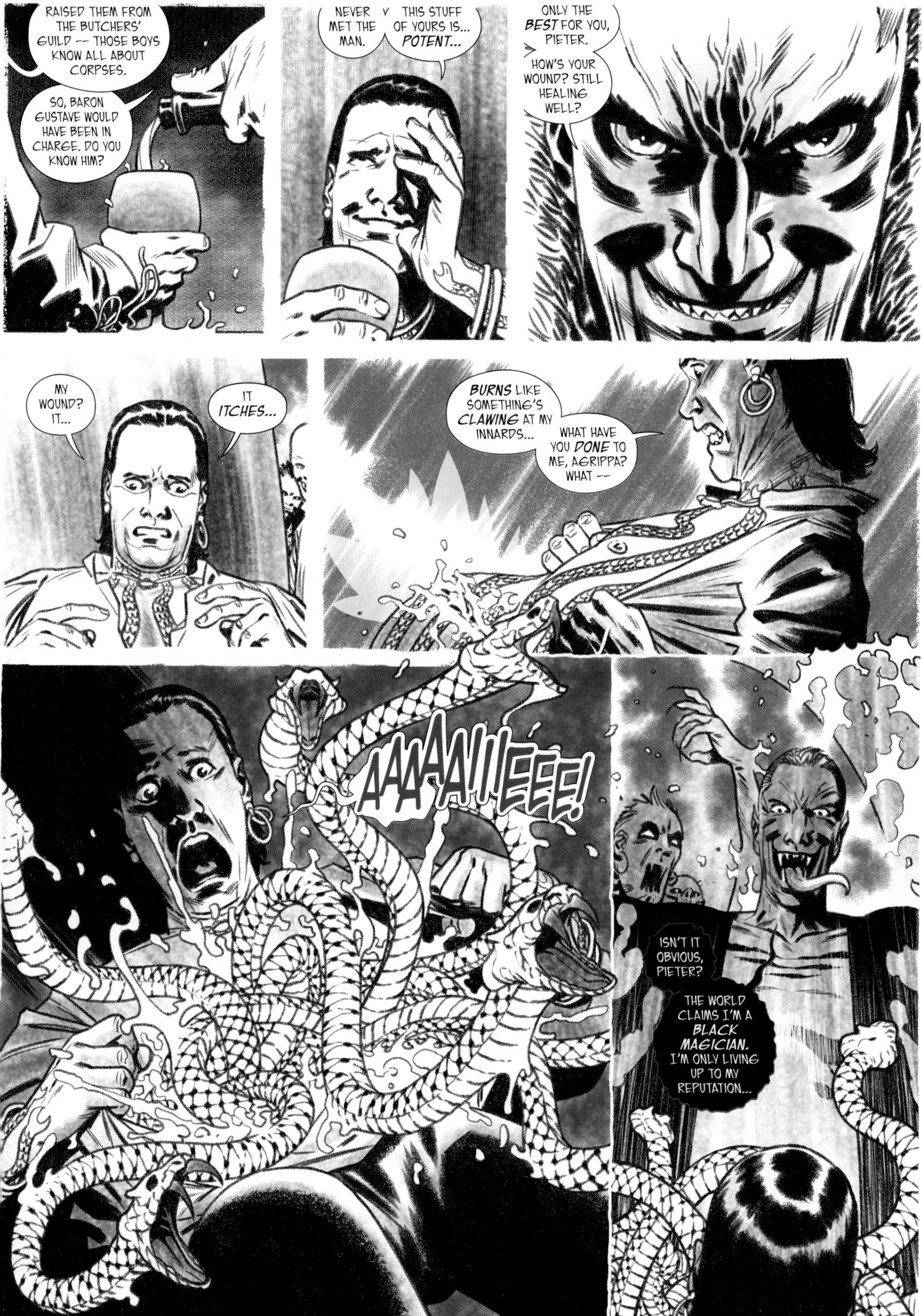
RAISED THEM FROM THE BUTCHERS' GUILD -- THOSE BOYS KNOW ALL ABOUT CORPSES.
SO, BARON GUSTAVE WOULD HAVE BEEN IN CHARGE. DO YOU KNOW HIM?
NEVER MET THE MAN.
THIS STUFF OF YOURS IS... POTENT...
ONLY THE BEST FOR YOU, PIETER.
HOW'S YOUR WOUND? STILL HEALING WELL?
MY WOUND? IT...
IT ITCHES...
BURNS LIKE SOMETHING'S CLAWING AT MY INNARDS...
WHAT HAVE YOU DONE TO ME, AGRIPPA? WHAT --
AAAAAIIIEEEE!
ISN'T IT OBVIOUS, PIETER?
THE WORLD CLAIMS I'M A BLACK MAGICIAN. I'M ONLY LIVING UP TO MY REPUTATION...

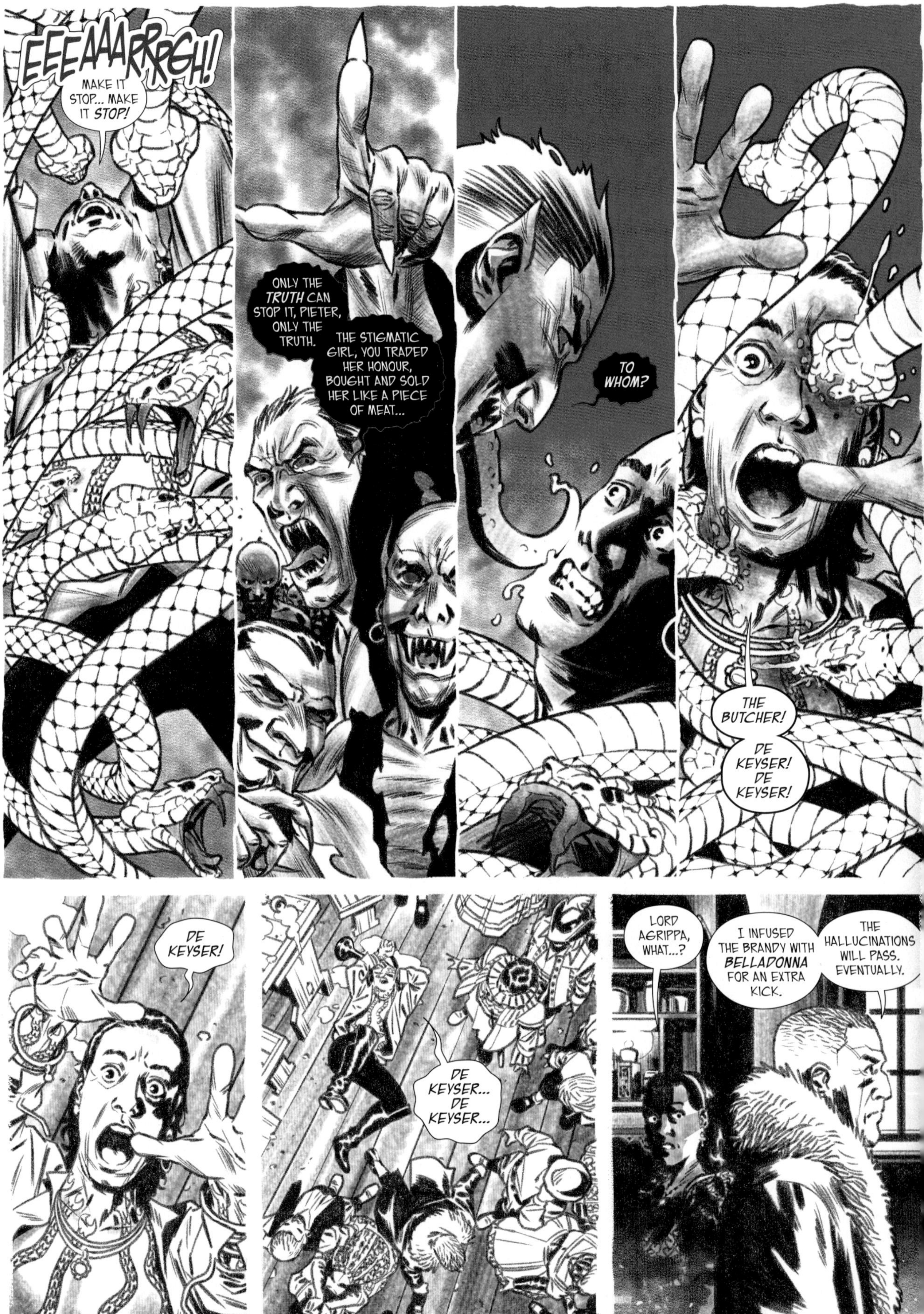
EEEAAARRRGH!
MAKE IT STOP... MAKE IT STOP!
ONLY THE TRUTH CAN STOP IT, PIETER, ONLY THE TRUTH.
THE STIGMATIC GIRL, YOU TRADED HER HONOUR, BOUGHT AND SOLD HER LIKE A PIECE OF MEAT...
TO WHOM?
THE BUTCHER!
DE KEYSER! DE KEYSER!
DE KEYSER!
DE KEYSER... DE KEYSER...
LORD AGRIPPA, WHAT...?
I INFUSED THE BRANDY WITH BELLADONNA FOR AN EXTRA KICK.
THE HALLUCINATIONS WILL PASS. EVENTUALLY.

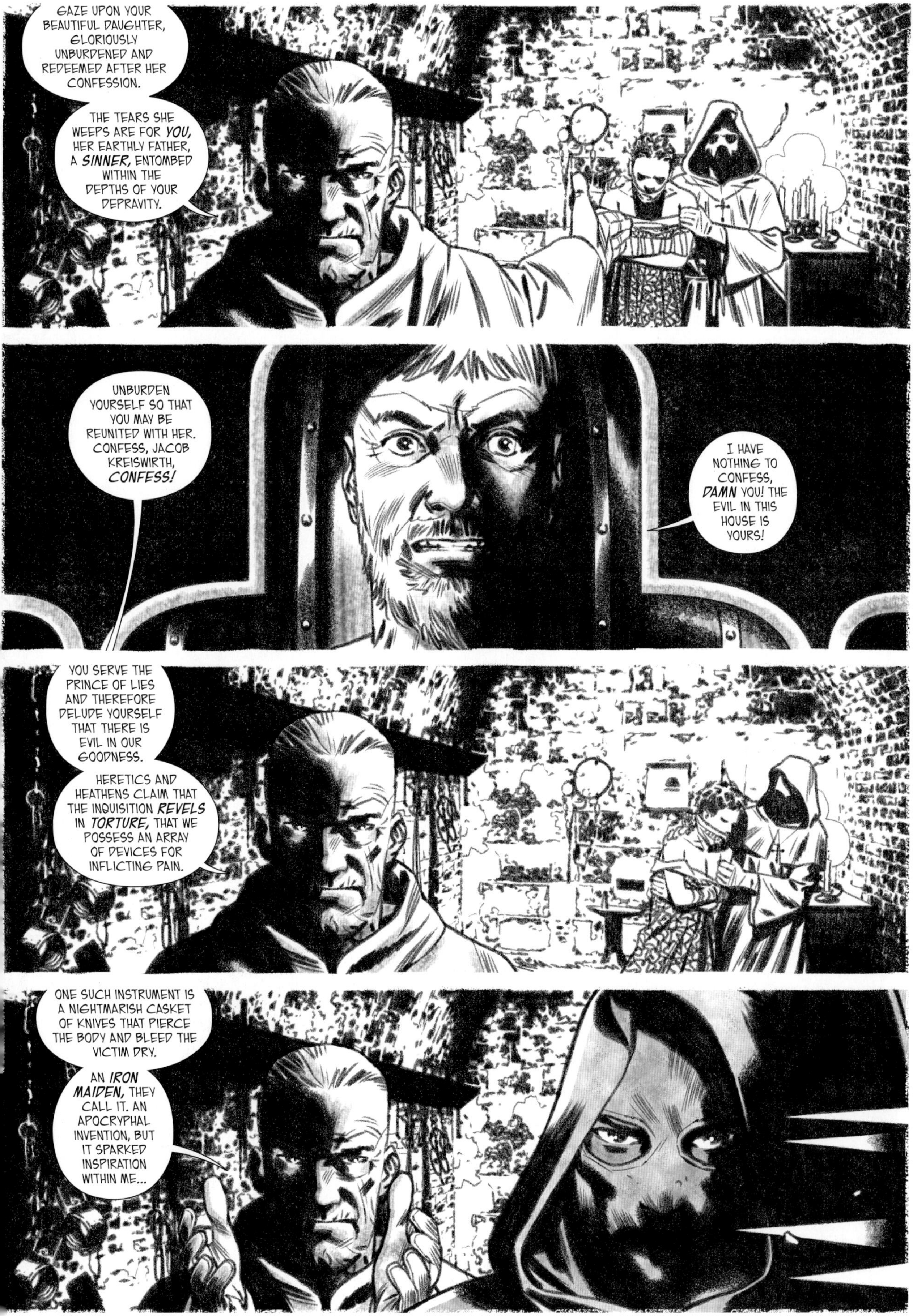
GAZE UPON YOUR BEAUTIFUL DAUGHTER, GLORIOUSLY UNBURDENED AND REDEEMED AFTER HER CONFESSION.
THE TEARS SHE WEEPS ARE FOR YOU, HER EARTHLY FATHER, A SINNER, ENTOMBED WITHIN THE DEPTHS OF YOUR DEPRAVITY.
UNBURDEN YOURSELF SO THAT YOU MAY BE REUNITED WITH HER. CONFESS, JACOB KREISWIRTH, CONFESS!
I HAVE NOTHING TO CONFESS, DAMN YOU! THE EVIL IN THIS HOUSE IS YOURS!
YOU SERVE THE PRINCE OF LIES AND THEREFORE DELUDE YOURSELF THAT THERE IS EVIL IN OUR GOODNESS.
HERETICS AND HEATHENS CLAIM THAT THE INQUISITION REVELS IN TORTURE, THAT WE POSSESS AN ARRAY OF DEVICES FOR INFLICTING PAIN.
ONE SUCH INSTRUMENT IS A NIGHTMARISH CASKET OF KNIVES THAT PIERCE THE BODY AND BLEED THE VICTIM DRY.
AN IRON MAIDEN, THEY CALL IT. AN APOCRYPHAL INVENTION, BUT IT SPARKED INSPIRATION WITHIN ME...

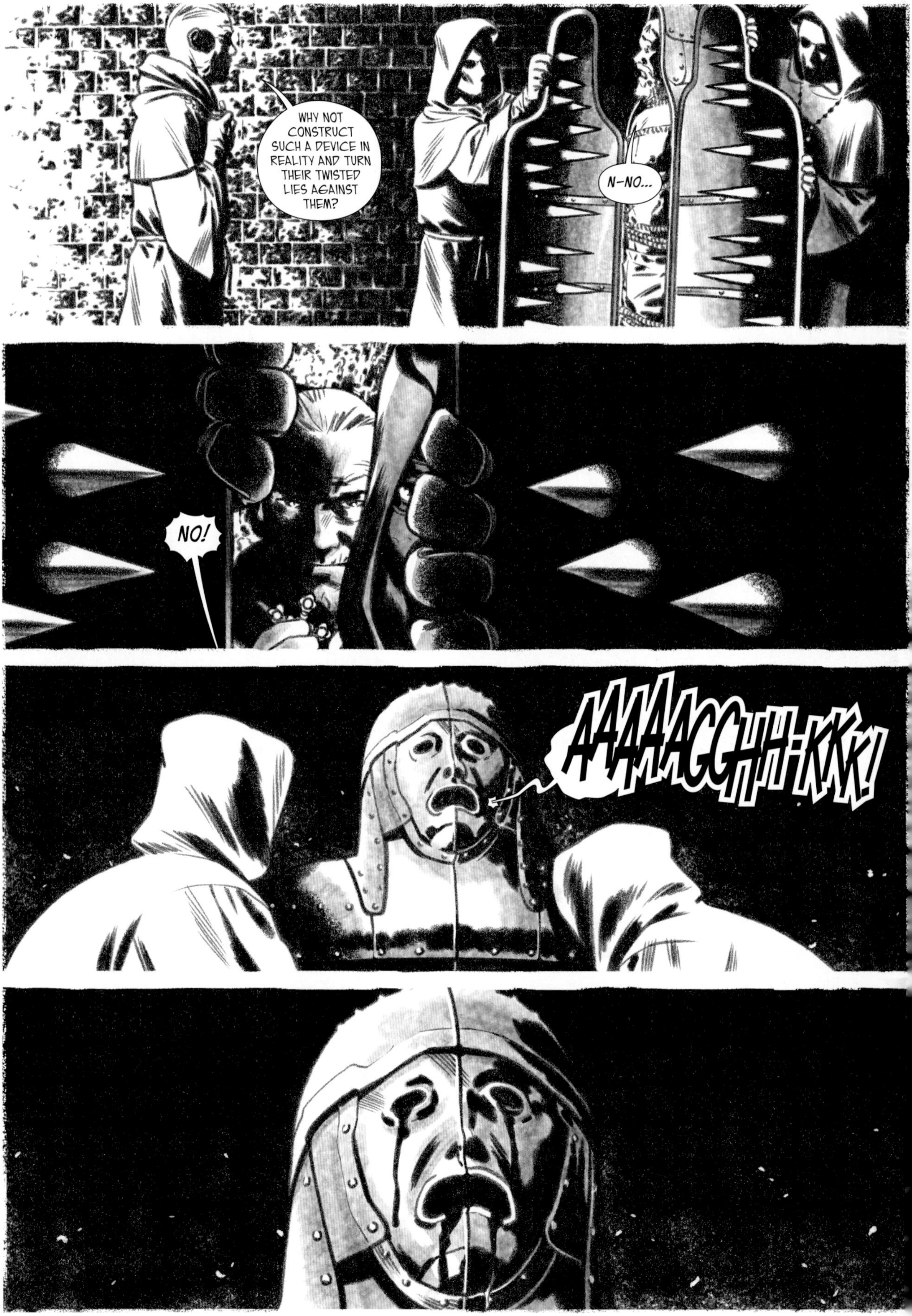
WHY NOT CONSTRUCT SUCH A DEVICE IN REALITY AND TURN THEIR TWISTED LIES AGAINST THEM?
N-NO...
NO!
AAAAAGGHH-KKK!

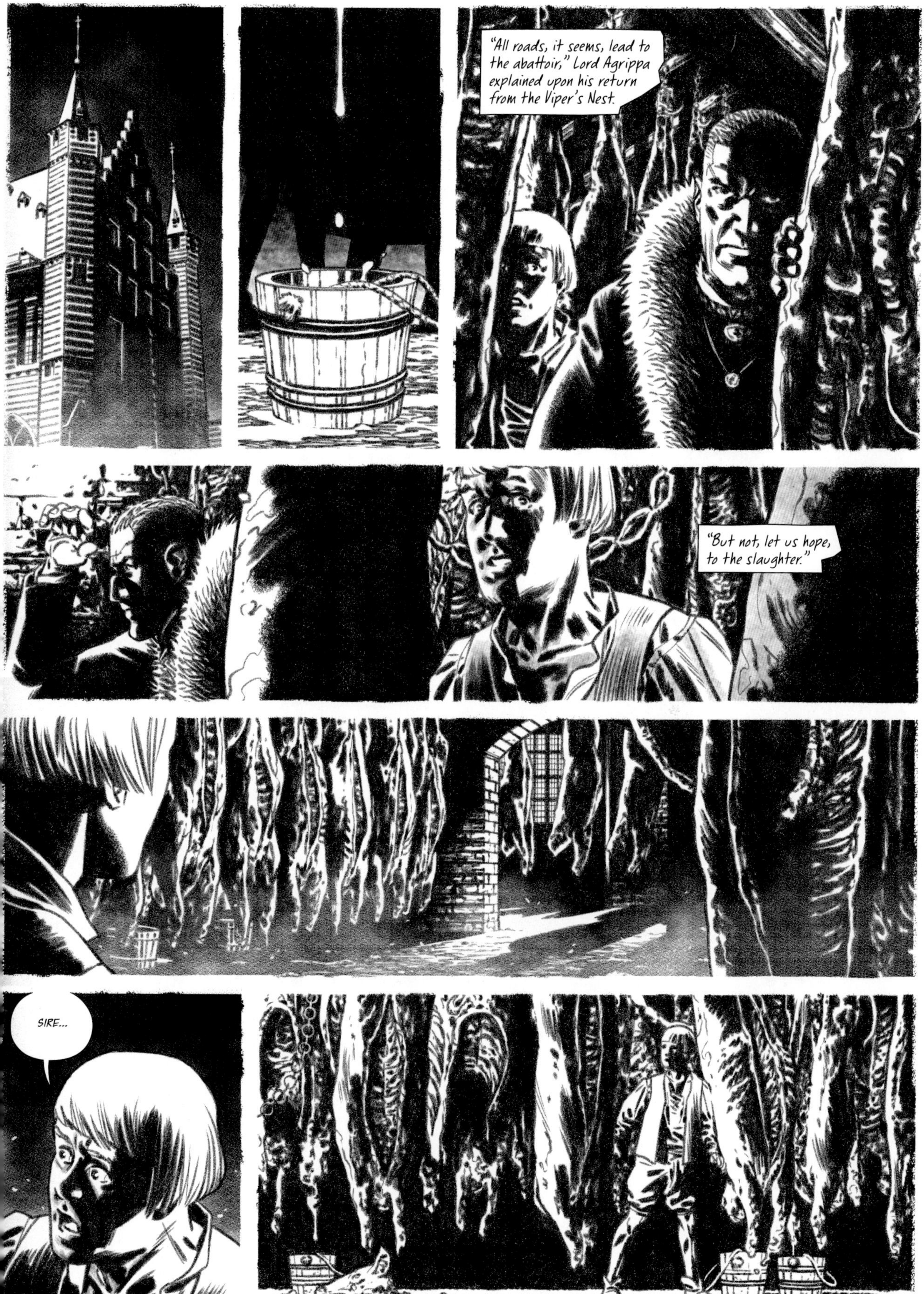
"All roads, it seems, lead to the abattoir," Lord Agrippa explained upon his return from the Viper's Nest.
"But not, let us hope, to the slaughter."
SIRE...

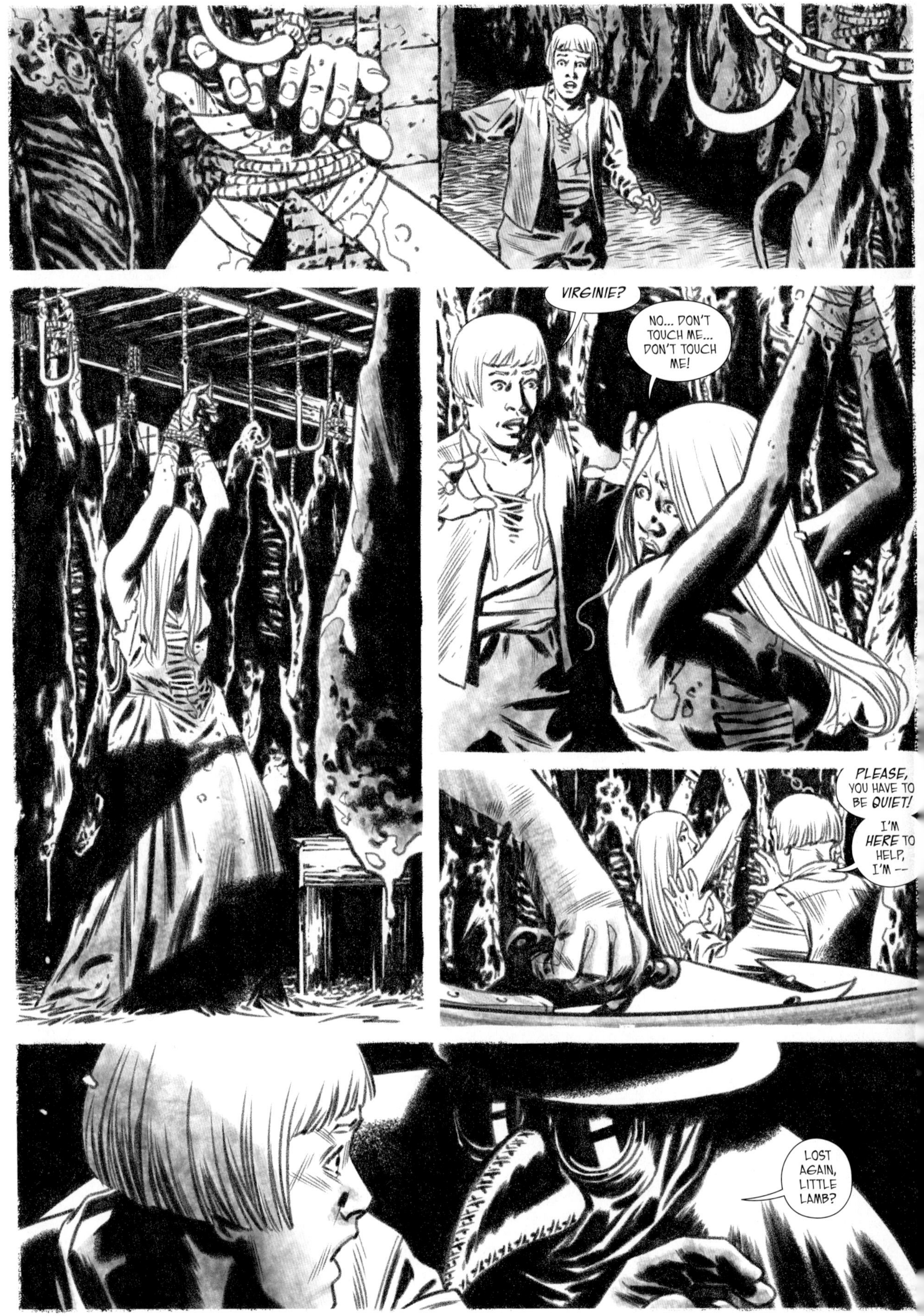
VIRGINIE?
NO... DON'T TOUCH ME... DON'T TOUCH ME!
PLEASE, YOU HAVE TO BE QUIET!
I'M HERE TO HELP, I'M --
LOST AGAIN, LITTLE LAMB?

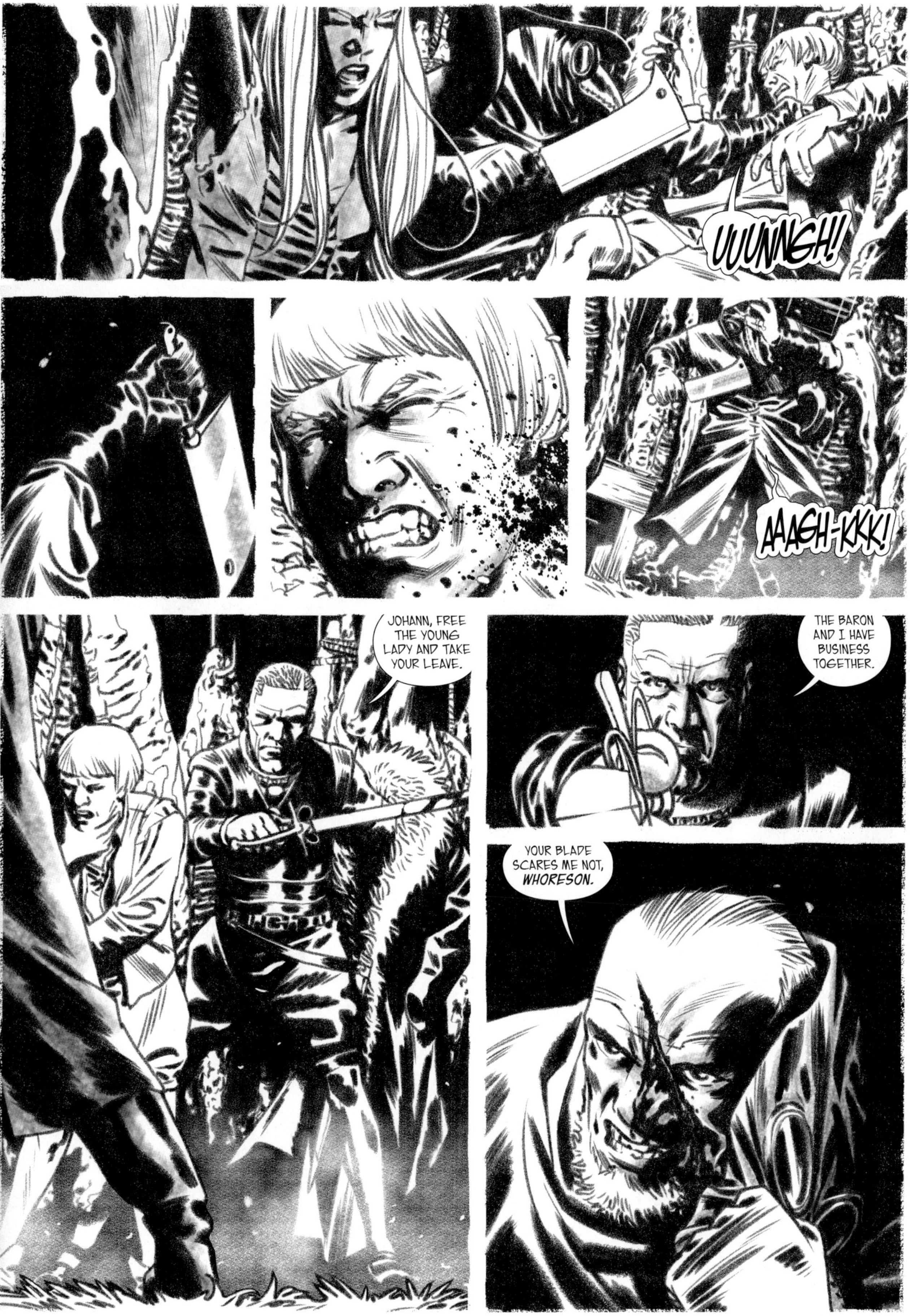
UUUNNGH!
AAAGH-KKK!
JOHANN, FREE THE YOUNG LADY AND TAKE YOUR LEAVE.
THE BARON AND I HAVE BUSINESS TOGETHER.
YOUR BLADE SCARES ME NOT, *WHORESON.*

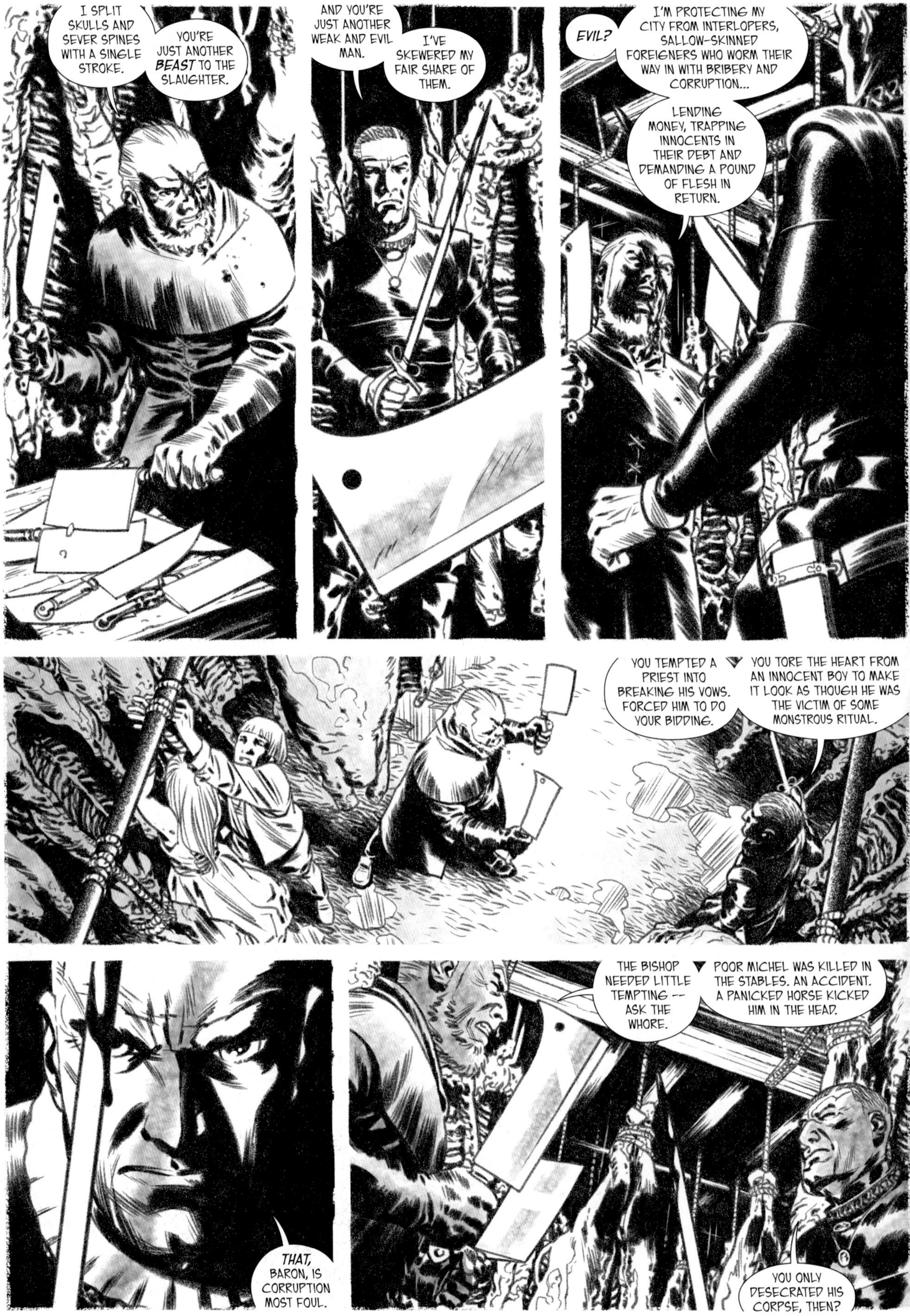
I SPLIT SKULLS AND SEVER SPINES WITH A SINGLE STROKE.
YOU'RE JUST ANOTHER BEAST TO THE SLAUGHTER.
AND YOU'RE JUST ANOTHER WEAK AND EVIL MAN.
I'VE SKEWERED MY FAIR SHARE OF THEM.
EVIL?
I'M PROTECTING MY CITY FROM INTERLOPERS, SALLOW-SKINNED FOREIGNERS WHO WORM THEIR WAY IN WITH BRIBERY AND CORRUPTION...
LENDING MONEY, TRAPPING INNOCENTS IN THEIR DEBT AND DEMANDING A POUND OF FLESH IN RETURN.
YOU TEMPTED A PRIEST INTO BREAKING HIS VOWS. FORCED HIM TO DO YOUR BIDDING.
YOU TORE THE HEART FROM AN INNOCENT BOY TO MAKE IT LOOK AS THOUGH HE WAS THE VICTIM OF SOME MONSTROUS RITUAL.
THAT, BARON, IS CORRUPTION MOST FOUL.
THE BISHOP NEEDED LITTLE TEMPTING -- ASK THE WHORE.
POOR MICHEL WAS KILLED IN THE STABLES. AN ACCIDENT. A PANICKED HORSE KICKED HIM IN THE HEAD.
YOU ONLY DESECRATED HIS CORPSE, THEN?

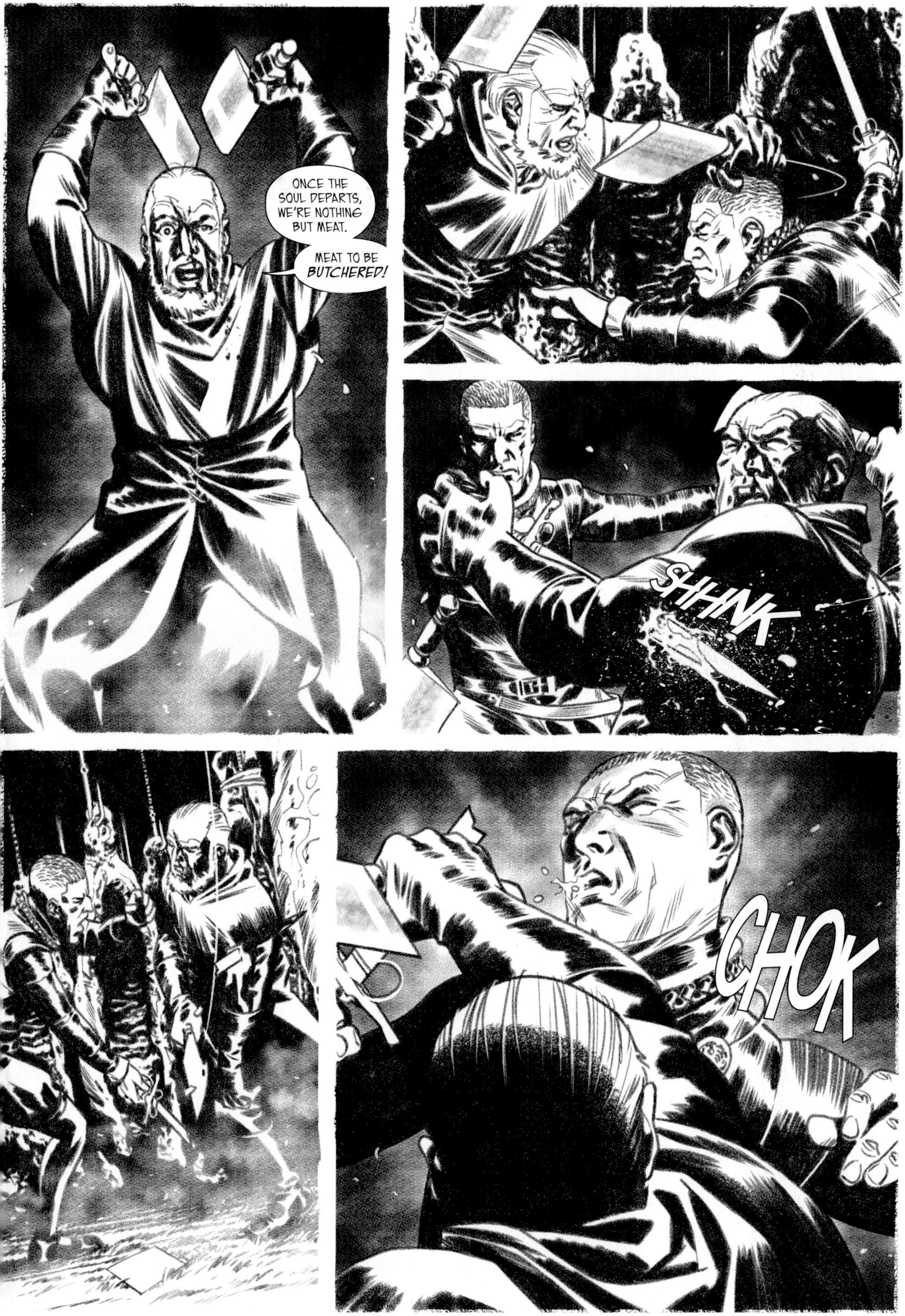
ONCE THE SOUL DEPARTS, WE'RE NOTHING BUT MEAT.
MEAT TO BE *BUTCHERED!*
SHHNK
CHOK

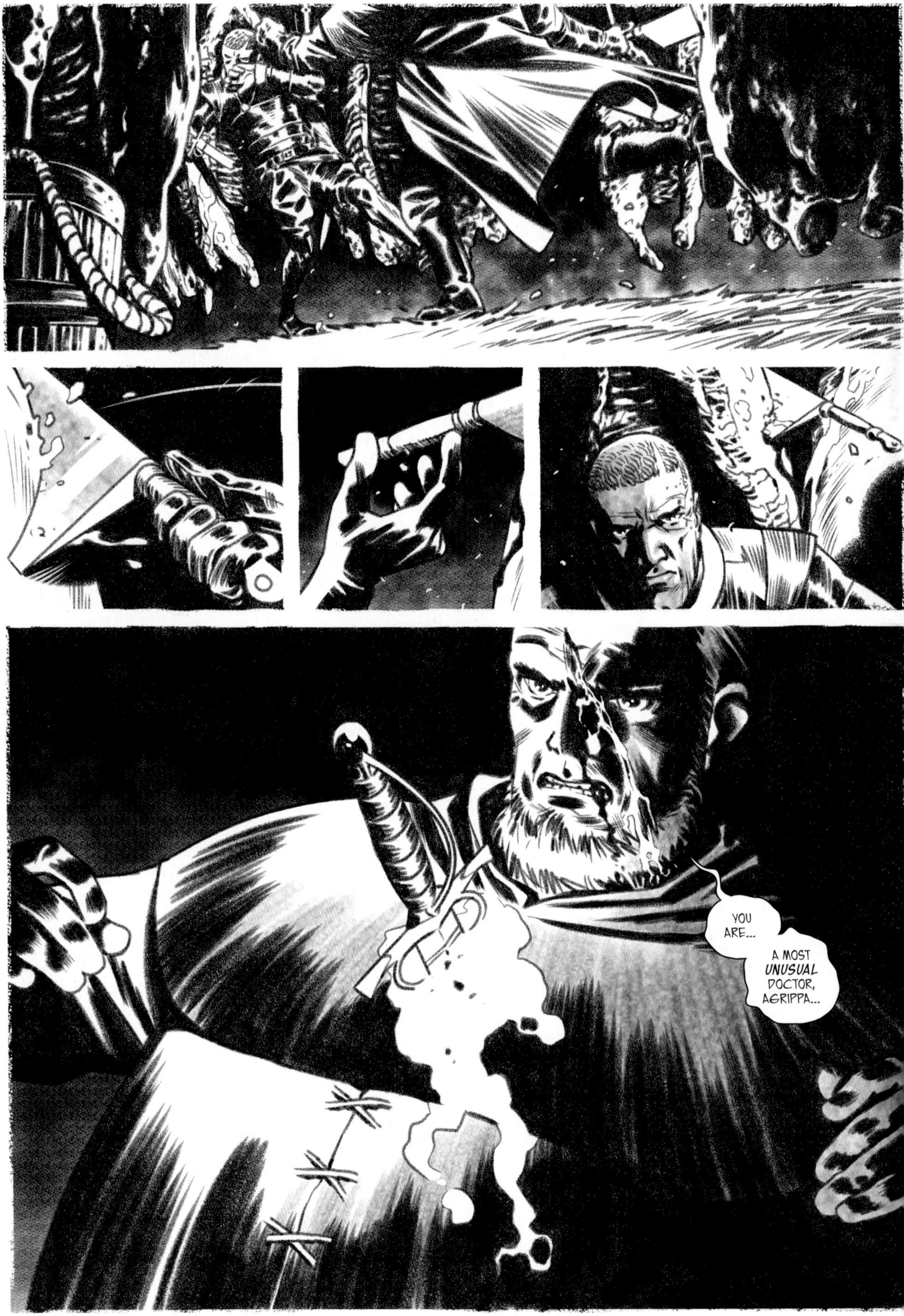
YOU ARE...
A MOST UNUSUAL DOCTOR, AGRIPPA...

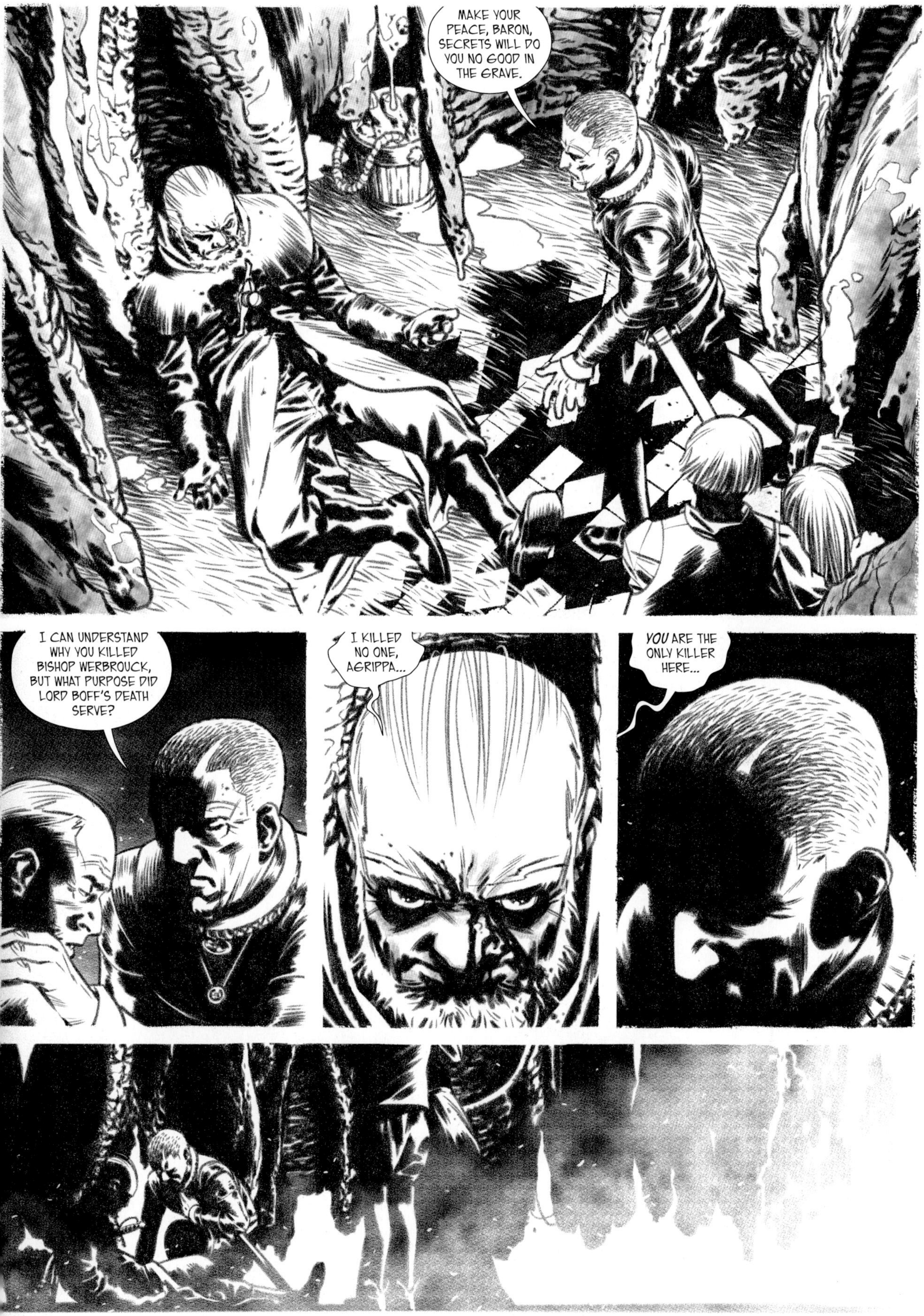
MAKE YOUR PEACE, BARON, SECRETS WILL DO YOU NO GOOD IN THE GRAVE.
I CAN UNDERSTAND WHY YOU KILLED BISHOP WERBROUCK, BUT WHAT PURPOSE DID LORD BOFF'S DEATH SERVE?
I KILLED NO ONE, AGRIPPA...
YOU ARE THE ONLY KILLER HERE...

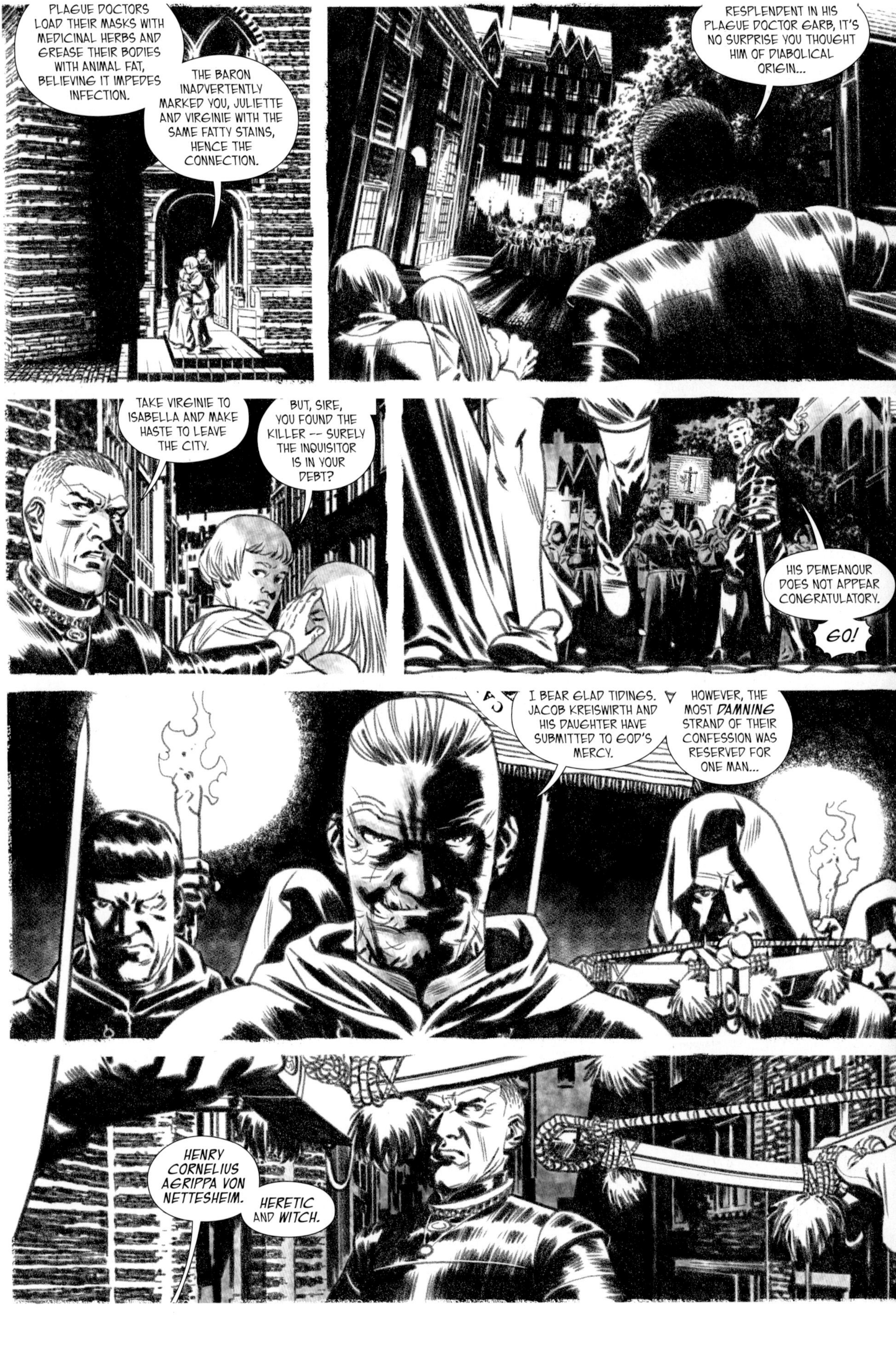
PLAGUE DOCTORS LOAD THEIR MASKS WITH MEDICINAL HERBS AND GREASE THEIR BODIES WITH ANIMAL FAT, BELIEVING IT IMPEDES INFECTION.
THE BARON INADVERTENTLY MARKED YOU, JULIETTE AND VIRGINIE WITH THE SAME FATTY STAINS, HENCE THE CONNECTION.
RESPLENDENT IN HIS PLAGUE DOCTOR GARB, IT'S NO SURPRISE YOU THOUGHT HIM OF DIABOLICAL ORIGIN...
TAKE VIRGINIE TO ISABELLA AND MAKE HASTE TO LEAVE THE CITY.
BUT, SIRE, YOU FOUND THE KILLER -- SURELY THE INQUISITOR IS IN YOUR DEBT?
HIS DEMEANOUR DOES NOT APPEAR CONGRATULATORY.
GO!
I BEAR GLAD TIDINGS. JACOB KREISWIRTH AND HIS DAUGHTER HAVE SUBMITTED TO GOD'S MERCY.
HOWEVER, THE MOST DAMNING STRAND OF THEIR CONFESSION WAS RESERVED FOR ONE MAN...
HENRY CORNELIUS AGRIPPA VON NETTESHEIM.
HERETIC AND WITCH.

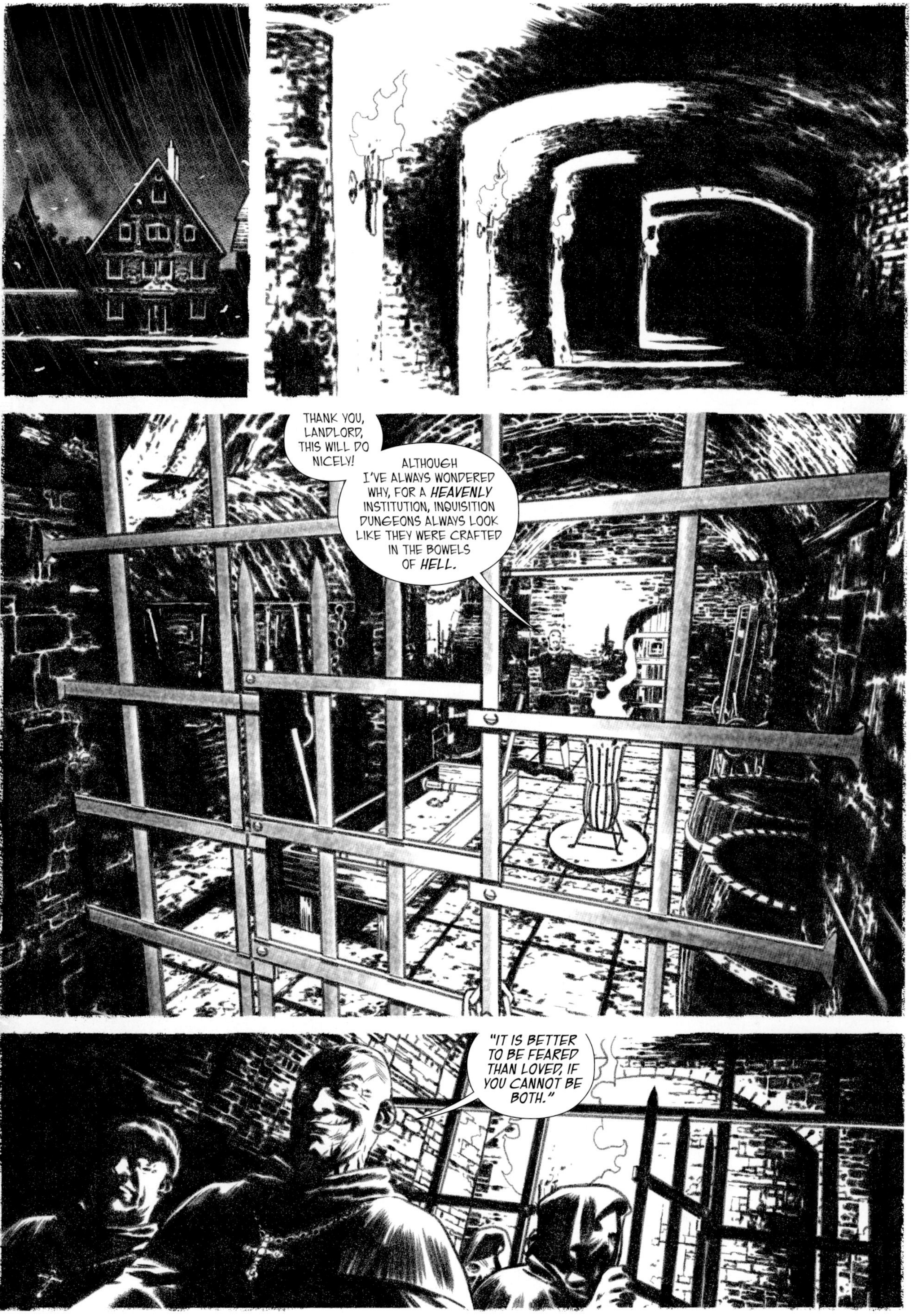
THANK YOU, LANDLORD, THIS WILL DO NICELY!
ALTHOUGH I'VE ALWAYS WONDERED WHY, FOR A HEAVENLY INSTITUTION, INQUISITION DUNGEONS ALWAYS LOOK LIKE THEY WERE CRAFTED IN THE BOWELS OF HELL.
"IT IS BETTER TO BE FEARED THAN LOVED, IF YOU CANNOT BE BOTH."

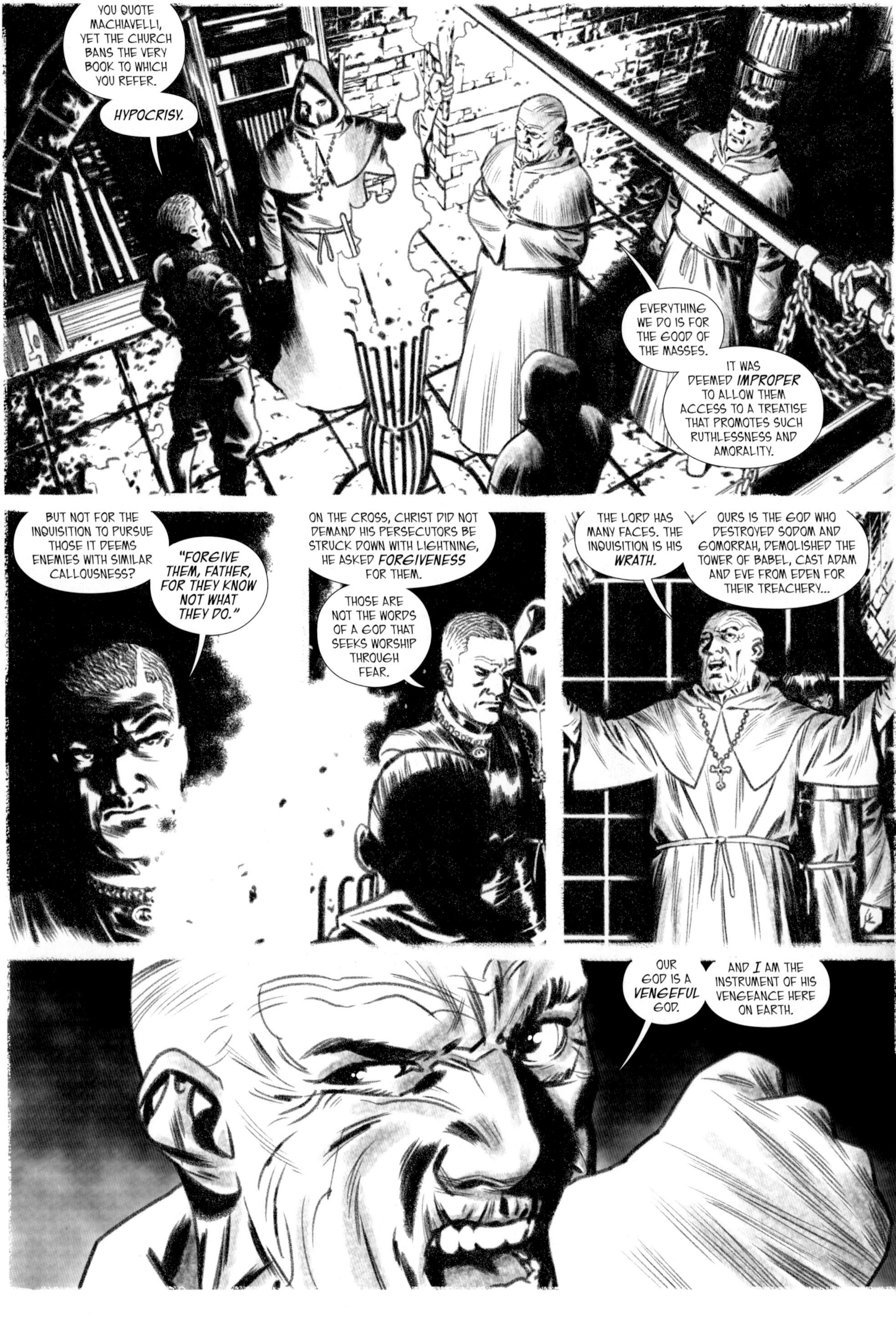
YOU QUOTE MACHIAVELLI, YET THE CHURCH BANS THE VERY BOOK TO WHICH YOU REFER.
HYPOCRISY.
EVERYTHING WE DO IS FOR THE GOOD OF THE MASSES.
IT WAS DEEMED IMPROPER TO ALLOW THEM ACCESS TO A TREATISE THAT PROMOTES SUCH RUTHLESSNESS AND AMORALITY.
BUT NOT FOR THE INQUISITION TO PURSUE THOSE IT DEEMS ENEMIES WITH SIMILAR CALLOUSNESS?
"FORGIVE THEM, FATHER, FOR THEY KNOW NOT WHAT THEY DO."
ON THE CROSS, CHRIST DID NOT DEMAND HIS PERSECUTORS BE STRUCK DOWN WITH LIGHTNING, HE ASKED FORGIVENESS FOR THEM.
THOSE ARE NOT THE WORDS OF A GOD THAT SEEKS WORSHIP THROUGH FEAR.
THE LORD HAS MANY FACES. THE INQUISITION IS HIS WRATH.
OURS IS THE GOD WHO DESTROYED SODOM AND GOMORRAH, DEMOLISHED THE TOWER OF BABEL, CAST ADAM AND EVE FROM EDEN FOR THEIR TREACHERY...
OUR GOD IS A VENGEFUL GOD.
AND I AM THE INSTRUMENT OF HIS VENGEANCE HERE ON EARTH.

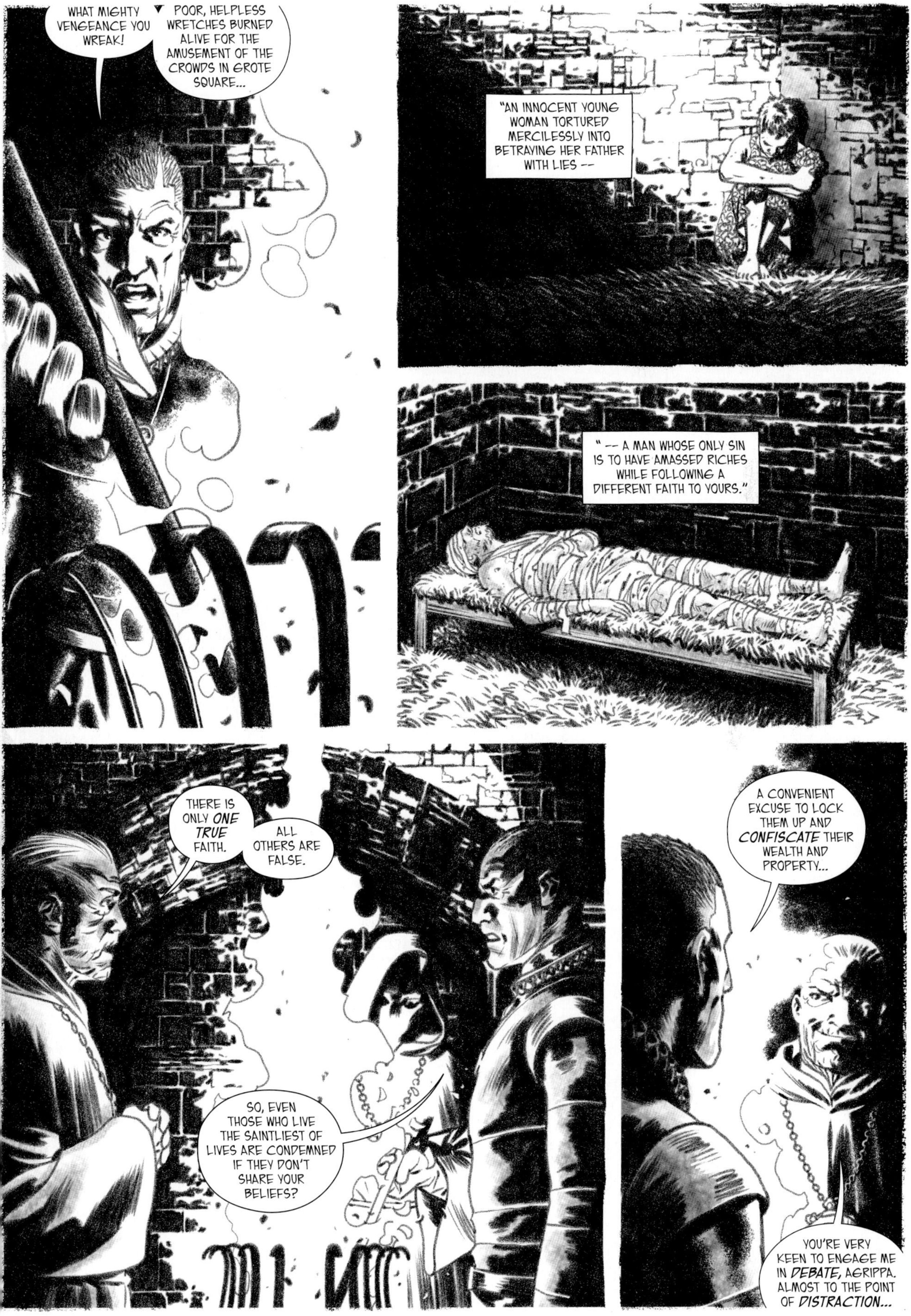
WHAT MIGHTY VENGEANCE YOU WREAK!
POOR, HELPLESS WRETCHES BURNED ALIVE FOR THE AMUSEMENT OF THE CROWDS IN GROTE SQUARE...
"AN INNOCENT YOUNG WOMAN TORTURED MERCILESSLY INTO BETRAYING HER FATHER WITH LIES --
" -- A MAN WHOSE ONLY SIN IS TO HAVE AMASSED RICHES WHILE FOLLOWING A DIFFERENT FAITH TO YOURS."
THERE IS ONLY *ONE TRUE* FAITH.
ALL OTHERS ARE FALSE.
SO, EVEN THOSE WHO LIVE THE SAINTLIEST OF LIVES ARE CONDEMNED IF THEY DON'T SHARE YOUR BELIEFS?
A CONVENIENT EXCUSE TO LOCK THEM UP AND *CONFISCATE* THEIR WEALTH AND PROPERTY...
YOU'RE VERY KEEN TO ENGAGE ME IN *DEBATE*, AGRIPPA. ALMOST TO THE POINT OF *DISTRACTION*...

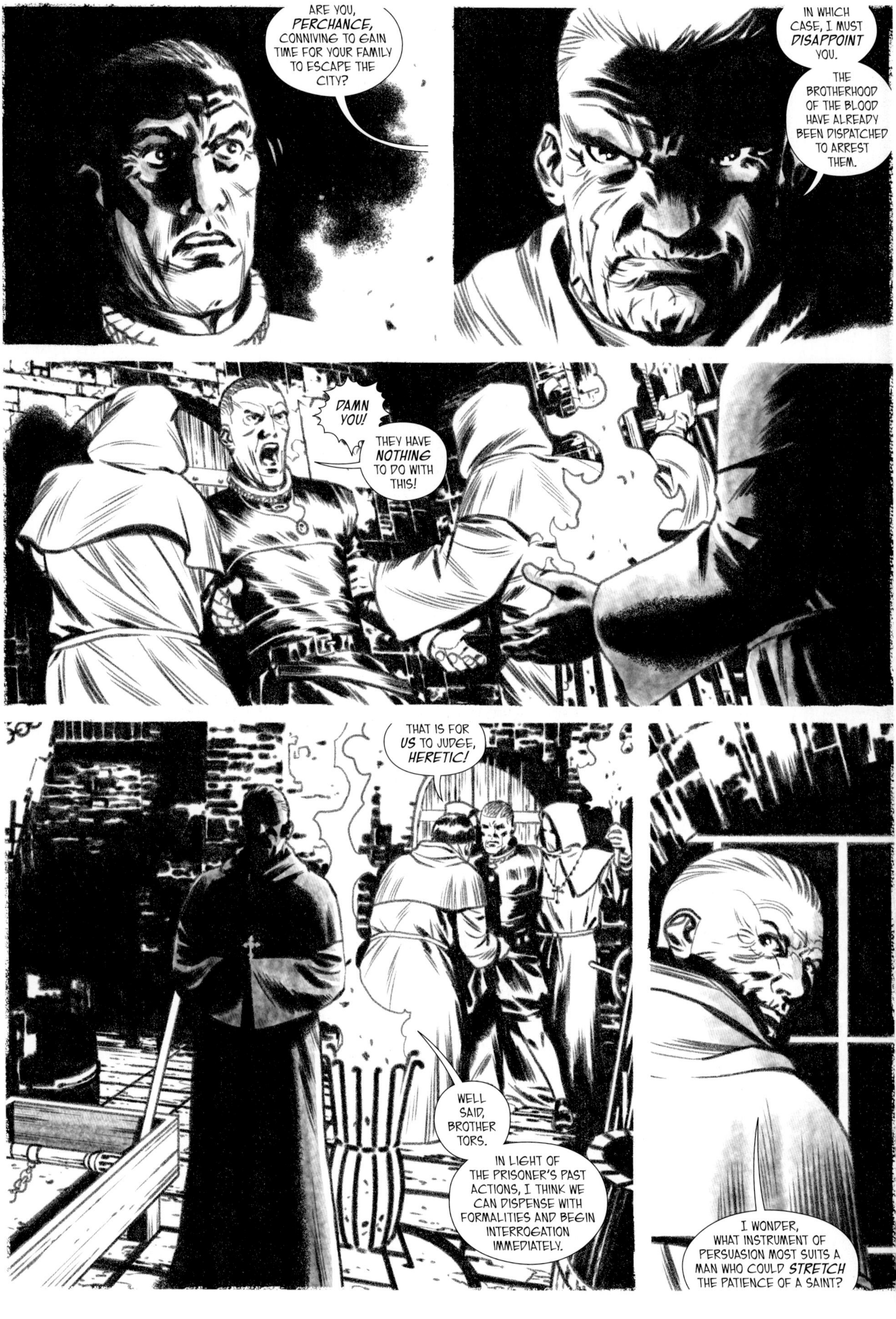
ARE YOU, *PERCHANCE,* CONNIVING TO GAIN TIME FOR YOUR FAMILY TO ESCAPE THE CITY?
IN WHICH CASE, I MUST *DISAPPOINT* YOU.
THE BROTHERHOOD OF THE BLOOD HAVE ALREADY BEEN DISPATCHED TO ARREST THEM.
DAMN YOU!
THEY HAVE *NOTHING* TO DO WITH THIS!
THAT IS FOR *US* TO JUDGE, *HERETIC!*
WELL SAID, BROTHER TORS.
IN LIGHT OF THE PRISONER'S PAST ACTIONS, I THINK WE CAN DISPENSE WITH FORMALITIES AND BEGIN INTERROGATION IMMEDIATELY.
I WONDER, WHAT INSTRUMENT OF PERSUASION MOST SUITS A MAN WHO COULD *STRETCH* THE PATIENCE OF A SAINT?

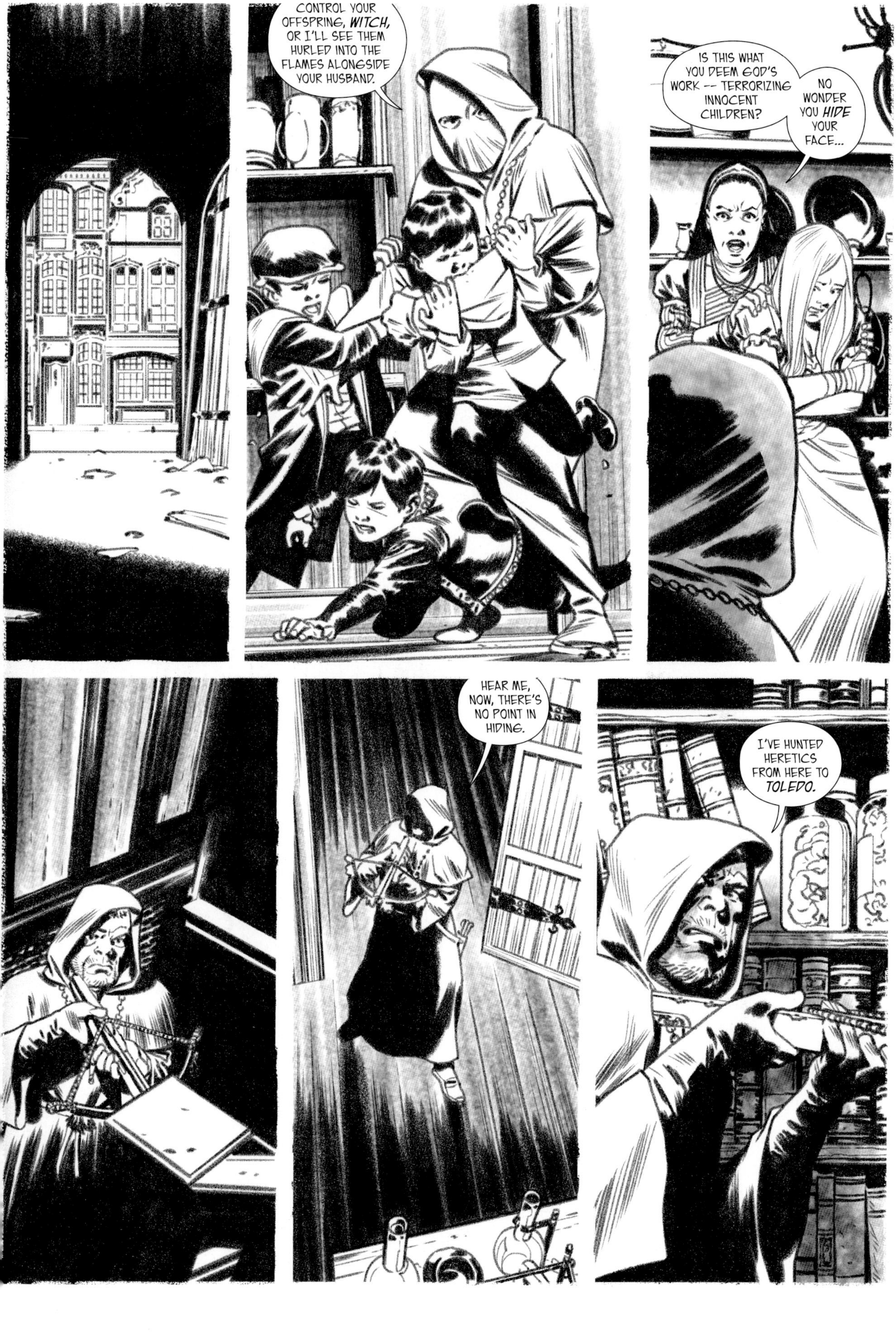
CONTROL YOUR OFFSPRING, WITCH, OR I'LL SEE THEM HURLED INTO THE FLAMES ALONGSIDE YOUR HUSBAND.
IS THIS WHAT YOU DEEM GOD'S WORK -- TERRORIZING INNOCENT CHILDREN?
NO WONDER YOU HIDE YOUR FACE...
HEAR ME, NOW, THERE'S NO POINT IN HIDING.
I'VE HUNTED HERETICS FROM HERE TO TOLEDO.

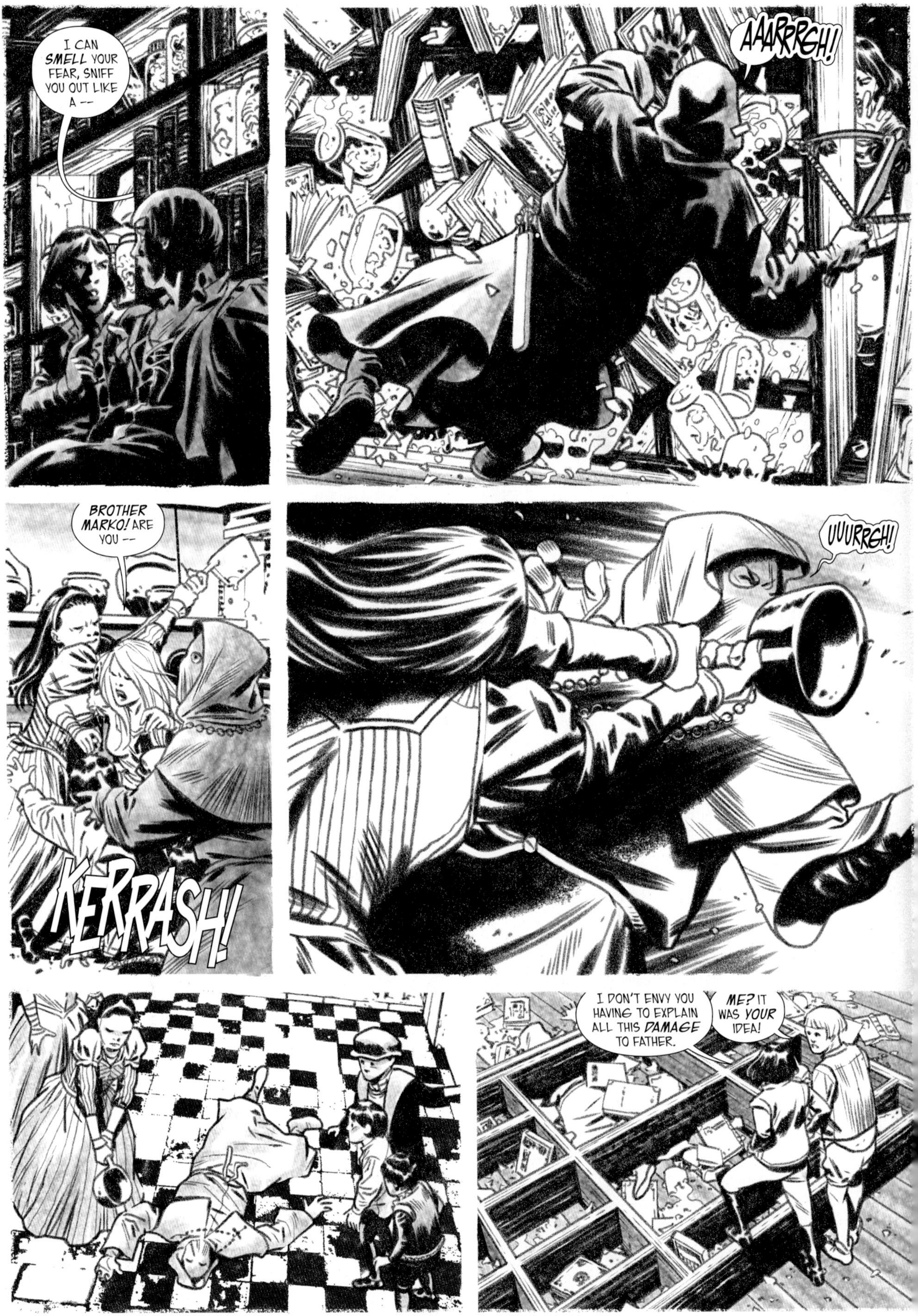
I CAN SMELL YOUR FEAR, SNIFF YOU OUT LIKE A --
AAARRRGH!
BROTHER MARKO! ARE YOU --
KERRASH!
UUURRGH!
I DON'T ENVY YOU HAVING TO EXPLAIN ALL THIS DAMAGE TO FATHER.
ME? IT WAS YOUR IDEA!

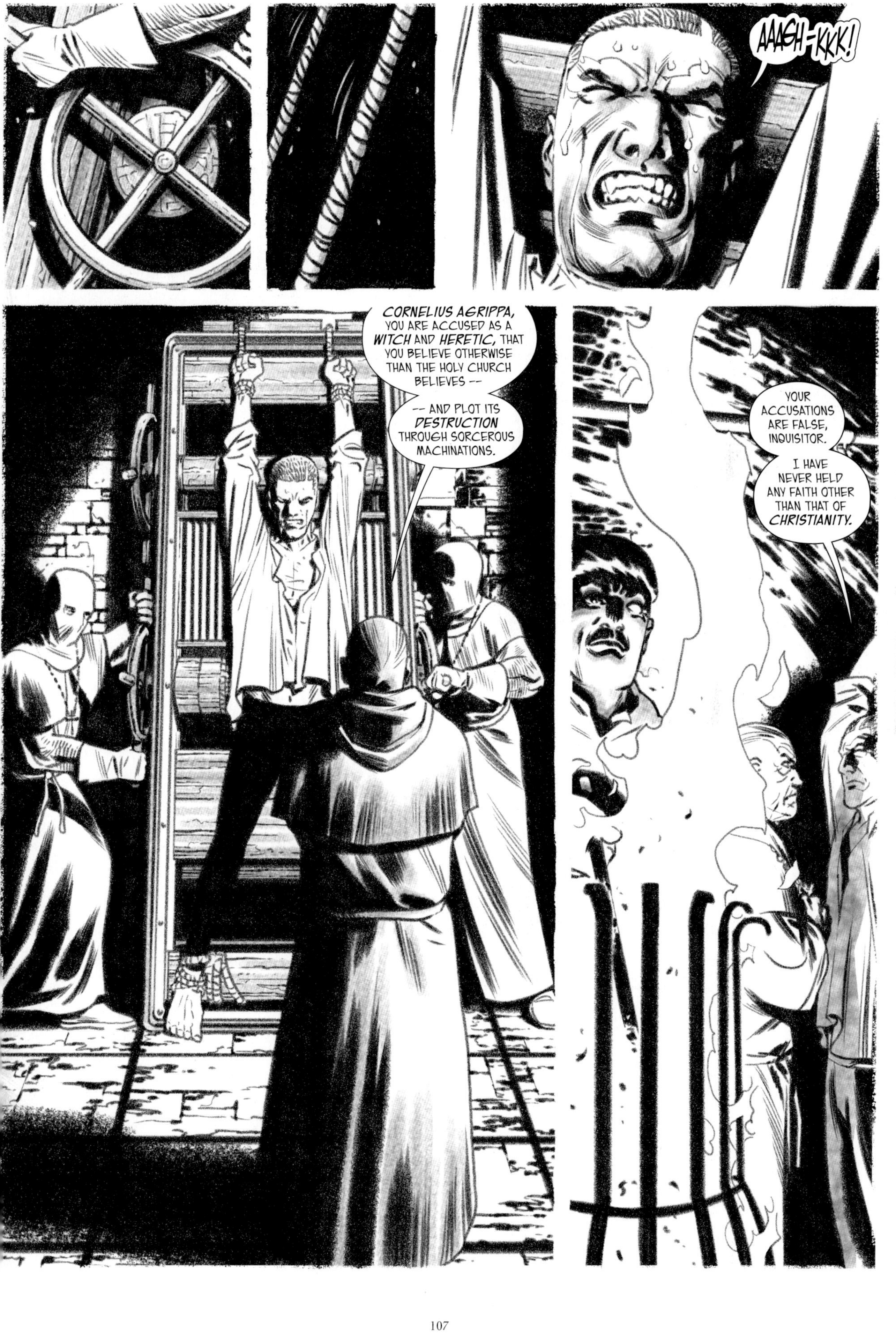
AAAGH-KKK!
CORNELIUS AGRIPPA, YOU ARE ACCUSED AS A WITCH AND HERETIC, THAT YOU BELIEVE OTHERWISE THAN THE HOLY CHURCH BELIEVES --
-- AND PLOT ITS DESTRUCTION THROUGH SORCEROUS MACHINATIONS.
YOUR ACCUSATIONS ARE FALSE, INQUISITOR.
I HAVE NEVER HELD ANY FAITH OTHER THAN THAT OF CHRISTIANITY.

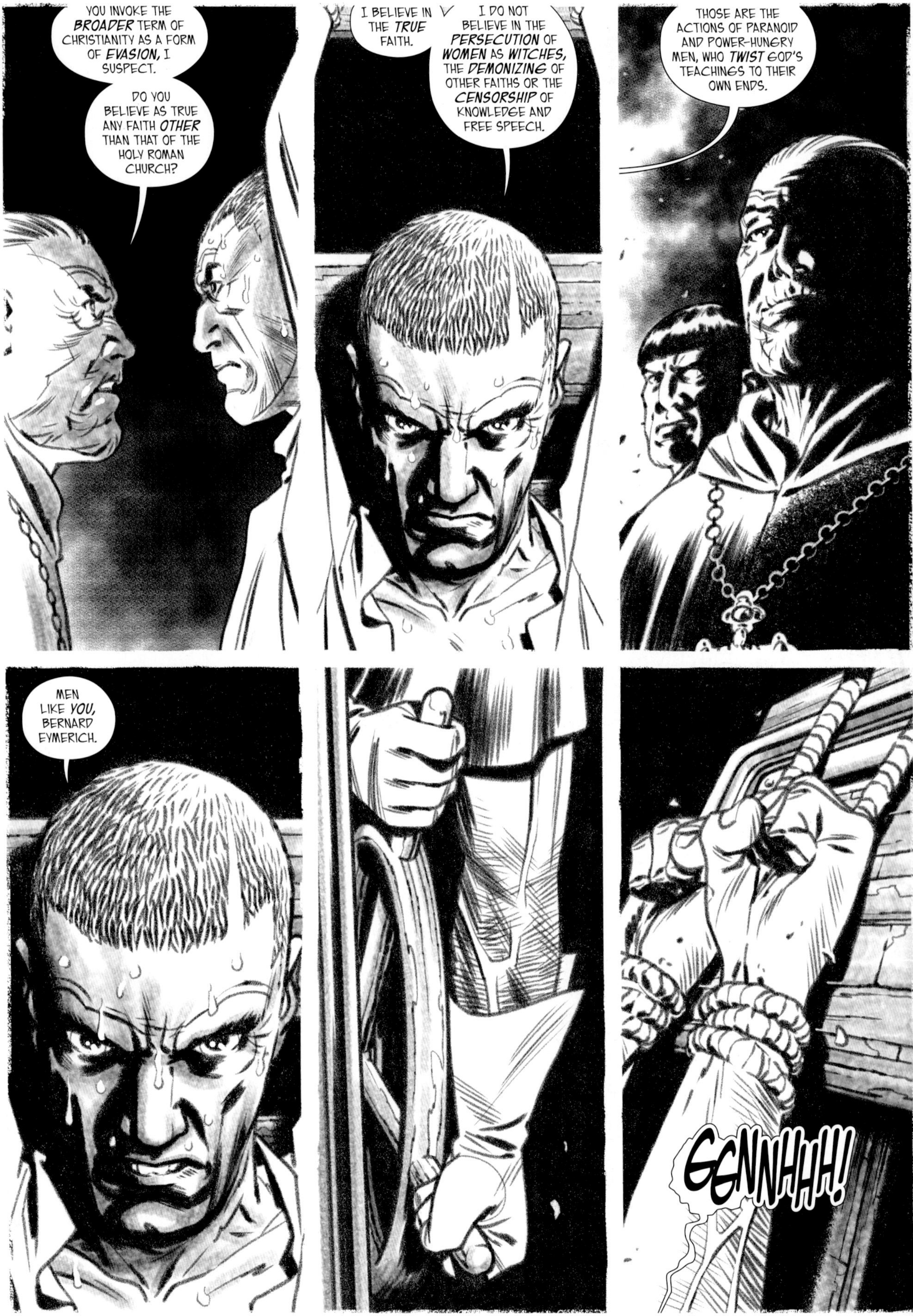

YOU INVOKE THE BROADER TERM OF CHRISTIANITY AS A FORM OF EVASION, I SUSPECT.
DO YOU BELIEVE AS TRUE ANY FAITH OTHER THAN THAT OF THE HOLY ROMAN CHURCH?
I BELIEVE IN THE TRUE FAITH.
I DO NOT BELIEVE IN THE PERSECUTION OF WOMEN AS WITCHES, THE DEMONIZING OF OTHER FAITHS OR THE CENSORSHIP OF KNOWLEDGE AND FREE SPEECH.
THOSE ARE THE ACTIONS OF PARANOID AND POWER-HUNGRY MEN, WHO TWIST GOD'S TEACHINGS TO THEIR OWN ENDS.
MEN LIKE YOU, BERNARD EYMERICH.
GGNNHHH!

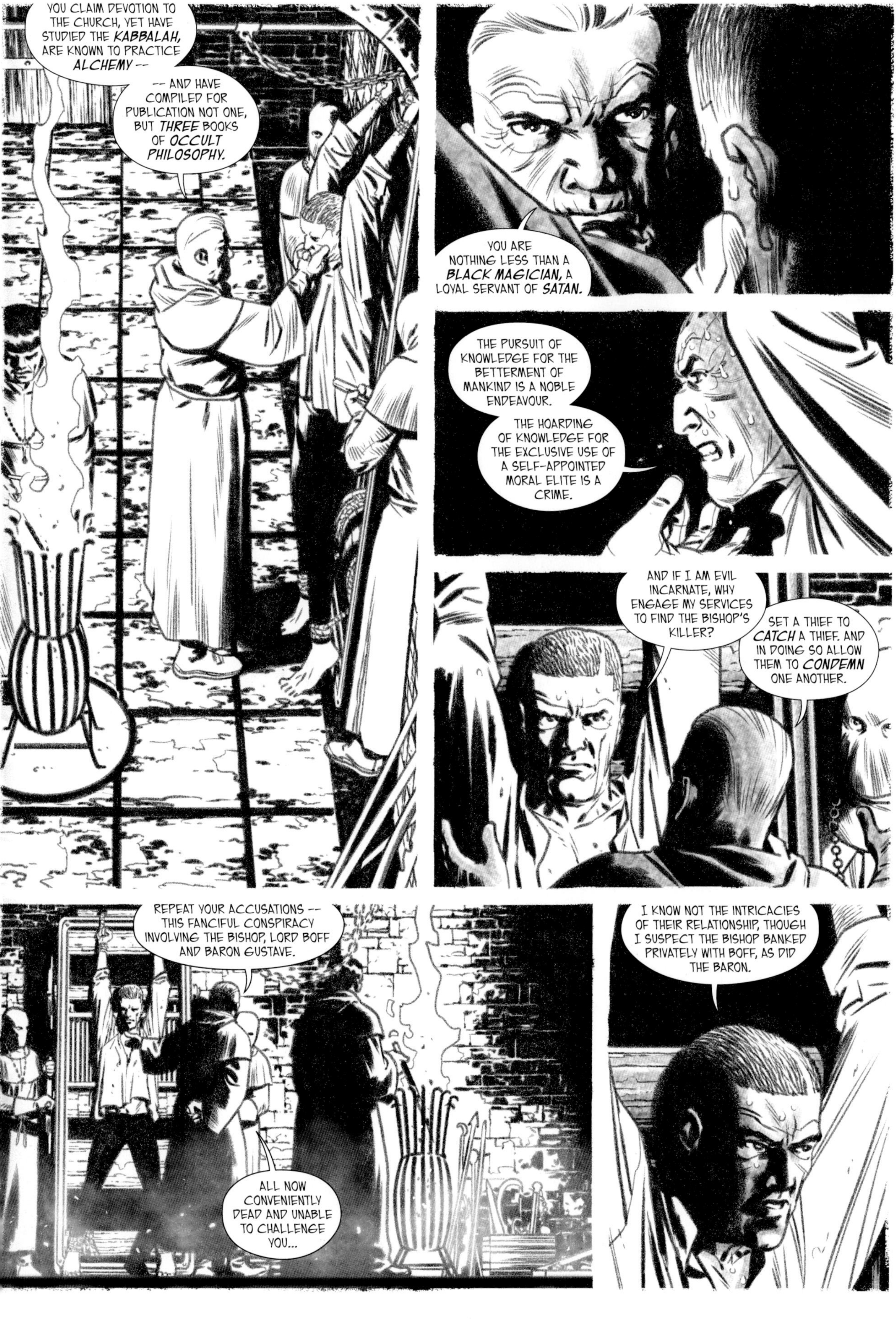

YOU CLAIM DEVOTION TO THE CHURCH, YET HAVE STUDIED THE KABBALAH, ARE KNOWN TO PRACTICE ALCHEMY --
-- AND HAVE COMPILED FOR PUBLICATION NOT ONE, BUT THREE BOOKS OF OCCULT PHILOSOPHY.
YOU ARE NOTHING LESS THAN A BLACK MAGICIAN, A LOYAL SERVANT OF SATAN.
THE PURSUIT OF KNOWLEDGE FOR THE BETTERMENT OF MANKIND IS A NOBLE ENDEAVOUR.
THE HOARDING OF KNOWLEDGE FOR THE EXCLUSIVE USE OF A SELF-APPOINTED MORAL ELITE IS A CRIME.
AND IF I AM EVIL INCARNATE, WHY ENGAGE MY SERVICES TO FIND THE BISHOP'S KILLER?
SET A THIEF TO CATCH A THIEF. AND IN DOING SO ALLOW THEM TO CONDEMN ONE ANOTHER.
REPEAT YOUR ACCUSATIONS -- THIS FANCIFUL CONSPIRACY INVOLVING THE BISHOP, LORD BOFF AND BARON GUSTAVE.
ALL NOW CONVENIENTLY DEAD AND UNABLE TO CHALLENGE YOU...
I KNOW NOT THE INTRICACIES OF THEIR RELATIONSHIP, THOUGH I SUSPECT THE BISHOP BANKED PRIVATELY WITH BOFF, AS DID THE BARON.

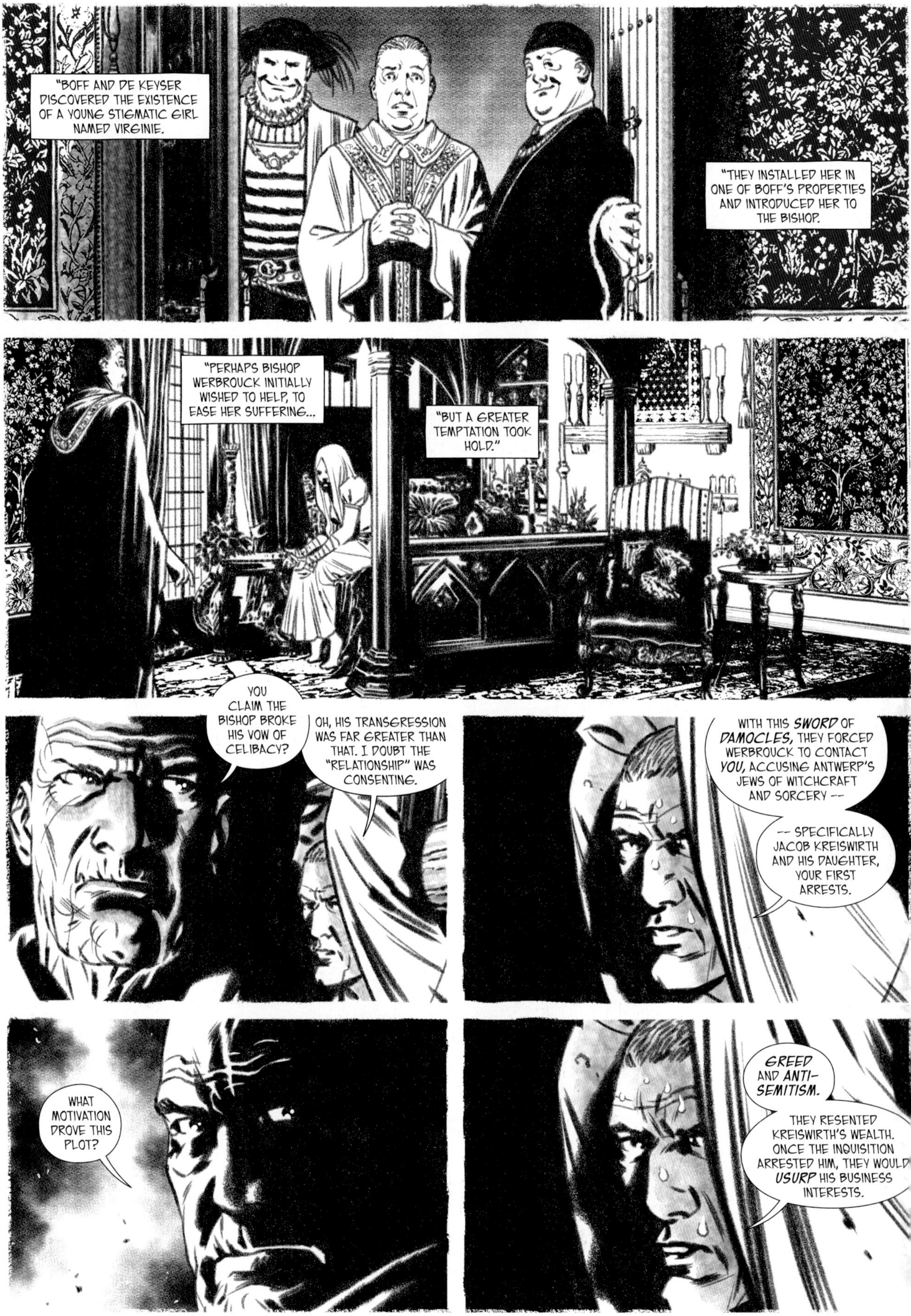
"BOFF AND DE KEYSER DISCOVERED THE EXISTENCE OF A YOUNG STIGMATIC GIRL NAMED VIRGINIE.
"THEY INSTALLED HER IN ONE OF BOFF'S PROPERTIES AND INTRODUCED HER TO THE BISHOP.
"PERHAPS BISHOP WERBROUCK INITIALLY WISHED TO HELP, TO EASE HER SUFFERING...
"BUT A GREATER TEMPTATION TOOK HOLD."
YOU CLAIM THE BISHOP BROKE HIS VOW OF CELIBACY?
OH, HIS TRANSGRESSION WAS FAR GREATER THAN THAT. I DOUBT THE "RELATIONSHIP" WAS CONSENTING.
WITH THIS SWORD OF DAMOCLES, THEY FORCED WERBROUCK TO CONTACT YOU, ACCUSING ANTWERP'S JEWS OF WITCHCRAFT AND SORCERY --
-- SPECIFICALLY JACOB KREISWIRTH AND HIS DAUGHTER, YOUR FIRST ARRESTS.
WHAT MOTIVATION DROVE THIS PLOT?
GREED AND ANTI-SEMITISM.
THEY RESENTED KREISWIRTH'S WEALTH. ONCE THE INQUISITION ARRESTED HIM, THEY WOULD USURP HIS BUSINESS INTERESTS.

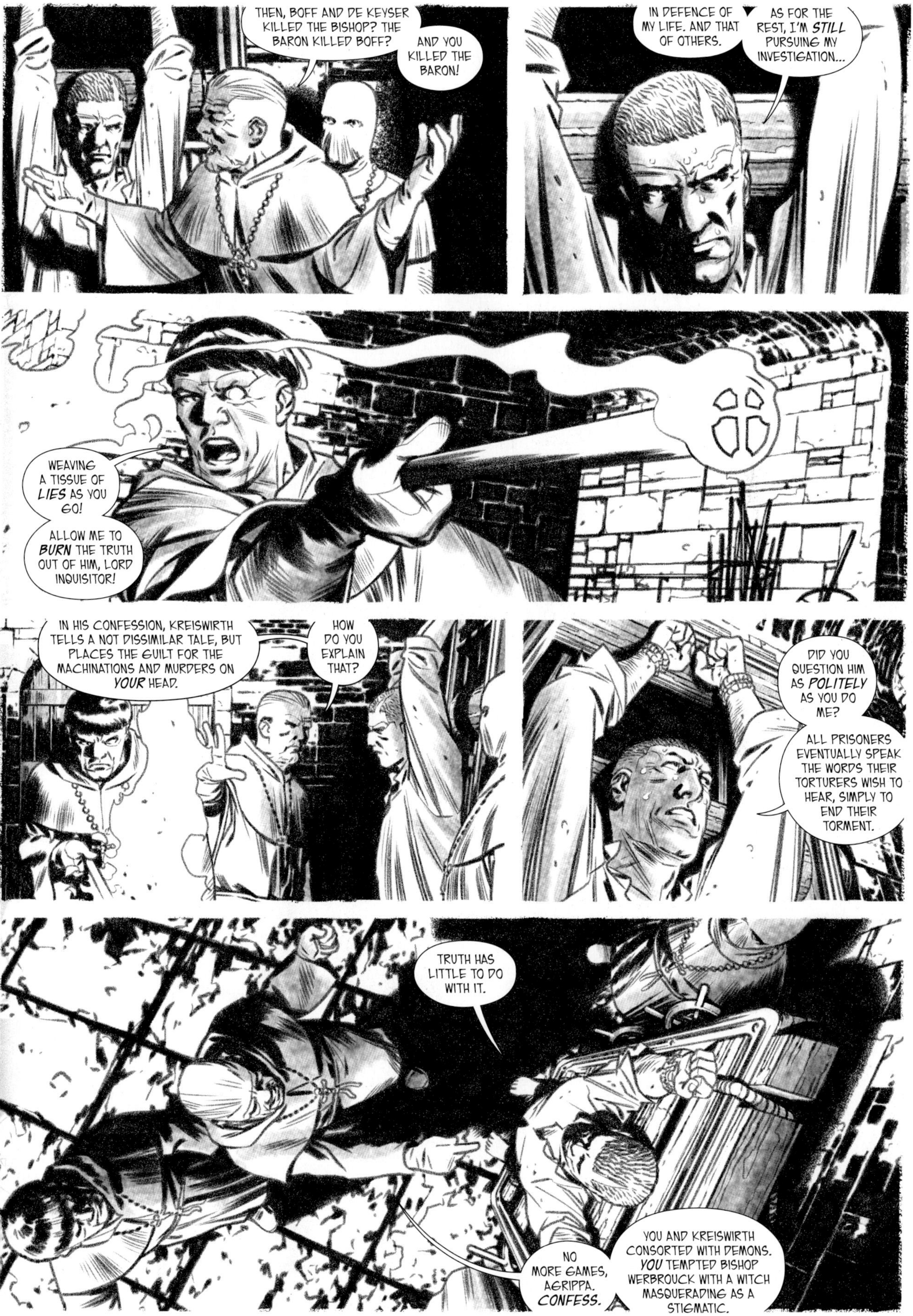
THEN, BOFF AND DE KEYSER KILLED THE BISHOP? THE BARON KILLED BOFF?
AND YOU KILLED THE BARON!
IN DEFENCE OF MY LIFE. AND THAT OF OTHERS.
AS FOR THE REST, I'M STILL PURSUING MY INVESTIGATION...
WEAVING A TISSUE OF LIES AS YOU GO!
ALLOW ME TO BURN THE TRUTH OUT OF HIM, LORD INQUISITOR!
IN HIS CONFESSION, KREISWIRTH TELLS A NOT DISSIMILAR TALE, BUT PLACES THE GUILT FOR THE MACHINATIONS AND MURDERS ON YOUR HEAD.
HOW DO YOU EXPLAIN THAT?
DID YOU QUESTION HIM AS POLITELY AS YOU DO ME?
ALL PRISONERS EVENTUALLY SPEAK THE WORDS THEIR TORTURERS WISH TO HEAR, SIMPLY TO END THEIR TORMENT.
TRUTH HAS LITTLE TO DO WITH IT.
NO MORE GAMES, AGRIPPA. CONFESS.
YOU AND KREISWIRTH CONSORTED WITH DEMONS. YOU TEMPTED BISHOP WERBROUCK WITH A WITCH MASQUERADING AS A STIGMATIC.

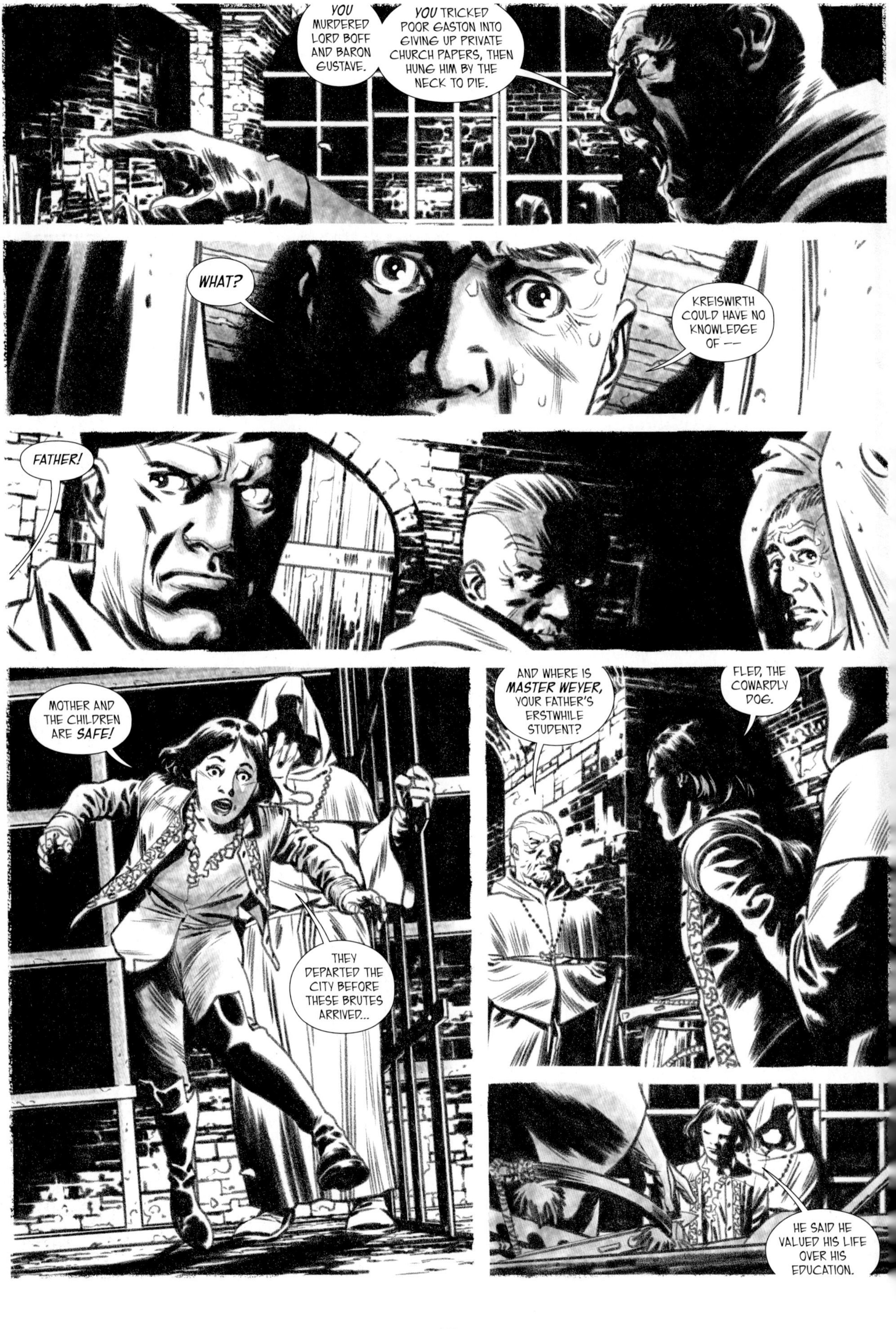
YOU MURDERED LORD BOFF AND BARON GUSTAVE.
YOU TRICKED POOR GASTON INTO GIVING UP PRIVATE CHURCH PAPERS, THEN HUNG HIM BY THE NECK TO DIE.
WHAT?
KREISWIRTH COULD HAVE NO KNOWLEDGE OF --
FATHER!
MOTHER AND THE CHILDREN ARE SAFE!
THEY DEPARTED THE CITY BEFORE THESE BRUTES ARRIVED...
AND WHERE IS MASTER WEYER, YOUR FATHER'S ERSTWHILE STUDENT?
FLED, THE COWARDLY DOG.
HE SAID HE VALUED HIS LIFE OVER HIS EDUCATION.

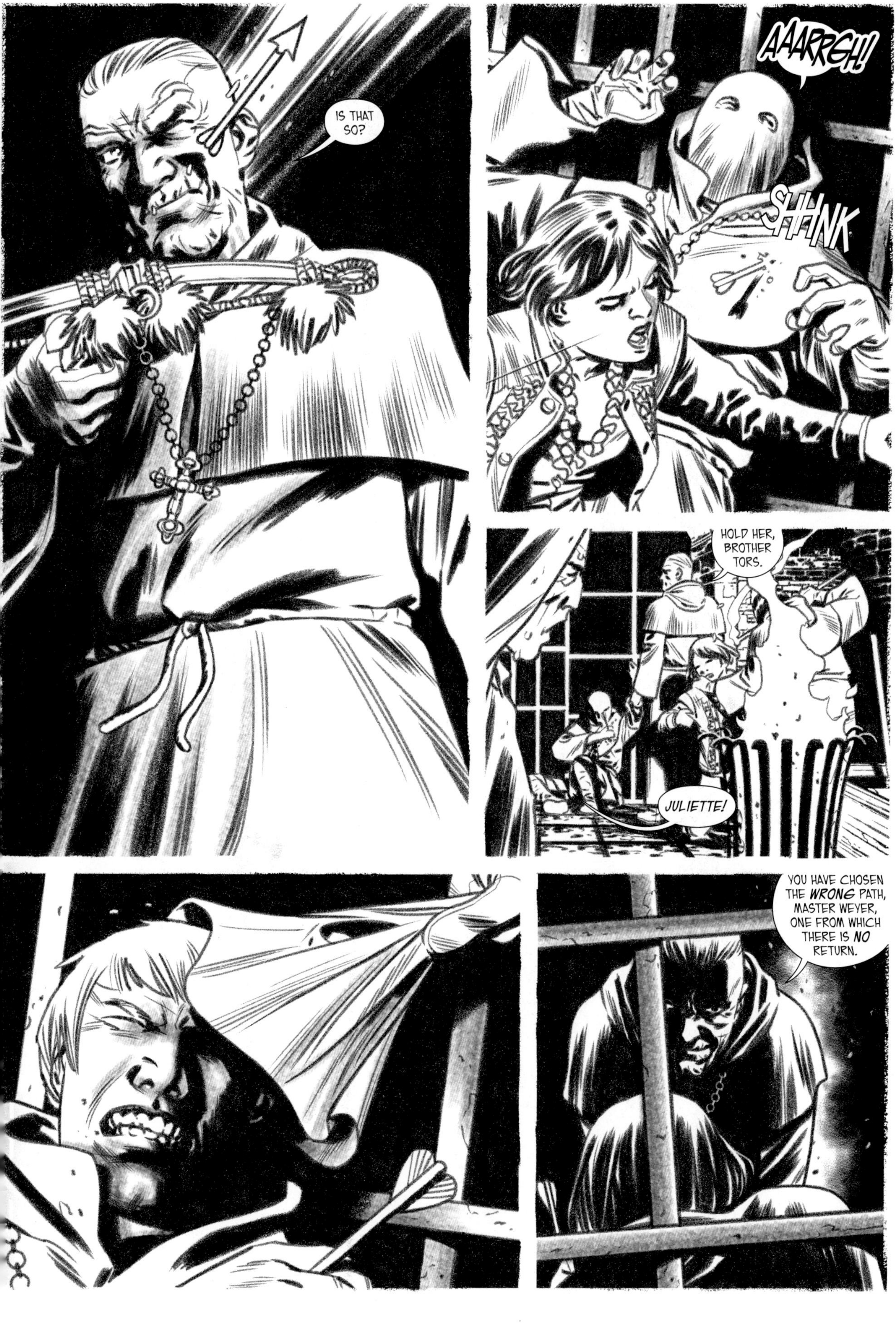
IS THAT SO?
AAARRGH!
SHHNK
HOLD HER, BROTHER TORS.
JULIETTE!
YOU HAVE CHOSEN THE WRONG PATH, MASTER WEYER, ONE FROM WHICH THERE IS NO RETURN.

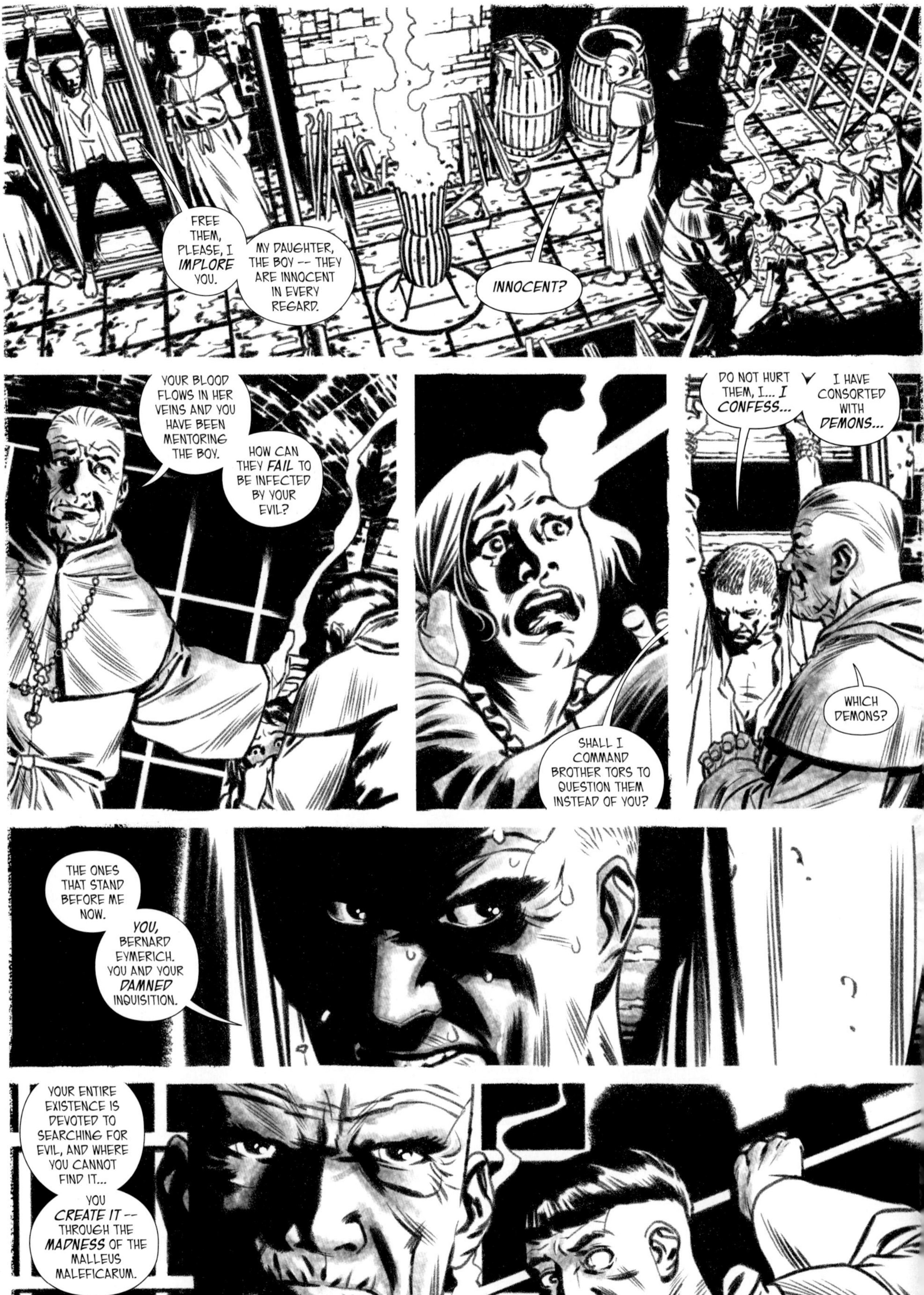
FREE THEM, PLEASE, I IMPLORE YOU.
MY DAUGHTER, THE BOY -- THEY ARE INNOCENT IN EVERY REGARD.
INNOCENT?
YOUR BLOOD FLOWS IN HER VEINS AND YOU HAVE BEEN MENTORING THE BOY.
HOW CAN THEY FAIL TO BE INFECTED BY YOUR EVIL?
SHALL I COMMAND BROTHER TORS TO QUESTION THEM INSTEAD OF YOU?
DO NOT HURT THEM, I... I CONFESS...
I HAVE CONSORTED WITH DEMONS...
WHICH DEMONS?
THE ONES THAT STAND BEFORE ME NOW.
YOU, BERNARD EYMERICH. YOU AND YOUR DAMNED INQUISITION.
YOUR ENTIRE EXISTENCE IS DEVOTED TO SEARCHING FOR EVIL, AND WHERE YOU CANNOT FIND IT...
YOU CREATE IT -- THROUGH THE MADNESS OF THE MALLEUS MALEFICARUM.

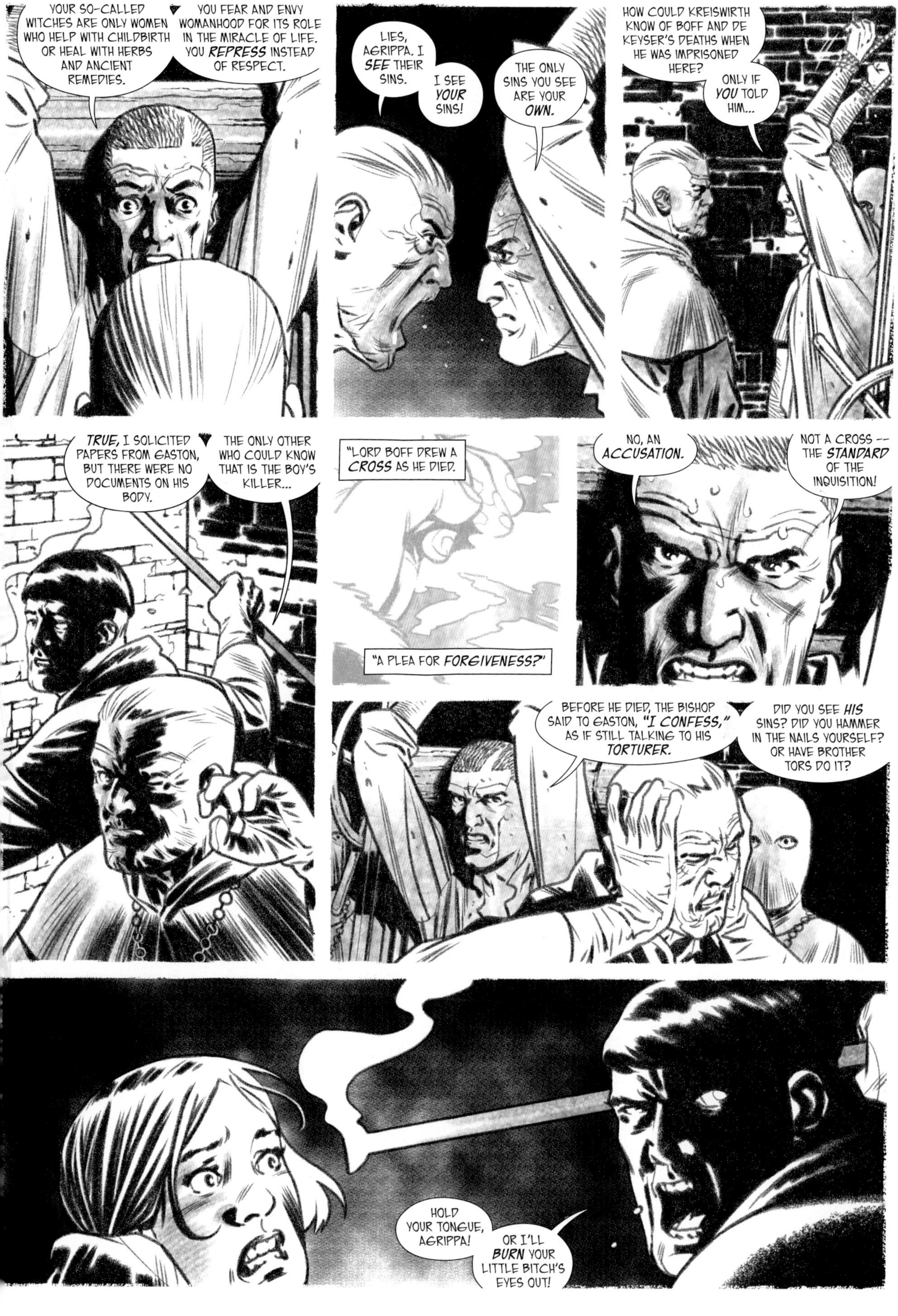
YOUR SO-CALLED WITCHES ARE ONLY WOMEN WHO HELP WITH CHILDBIRTH OR HEAL WITH HERBS AND ANCIENT REMEDIES.
YOU FEAR AND ENVY WOMANHOOD FOR ITS ROLE IN THE MIRACLE OF LIFE. YOU REPRESS INSTEAD OF RESPECT.
LIES, AGRIPPA. I SEE THEIR SINS.
I SEE YOUR SINS!
THE ONLY SINS YOU SEE ARE YOUR OWN.
HOW COULD KREISWIRTH KNOW OF BOFF AND DE KEYSER'S DEATHS WHEN HE WAS IMPRISONED HERE?
ONLY IF YOU TOLD HIM...
TRUE, I SOLICITED PAPERS FROM GASTON, BUT THERE WERE NO DOCUMENTS ON HIS BODY.
THE ONLY OTHER WHO COULD KNOW THAT IS THE BOY'S KILLER...
"LORD BOFF DREW A CROSS AS HE DIED.
"A PLEA FOR FORGIVENESS?"
NO, AN ACCUSATION.
NOT A CROSS -- THE STANDARD OF THE INQUISITION!
BEFORE HE DIED, THE BISHOP SAID TO GASTON, "I CONFESS," AS IF STILL TALKING TO HIS TORTURER.
DID YOU SEE HIS SINS? DID YOU HAMMER IN THE NAILS YOURSELF? OR HAVE BROTHER TORS DO IT?
HOLD YOUR TONGUE, AGRIPPA!
OR I'LL BURN YOUR LITTLE BITCH'S EYES OUT!

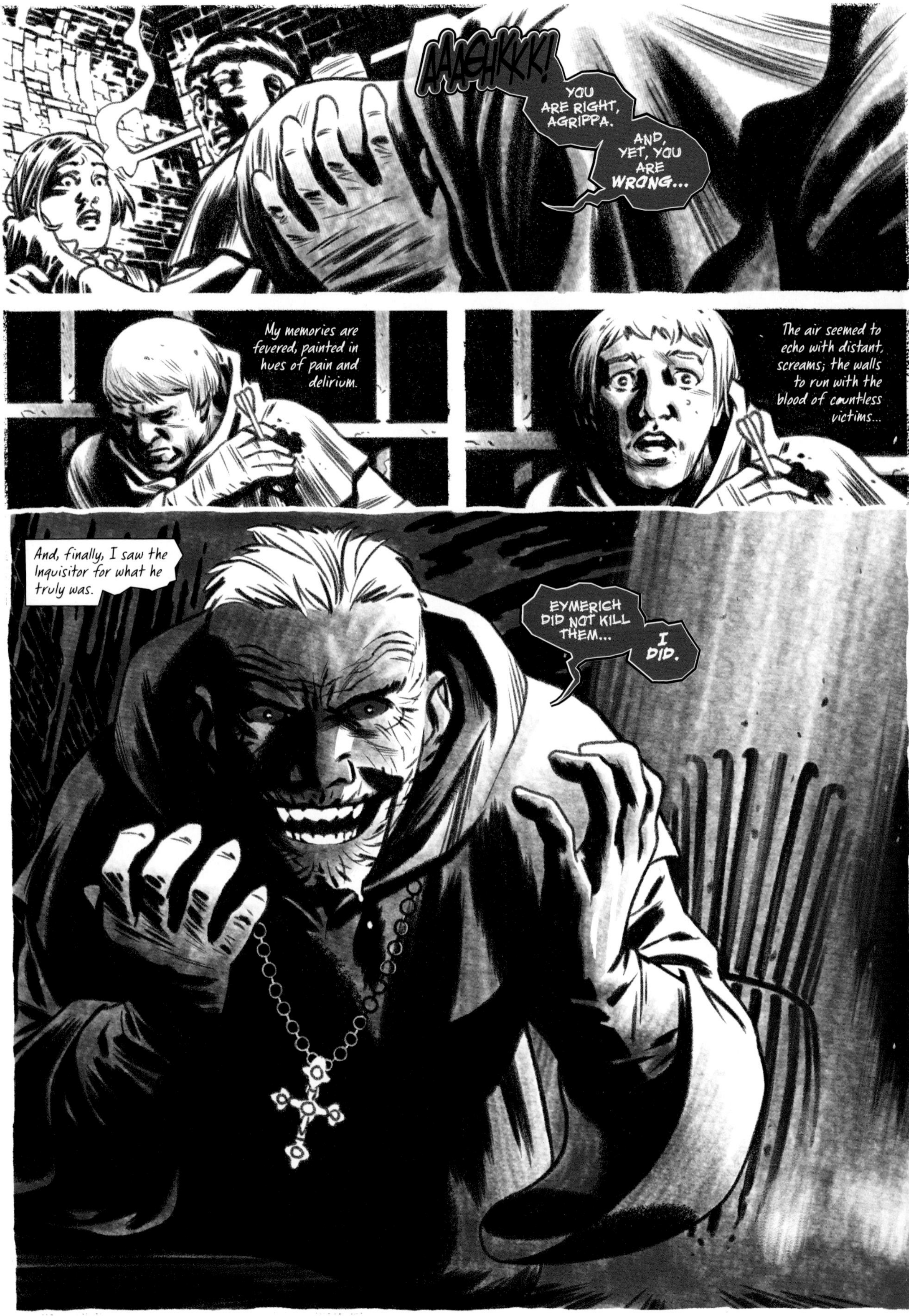
AAAGHKKK!
YOU ARE RIGHT, AGRIPPA.
AND, YET, YOU ARE WRONG...
My memories are fevered, painted in hues of pain and delirium.
The air seemed to echo with distant screams; the walls to run with the blood of countless victims...
And, finally, I saw the Inquisitor for what he truly was.
EYMERICH DID NOT KILL THEM...
I DID.

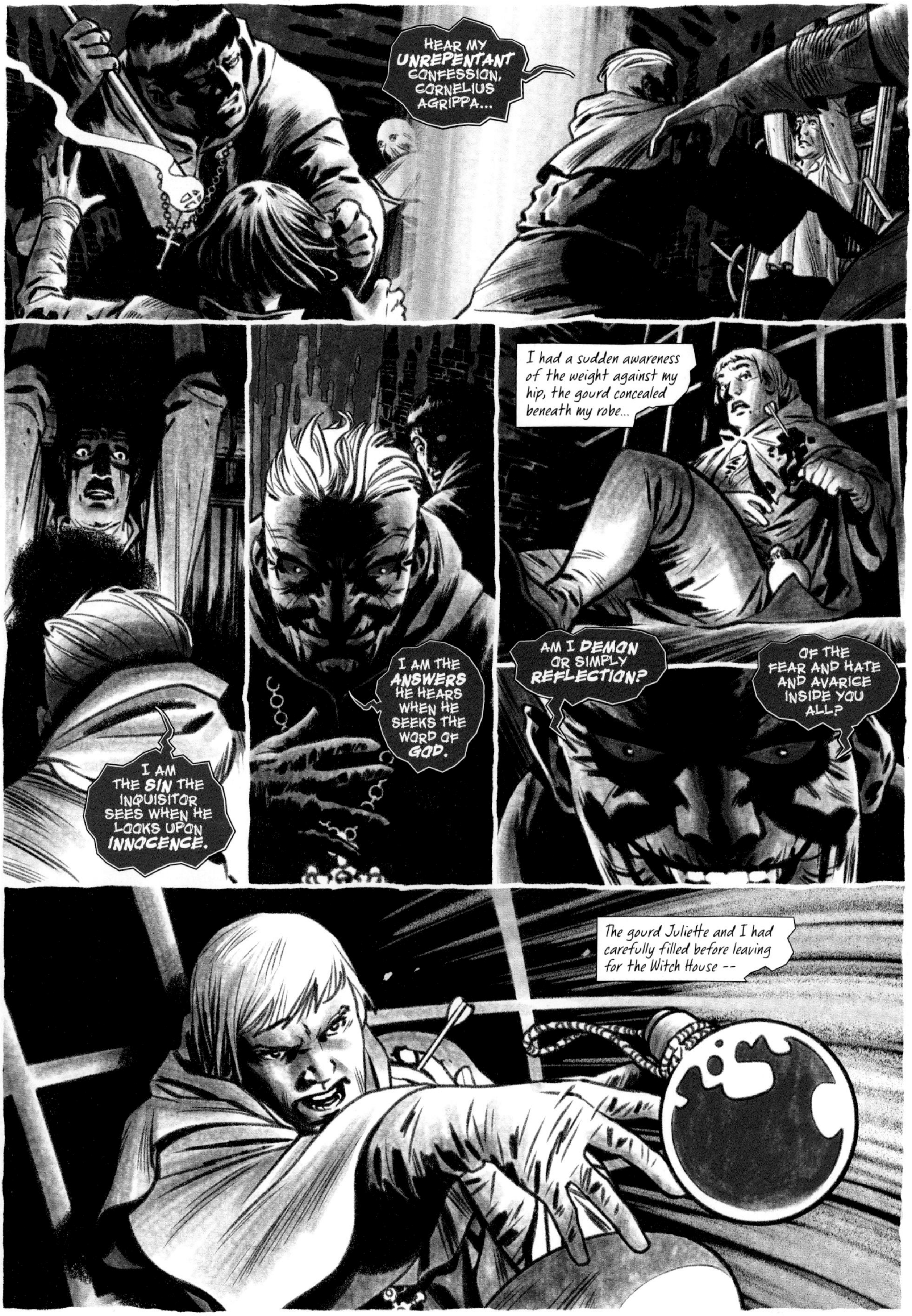
HEAR MY UNREPENTANT CONFESSION, CORNELIUS AGRIPPA...
I AM THE SIN THE INQUISITOR SEES WHEN HE LOOKS UPON INNOCENCE.
I AM THE ANSWERS HE HEARS WHEN HE SEEKS THE WORD OF GOD.
I had a sudden awareness of the weight against my hip, the gourd concealed beneath my robe...
AM I DEMON OR SIMPLY REFLECTION?
OF THE FEAR AND HATE AND AVARICE INSIDE YOU ALL?
The gourd Juliette and I had carefully filled before leaving for the Witch House --

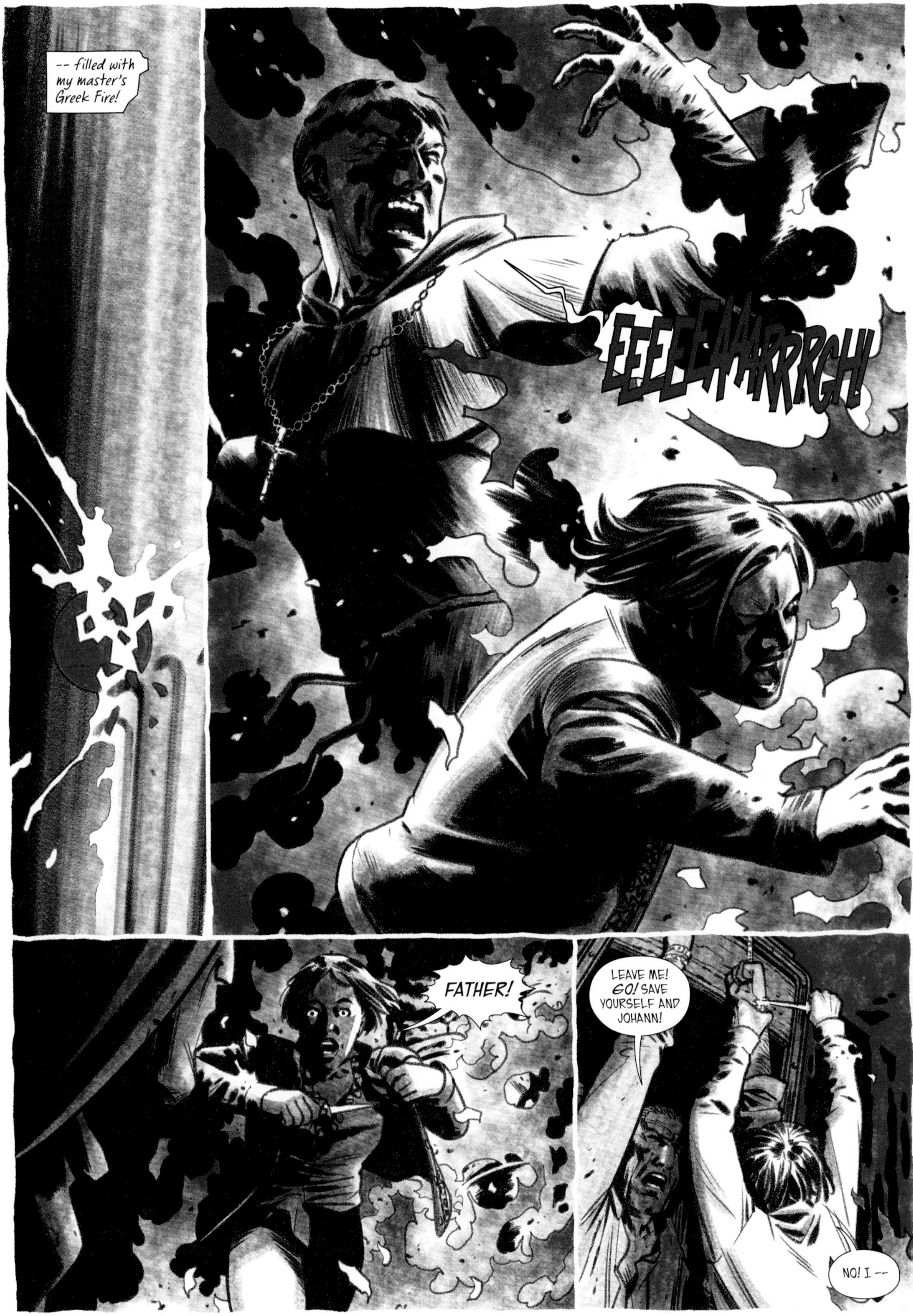
-- filled with my master's Greek Fire!
EEEEEAAARRRGH!
FATHER!
LEAVE ME! GO! SAVE YOURSELF AND JOHANN!
NO! I --

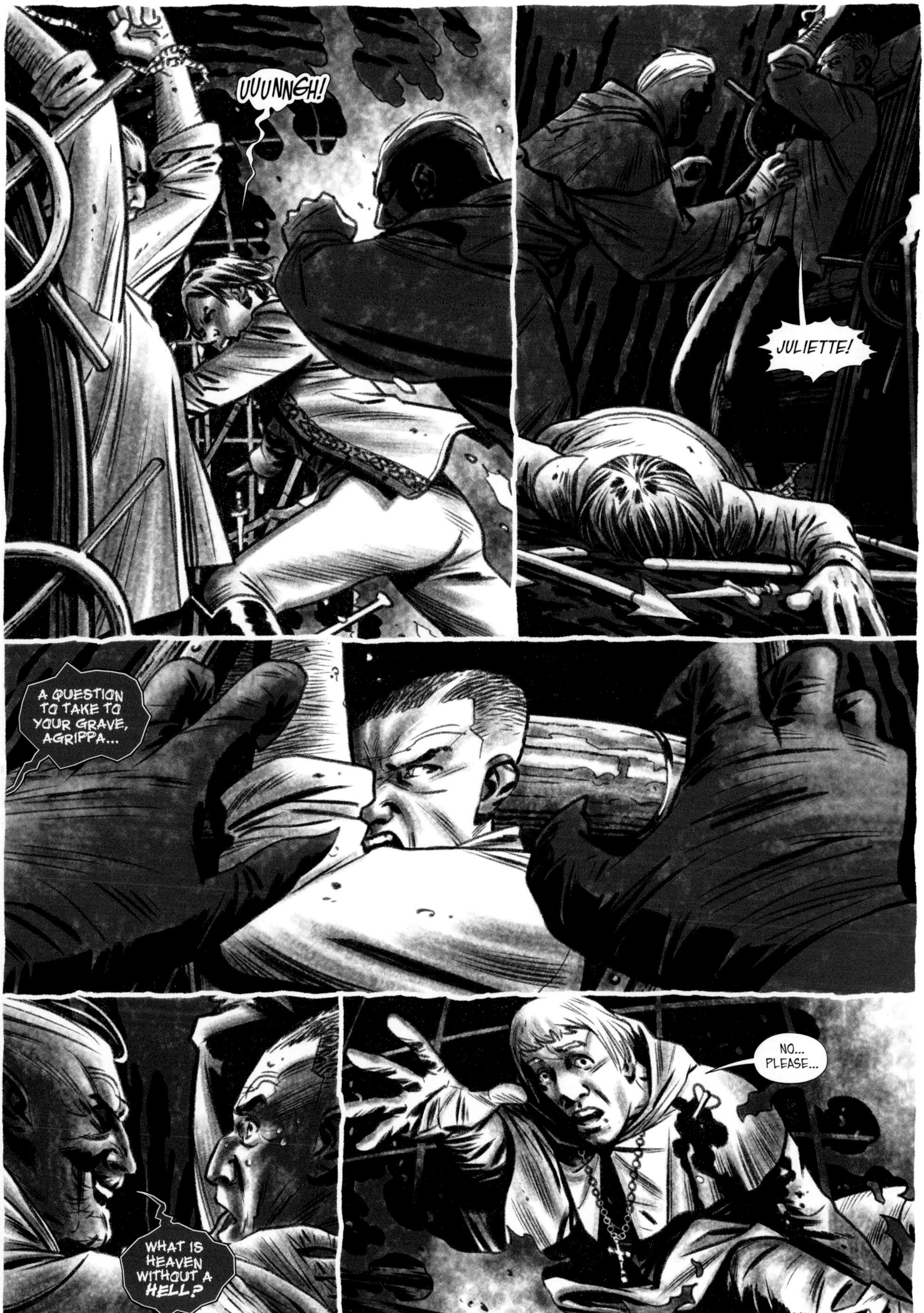
UUUNNGH!
JULIETTE!
A QUESTION TO TAKE TO YOUR GRAVE, AGRIPPA...
WHAT IS HEAVEN WITHOUT A HELL?
NO... PLEASE...

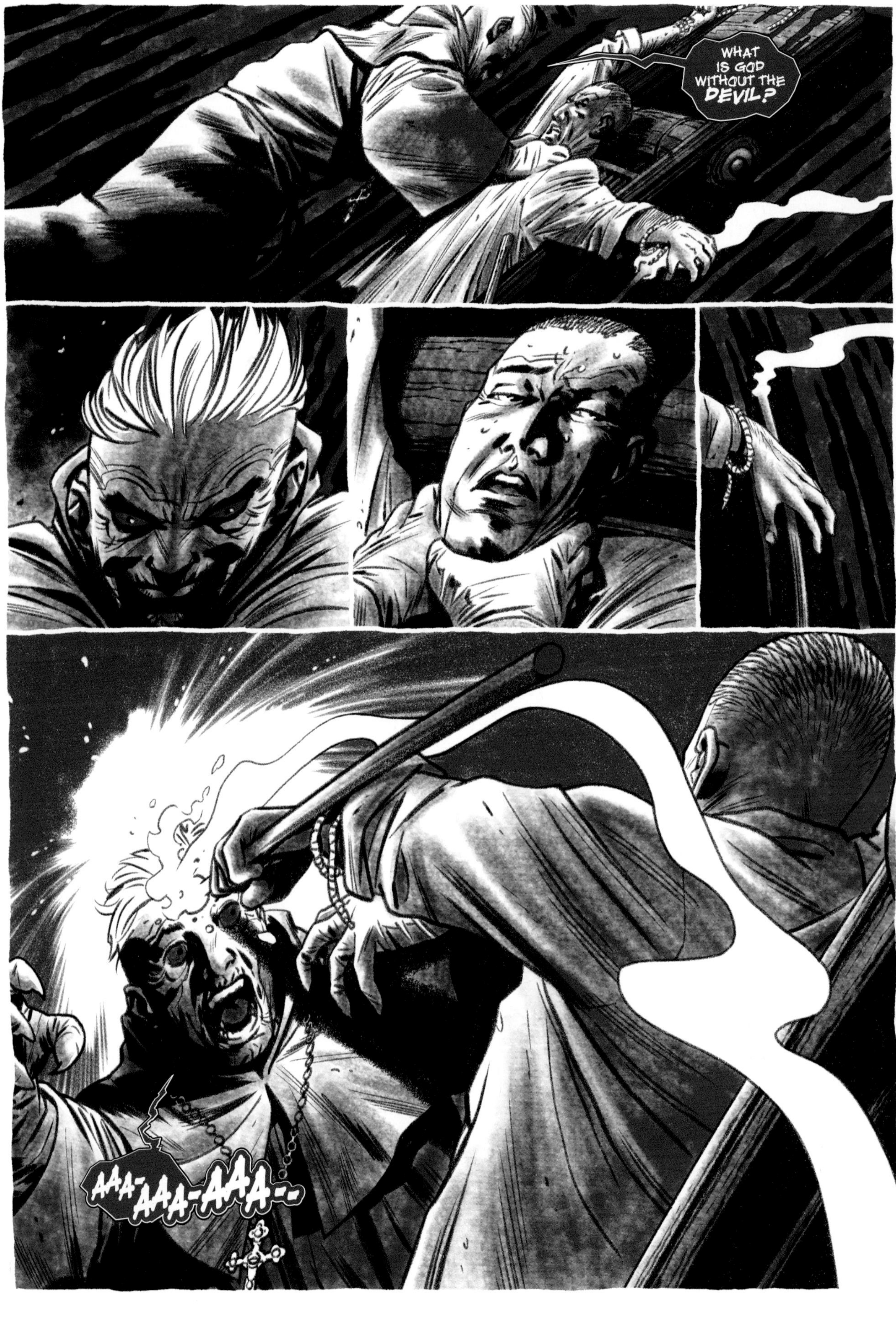
WHAT IS GOD WITHOUT THE DEVIL?
AAA-AAA-AAA--

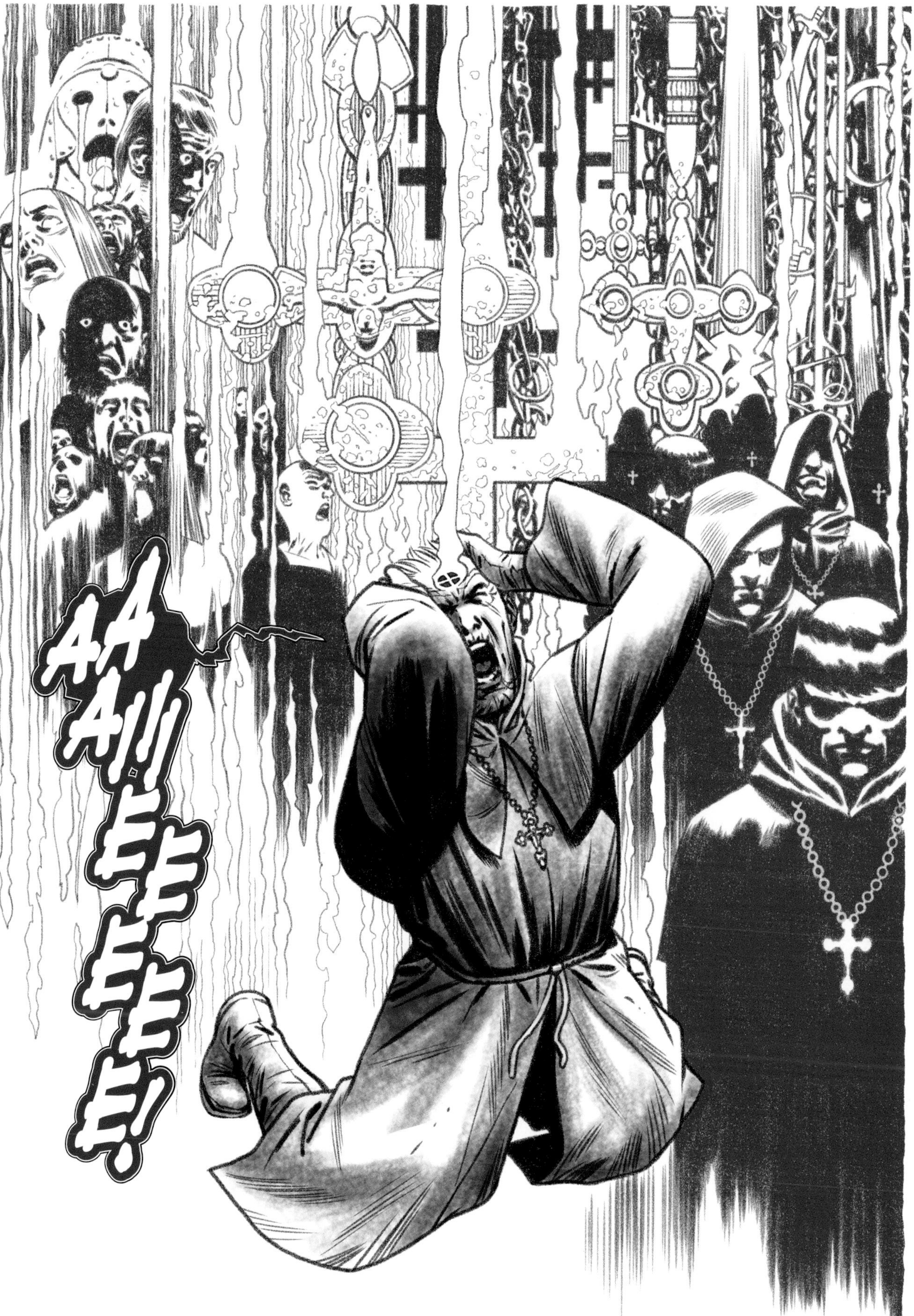
AAAIIIEEEEEE!

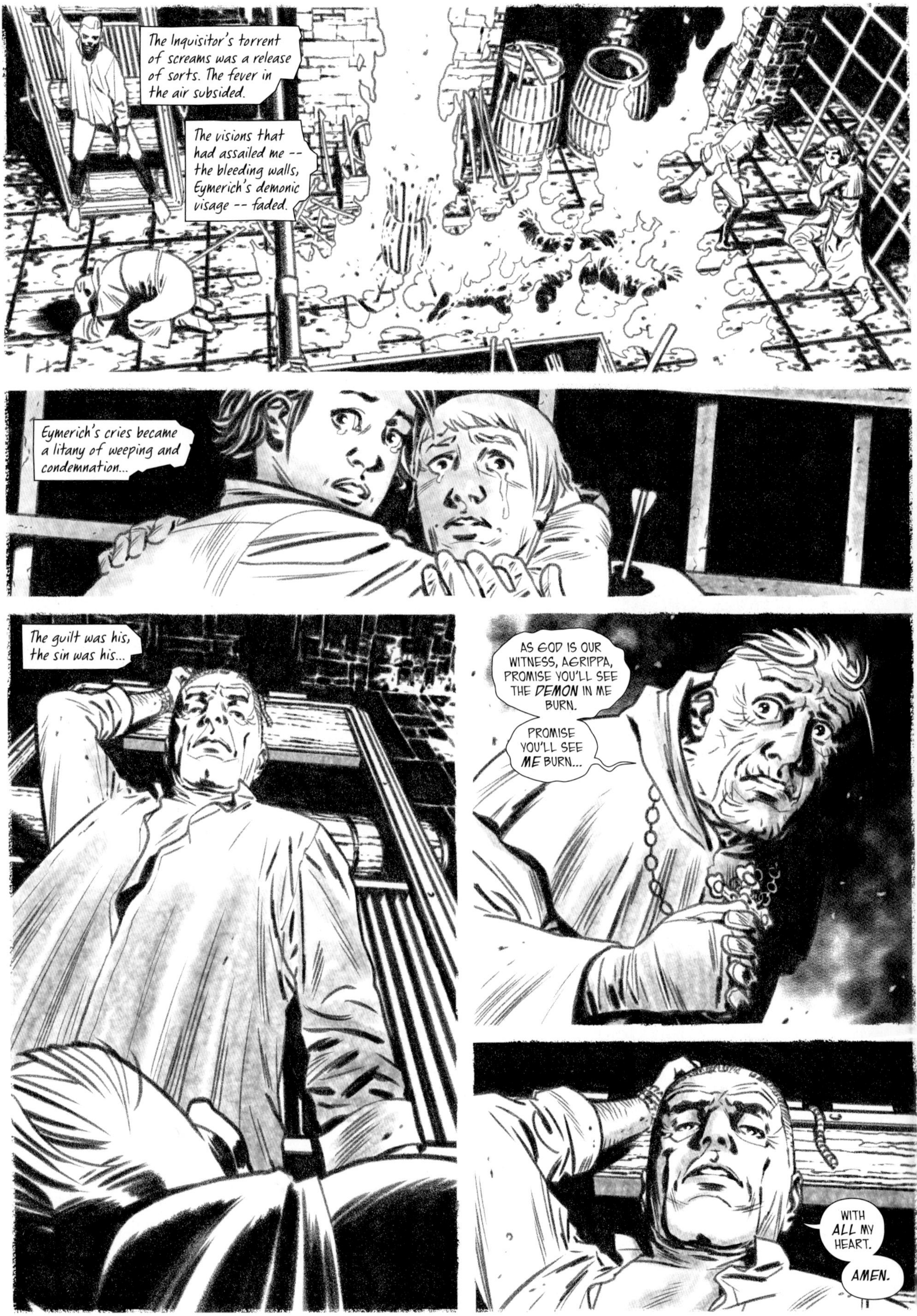
The Inquisitor's torrent of screams was a release of sorts. The fever in the air subsided.
The visions that had assailed me -- the bleeding walls, Eymerich's demonic visage -- faded.
Eymerich's cries became a litany of weeping and condemnation...
The guilt was his, the sin was his...
AS GOD IS OUR WITNESS, AGRIPPA, PROMISE YOU'LL SEE THE DEMON IN ME BURN.
PROMISE YOU'LL SEE ME BURN...
WITH ALL MY HEART.
AMEN.

CONSIGN ME TO THE FLAMES.

I WELCOME GOD'S JUDGMENT.

Bernard Eymerich's final act as Chief Inquisitor was to declare himself a witch and a heretic --

-- and order that he be burned at the stake like his countless victims.

Jacob Kreiswirth arranged for Virginie to be adopted as his ward.

Thanks to the Regent Margaret's intervention, he and his daughter Rebecca were granted full pardons within days.

Their scars, inside and out, would take longer to heal, if ever.

As the flames rose, Lord Agrippa turned to me and, his voice edged with despair, spoke words no other could hear...

PERHAPS ALL DEMONS ARE OF OUR OWN CREATION. AND GODS.

PERHAPS, IN THE END, THERE'S ONLY US.

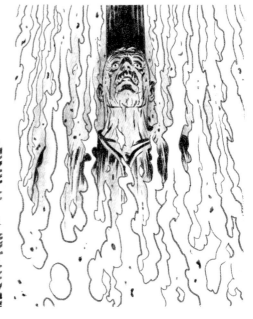

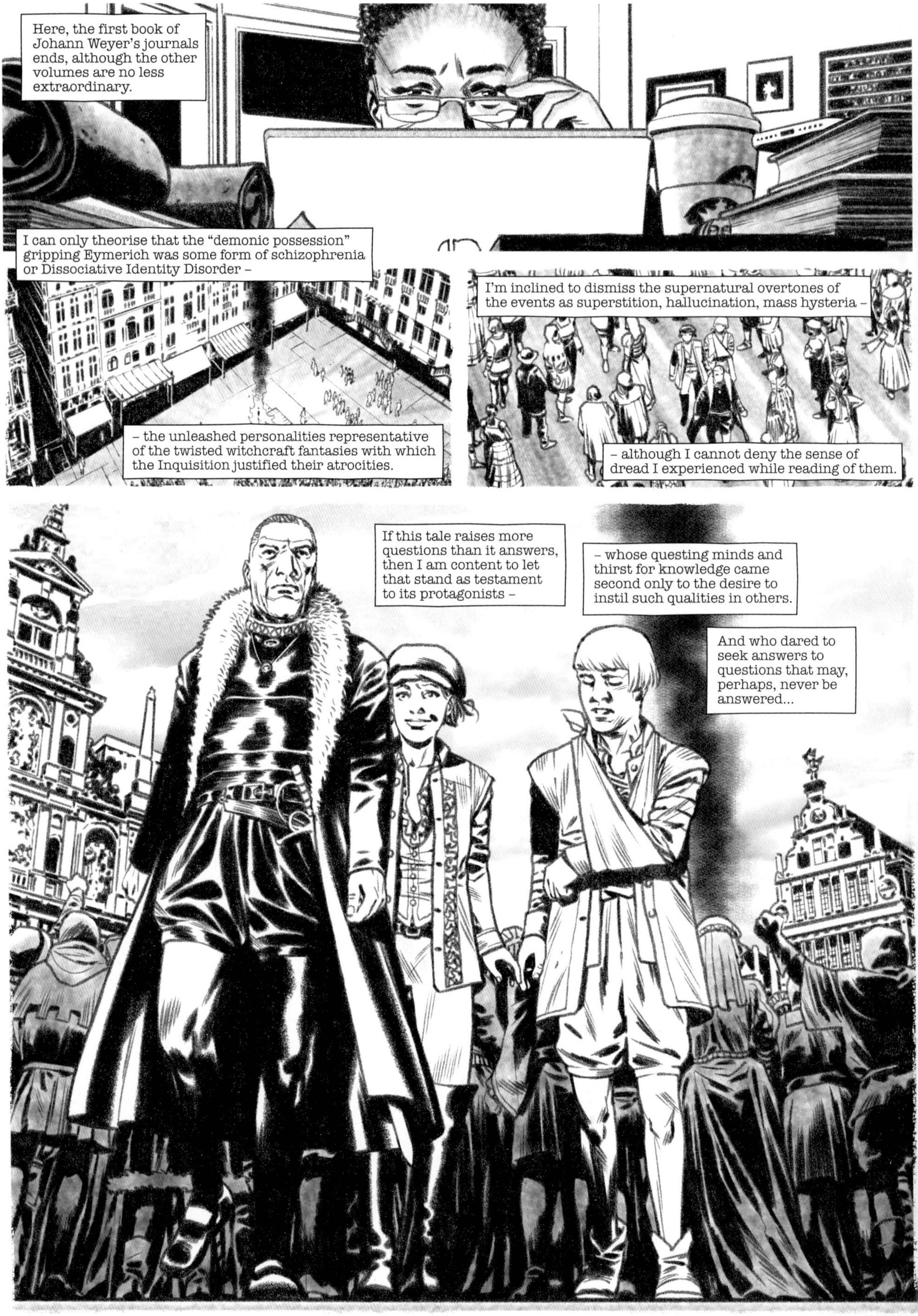
Here, the first book of Johann Weyer's journals ends, although the other volumes are no less extraordinary.
I can only theorise that the "demonic possession" gripping Eymerich was some form of schizophrenia or Dissociative Identity Disorder –
– the unleashed personalities representative of the twisted witchcraft fantasies with which the Inquisition justified their atrocities.
I'm inclined to dismiss the supernatural overtones of the events as superstition, hallucination, mass hysteria –
– although I cannot deny the sense of dread I experienced while reading of them.
If this tale raises more questions than it answers, then I am content to let that stand as testament to its protagonists –
– whose questing minds and thirst for knowledge came second only to the desire to instil such qualities in others.
And who dared to seek answers to questions that may, perhaps, never be answered...

THE END.

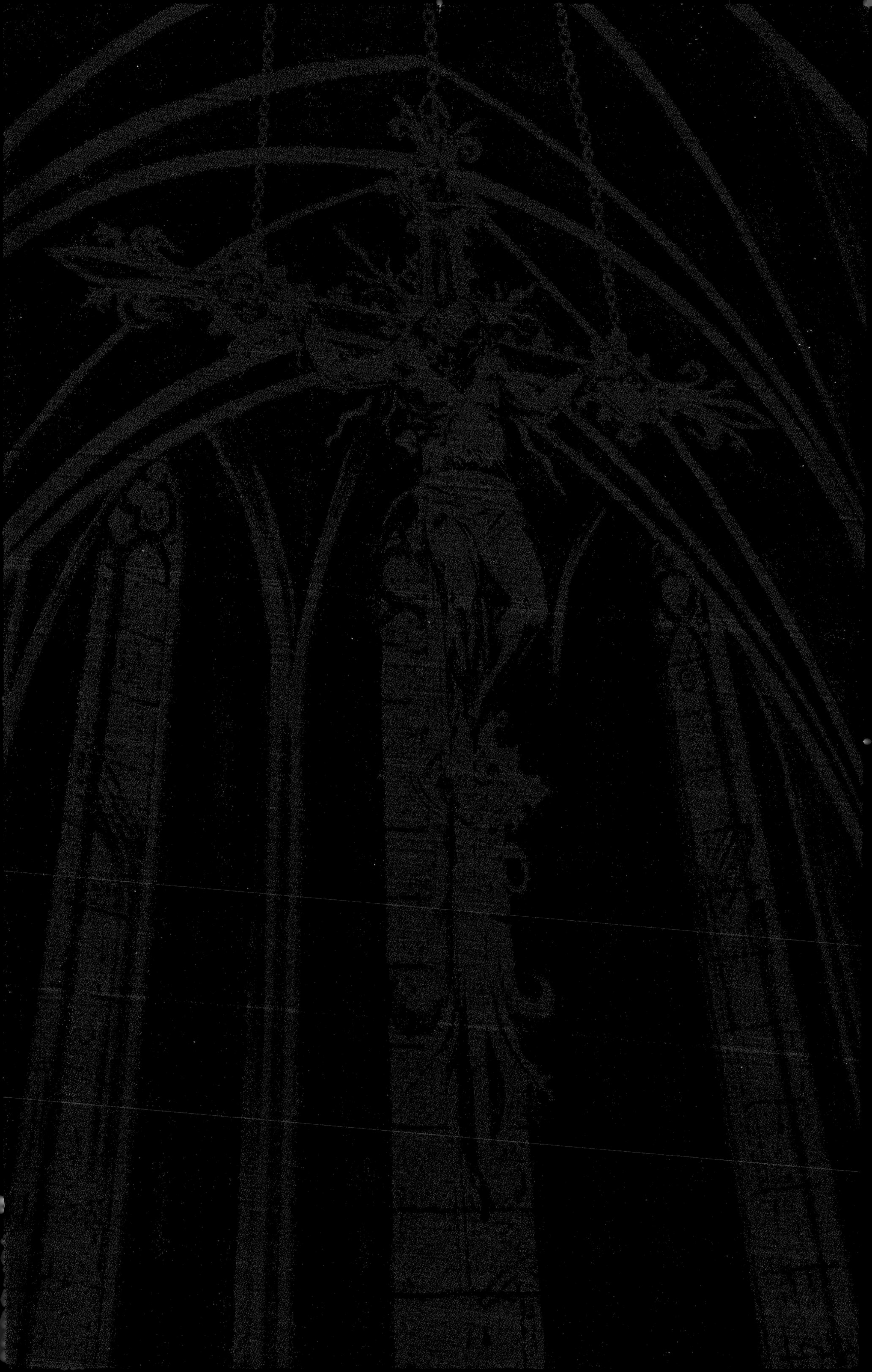

AFTERWORD

The Renaissance was a period in which many elements of modern society were forged, from science, education and philosophy to the political structure of governments and other institutions. Paradoxically, it was also a time in which the pursuit of knowledge was brutally censored by Church and State, who, anxious to maintain power and control, feared the change such awareness could bring about.

Those who dared challenge accepted views and opinions were branded heretics or witches by the all-powerful Inquisition. Claiming to act in the name of God, the Inquisition inflicted torture and execution upon enemies of the Church, their centuries-long terror culminating in the great European witch-hunts and trials, which executed and confiscated the property of countless victims.

By the standards of any age, Henry Cornelius Agrippa von Nettesheim was a remarkable man. Possessed of immense knowledge, he had a varied career to say the least: knight, soldier and military entrepreneur, advocate, astrologer, cabalist, Doctor of Law and medicine, and reputedly a magician of great power.

Born in Cologne, Germany, Agrippa was a man of peace, yet fate made him a soldier. He led a tempestuous life of war and writing, study and adventure, wandering and persecution. One of the first people to publicly challenge the Inquisition, he successfully defended a woman accused of witchcraft in Metz, northern France, the start of an epic, decades-long duel with the Church.

Much of Agrippa's life remains a mystery; biographers and historians inevitably disagree upon the true character of such a notorious figure. Some view him as the greatest intellectual of his age, others a charlatan whose opportunistic schemes eventually backfired, costing him his reputation and, ultimately, his life.

Agrippa's writings were extensively published, his famous three-volume *De Occulta Philosophia* adding impetus to the Renaissance study of magic. The cynical *Declamation On the Vanity and Uncertainty of Arts and Sciences* is a scathing attack upon the corruption and greed of nobility and government, and upon the Church, which supported superstition and cruelty, and, through the Inquisition, destroyed all attempts at progress.

His controversial *Declamation on the Nobility and Preeminence of the Female Sex*, in which he argues that women are more than the equal of men, can be seen as an early feminist text. On a literary note, Agrippa and his works influence Victor Frankenstein in Mary Shelley's classic novel, and he even appears as a collectible card in *Harry Potter and the Philosopher's Stone*.

Johann Weyer, it's claimed, was acquainted with the supernatural from an early age. His home was seemingly shared with a *house cobold*, or poltergeist, the experience of which opened the boy's mind to the mysteries of the unknown. After studying medicine in Paris and Orleans, he became an equally illustrious, if less infamous, physician and scholar as Agrippa, and was one of the first serious opponents of the witch mania. Published at great risk, his *De Praestigiis Daemonum* is a passionate, logically argued plea against the barbarity of the witch trials and marked the first turning of the tide away from the tyranny of the Inquisition.

Weyer studied under Agrippa in Antwerp around 1529-1533, aged somewhere between 14 and 17. One can only imagine the philosophical, intellectual and moral debates these two great minds must have engaged in. The bond of respect, friendship and admiration between them was strong. As noted by Agrippa's biographer: "When it was almost heresy to say a good word for his early teacher, Weyer spoke of Agrippa lovingly, and ventured to defend his reputation."

* * *

It's fair to say that this book has been some time in the making. I first learned of Cornelius Agrippa and Johann Weyer almost thirty years ago, from the briefest of references in Adam Douglas's *The Beast Within*, a book about werewolf myths throughout history. Whatever werewolf-related story I was researching obviously came to nothing, but I couldn't shake the thought of the real-life figures Agrippa – arrogant, flamboyant, outspoken – and Weyer – naive, yet sometimes wiser than his mentor – pooling their powers of deduction, reasoning and scientific awareness like a Renaissance Holmes and Watson.

The idea percolated over the years like one of Agrippa's alchemical experiments, until I found the perfect collaborator for a tale of murder, magic and madness in my old friend and former Comics Laureate Charlie Adlard. Charlie's art oozes atmosphere, beautifully conjuring up the Renaissance world and the horrors of the Inquisition. Add the award-winning lettering of Rus Wooton, and I hope you'll agree the book was worth the wait.

While we've tried to stay true to the broad strokes of history, *Heretic* is a work of fiction and we have taken certain liberties for dramatic purposes, for example in the make-up of Agrippa's family, about which little is known, and in the styling of the plague doctor apparel, which is from a slightly later time period. Any other errors and inaccuracies are ours, and ours alone.

Finally, not every writer is fortunate enough to have a professional editor for a partner, and I'd like to thank my other half Deborah Tate for suggesting that *Heretic* would make a good project for Charlie and me in the first place.

ROBBIE MORRISON
JULY 2024

ROBBIE MORRISON is the author of the Inspector Jimmy Dreghorn crime thrillers, set in 1930s Glasgow. One of the most respected writers in the UK comic-book industry, he has scripted iconic characters such as Batman, Doctor Who and Judge Dredd, as well as his own creation Nikolai Dante, serialized for over 15 years in cult science-fiction comic *2000AD*. He is also the writer of the graphic novels *Drowntown* and *White Death*, also drawn by Charlie Adlard.

Edge of the Grave, the first Jimmy Dreghorn novel, won Bloody Scotland Debut Crime Novel in 2021, was shortlisted for the McIlvanney Prize, the Crime Writers' Association Historical Dagger and the Historical Writers' Association Debut Crown, and was a Waterstones Book of the Month (Scotland). *Cast a Cold Eye*, the follow-up, was shortlisted for the McIlvanney Prize and was Waterstones Book of the Month in Scotland, April '24.

Other books by Robbie Morrison:

THE JIMMY DREGHORN NOVELS

Edge of the Grave
Cast a Cold Eye

THE NIKOLAI DANTE SERIES
(Artists: Simon Fraser, John Burns & Others)

The Romanov Dynasty – The Great Game –
The Courtship of Jena Makarov – Tsar Wars Vol. 1 –
Tsar Wars Vol. 2 – Hell and High Water –
Sword of the Tsar - The Beast of Rudinshtein –
Amerika – Hero of the Revolution -
Sympathy for the Devil

SHAKARA! (Artist: Henry Flint)

The Bendatti Vendetta (Artist: John Burns)

Drowntown (Artist: Jim Murray)

White Death (Artist: Charlie Adlard)

CHARLIE ADLARD has been a "veteran" of the comic industry for over 30 years. He's spent the majority of his time since 2003 working on *The Walking Dead*, which finished in 2019, and has received many industry awards for his work on the series culminating in winning the Sergio Aragonés International Award for Excellence in Comic Art in 2019

Born on the 4th August 1966 in the town of Shrewsbury, England and, having moved away to study film and video at art college, eventually moved back and still resides there today. Before moving back to Shrewsbury, he spent a brief stint in London, finding out that the BA he'd earned at art college was pretty useless in getting a job in the film industry, and, after failing to set the world alight playing the drums in a rock band, eventually settled on the "third" option – which was comics. An option he finally realised should have been number one right from the beginning.

After spending two years back in Shrewsbury, working on a portfolio, he eventually found his first work at the *Judge Dredd Megazine* in 1992 and hasn't looked back since.

Other books by Charlie Adlard:

The Walking Dead (Writer: Robert Kirkman)

Damn Them All (Writer: Si Spurrier)

Altamont (Writer: Herik Hanna)

Vampire State Building (Writers: Ange Renault and Patrick Renault)

Breath Of The Wendigo (Writer: Mathieu Missoffe)

Savage (Writer: Pat Mills)

Rock Bottom (Writer: Joe Casey)

White Death (Writer: Robbie Morrison)

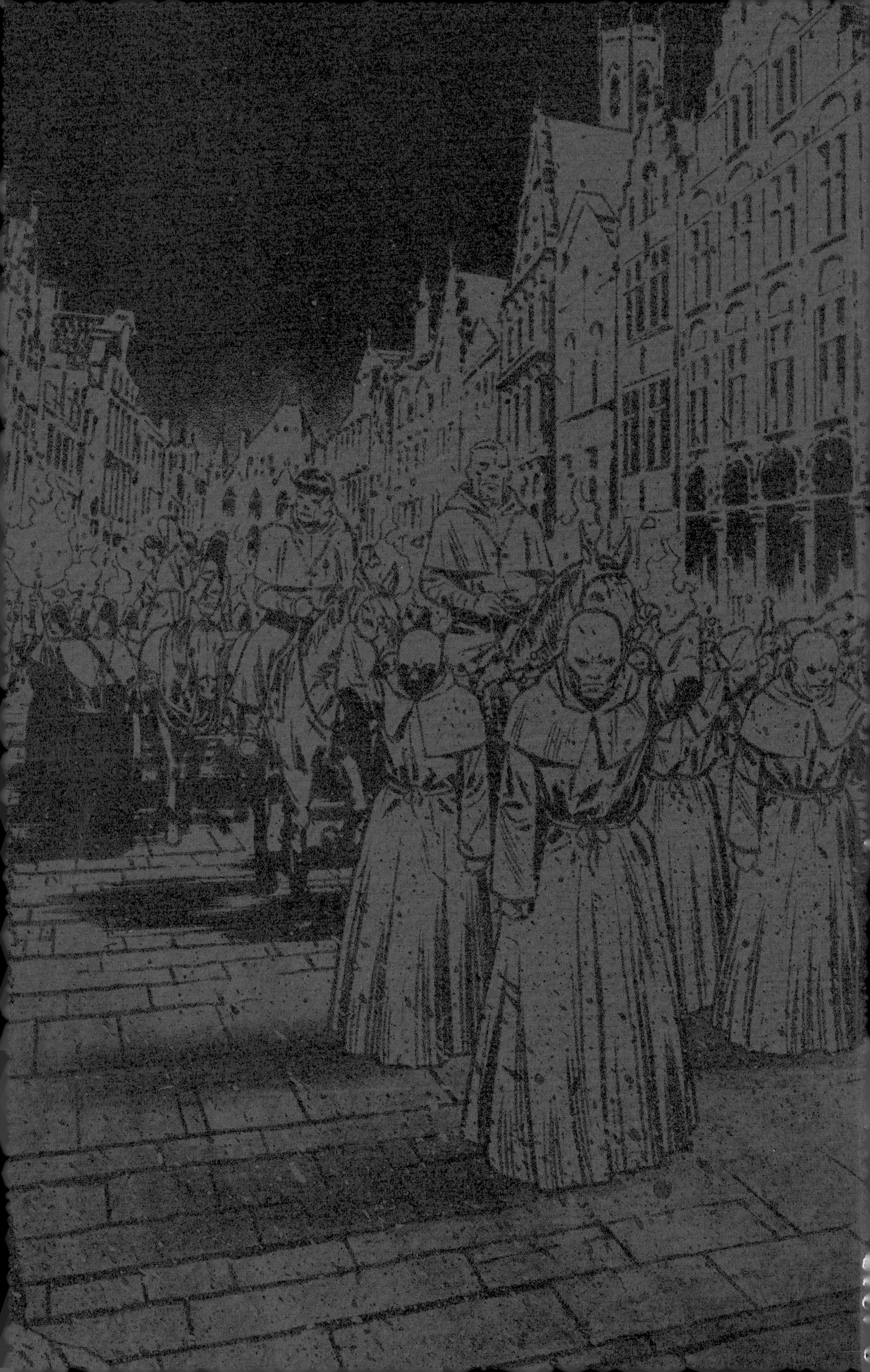